What people are saying about Barry Callen ...

"I'm one of those people who think outside the box. Our message strategy session with Barry Callen made me realize there is a zone beyond the space outside the box. This ain't your mama's marketing session."

—Deanna Springer, Nancy's Notions

"Brother Barry made our communications congregation see the light."

—Michael Bridgeman
Wisconsin Public Television

"Barry Callen received the highest praise and the highest marks ever recorded for a Super Stars Training session since we began in 1996."

—Theresa T.K. Timm
Mid-West Family Broadcasting

"Barry is one of the most insightful creatives I've worked with over my 25-year career. His ability to 'think like the customer' and to turn consumer insights into strategy is unmatched. In the 17 years I've known him, he has never failed to bring more value to the table than what he was paid."

—Scott W. Cooper
author, *The One-Day Marketing Plan*

"He provided clever and inexpensive strategies to solve real marketing problems as well as authentic methods to disarm those negative nellies among us. He's whip-smart, wickedly creative, and stylishly cool."

—Rolanda Taylor Enroth
Television Producer/Anchor

"Since we met in class a few weeks ago, I wanted to reemphasize how much I got out of your session. It was by far the most useful section of my series."

—Jennifer Janowski, GE Healthcare

Other titles in the Briefcase Books series include:

To learn more about titles in the Briefcase Books series go to
www.briefcasebooks.com

Manager's Guide to Marketing, Advertising, and Publicity

Barry Callen

New York Chicago San Francisco Lisbon
London Madrid Mexico City Milan New Delhi
San Juan Seoul Singapore Sydney Toronto

The McGraw·Hill Companies

1 2 3 4 5 6 7 8 9 0 DOC/DOC 0 1 0 9

ISBN : 978-0-07-162796-2
MHID :   0-07-162796-0

This is a CWL Publishing Enterprises book developed for McGraw-Hill by CWL Publishing Enterprises, Inc., Madison, Wisconsin, www.cwlpub.com.

McGraw-Hill books are available at special quantity discounts to use as premiums and sales promotions, or for use in corporate training programs. To contact a representative please e-mail us at bulksales@mcgraw-hill.com.

Contents

Preface

This book is written for business managers who know very little about the strange world of marketing communications but need to engage in that world. It is the result of 30 years of hands-on, frontline trial-and-error learning with hundreds of clients and thousands of marketing communications and millions of customers, with clients investing just under half a billion dollars in many kinds of media to achieve measurable results. It is founded on hard-won knowledge from many sectors: consumer, business-to-business, professional, non-profit, manufacturing, distribution, retail, established national brands, technology start-ups, and local businesses.

Marketing and advertising are best learned on the job, through apprenticeship. This is the book I wish I could have given my many clients who were just starting out, to keep them from wandering into the minefields of misunderstanding.

This book is written to use, not to impress. It is more of a handbook than a textbook. I have tried to write it in plain, conversational English. Because marketing is full of confusing jargon, definitions are included.

I have organized the book's chapters in their order of importance. When you build a house, you first need a strong foundation, then good framing, wiring, and plumbing, and then the finish carpentry and paint. And so it is with marketing. First you need the right attitudes and expectations, then the right strategies, and then the right tactics.

Most wrongheaded marketing has its roots in ignorance, greed, fear, and false beliefs about human behavior that are exaggerated by standard American business culture. So Chapters 1 through 4 are about the basics and benefits of marketing, realistic expectations, major mistakes to avoid, planning, and 14 basic principles of marketing communications strategy. If you read no other chapters, you'll get your money's worth if you read and learn from these. Another classic marketing mistake is to jump straight to tactics without a marketing strategy, as in "Let's get some free PR! That'll increase our sales."

Chapters 5 through 7 provide an overview of the key marketing and messaging strategies, disciplines, positioning and personality, and a simple method for developing a message strategy—stuff you will need regardless of the advertising media you use. But a strategy is only as good as its execution and most of your dollars will go toward execution. So Chapters 8 through 14 on are about specific types of communications you might find yourself purchasing or managing: creative, media, research, advertising, Web, and PR.

This book is written so you can pick subjects and chapters, but I strongly encourage you to read the whole book. That way you'll make your management decisions with a helicopter view of the whole battlefield.

Most marketing and marketing communications are done very poorly and achieve mediocre results. If you merely imitate your competitors, you will not surpass them—and you may even make matters worse for your company. A lot of the common beliefs about marketing held by business professionals outside of marketing are dead wrong—and often harmful.

In some ways, many of the things you learn that make you a good businessperson make you a lousy marketer. For example, if you are buying an ad, isn't it a waste to focus on one selling idea when you have room to list 10? The answer is no. In advertising, less is more, and the ad that focuses on one idea is more likely to be effective. This is the principle of "One ad/one idea" and it has been proven to work again and again. Marketing is filled with such anomalies because of the quirkiness of human perception.

Maybe you are a sales manager or engineer or controller or doctor or scientist who has been put in charge of the marketing department. Maybe you are a first-time brand manager. Maybe you have been charged with creating a marketing function within a manufacturing or sales-driven organization. Maybe you are being out-marketed or outspent by a competitor. Maybe you are a CEO or president or business owner who wants to understand what's possible for marketing communications to achieve. Maybe you're a student who wants to hit the ground running in a career in marketing or communications. Maybe you face declining market share, or a new competitor, or the need to launch a new product or restage an old brand. Maybe no one knows your company name or perhaps your product is far better than it's perceived to be. Maybe you are a business professional struggling to inspire and lead the creative types who write and design your communications. If any of these scenarios sound familiar, this book is written for you.

Done well, marketing and marketing communications can help you increase sales or donations, increase competitive market share, inoculate your customers against switching brands, make the public more forgiving during a crisis, increase the value of your stock, and provide an early warning system for customer problems.

But you can't manage what you don't understand. Use this book to help take full advantage of the power of marketing—and to avoid stepping on those land mines.

Finally, see the end of Chapters 5, 7, and 8 for special free whitepaper offers that extend the information in those chapters.

Special Features

The idea behind the books in the Briefcase Books series is to give you practical information written in a friendly, person-to-person style. The chapters deal with both strategic and tactical issues and include lots of examples and how-to information. They also feature numerous sidebars designed to give you specific types of information you can use. Here's a description of the boxes you'll find in this book.

KEY TERM Every subject has some special jargon, including this one, dealing with marketing and advertising. These boxes provide definitions of these terms and concepts.

SMART

MANAGING

These boxes do just what their name implies: give you tips and tactics for using the ideas in this book to intelligently manage and encourage sound marketing communications decisions and execution.

These boxes give you how-to and insider hints on techniques insiders use to create and execute marketing and advertising strategies and tactics in a variety of contexts.

It's always useful to have examples that show how the principles in the book are applied. These boxes provide descriptions of how managers and organizations have prospered from effective marketing.

These boxes provide warnings for where things could go wrong when you're planning and implementing your marketing and advertising strategy.

How can you make sure you won't make a mistake when you're trying to implement the techniques the book describes? You can't, but these boxes will give you practial advice on how to minimize the possibility of an error.

This icon identifies boxes where you'll find specific procedures or techniques you can follow to take advantage of the book's advice.

TOOLS

Acknowledgments

This book is the distilled essence of 30 years of mistakes, mentoring, and mayhem in the advertising and marketing business. It is designed to help you in situations of hellish pressure, eighty-hour weeks, stupid human tricks, recovering from rejection, meeting a payroll, and growing a business. There is sweat and blood on every lesson in this book. It is impossible to thank all the folks who taught me this stuff: clients, colleagues, bosses, authors, experts, artists, target audiences, and even competitors. Thousands of people. So instead of a group hug, here's a group thank you.

Thank you, my daughters, Lexie and Paige, for your tolerance and understanding of my time spent with this book at the computer instead of with you at the swimming pool. Writing pales in comparison to your sparkling creativity and laughter. You have made me a better man and shown me there is more to life than work. May you love yourself, and find the right balance of people, life, and work that you truly love. I love you most of all.

Thank you, Nell Weatherwax, for being my soulmate, true love, best friend, personal growth partner, creative colleague, and Feral Diva extraordinaire. I love teaching Corprov™ Corporate Improv classes with you, especially at that magic moment when we see our students get it. I encourage everyone to see you perform on YouTube, at Nellweatherwax.com, or in person. You are a world-class artist and an excellent teacher. Thank you for your support as this book so often intruded on our weekends together. Let's have a big life.

Thank you, God, the Cosmic Wink, Guardian Angels, Guidance, Spirit, Light, Ferd Berful, or whatever it is you call yourself, for helping me survive my stroke at the young age of 49, and for completely reinventing every aspect of my life: family, love, health, work, play, friends, spirit, intuition, creativity. Given my previous loathing of all things spiritual, I am living proof that God has a sense of humor. Thanks for the second chance. Thanks for the daily guidance. And a special thinks to ace market researcher Mike Pratzel for staying behind with me at the emergency room in Denver.

Thanks to my friends and mentors for being there when I needed you, and providing wise and loving counsel: Betty Marquardt for all the great conversations and prayers; Kim Lasdon for seeing me at my worst and sticking with me; Kim Shanehaar for safe loving massage; Kimberly Wilson (and Brian) for sticking by me through my divorce; my sister Linda for reconnecting with me at the moment of my father's death and for caring for my mom through her heart attack and beyond; Kay Plantes, Jo Lynn Rogers, Ben Wheatley, Nancy Bolts, Joan Gillman, and Jody Glynn Patrick for long-term friendship; and Jane Brotman, Jane Biondi, and Anne Simon-Wolf for wise, honest, tough, loving, lifesaving therapy, and life-coaching. Thanks to all my Hoffman Institute buddies, for love, and light, and (expletive) delight: Al, Carmen, Dena, Deb, Joey, Joy, Jude, Martha, Nancy, Sharon, Teri, and Tom. Thanks to my nutritionists, Kim Lasdon and Tracie Hittman, and to my personal trainer, Sarah Heezen, and to my doctor, Douglas Kutz, for helping me become younger, stronger, lighter, full of pleasure, and able to walk again. Thanks to all my contact improvisation dance buddies and my new musical friends Dave Schindele and Jen Logueflower. I am truly blessed by you all.

As for the book, I thank Scott Cooper of the Marketing Engine Group for introducing me to Linda Gorchels, of the U.W. Graduate School of Business, who gave me the opportunity to teach and led me to John Woods, president of CWL Publishing who approached me to write *Perfect Phrases for Sales and Marketing Copy*, and then this book, and managed the project from beginning to end, assembled the team, and herded the cats. I thank Bob Magnan, editor, especially for the sidebars in the media chapter and for his editing of the entire manuscript. I thank Knox Huston, acquisitions editor at McGraw-Hill, for having a cool name and for initiating the project. I thank Katie O'Brien, really really smart marketing strategist for agreeing at the last minute to ruthlessly slash 100 pages from the original manuscript (Contact her at k8obrien@charter.net). I thank Judy Duguid, proofreader, for changing who to whom and undoing my learning disabilities. I thank Kevin Campbell, indexer, for figuring out where it's all at.

I thank my contributors for writing the chapters that fall later in the book, and doing a much better job at it than I. I chose battle-tested veterans who know their stuff. You'd be crazy not to work with them. Barb Hernandez, P.R. and crisis communications wiz can be reached at hernandezbarbara39@yahoo.com or 608.235.1623. Nancy Bolts of Communicopia is a quadruple threat: writer, account executive, P.R. person, and media maven. Contact her at 919.324.5779 or boltsey@aol.com. Donna Fletcher is one of the few researchers with integrity who actually gets marketing strategy. Reach her at www.donnafletcherconsulting.com or 847.432.1972. Sandra Bradley has lived in the online world from the beginning, and has that rare mix of technical, creative, and business savvy that is so hard to find in one place, let alone one person. Contact her at www.linkedin.com/in/sandrabradley or 608-239-3122.

I'd like to thank my visionary client Judy Faulkner of Epic Systems for recommending me as a marketing consultant to my first solo client, the Health Care Information Management Systems Society, and secretly guaranteeing to refund my $25,000 payment if they were not completely satisfied. Thanks to Stephen Lieber and Norris Orms for taking Judy up on her offer, and for not requesting a refund. You guys helped me start my own business. Thanks to Dave Chew, Matt Jones, and Todd Hain of Kinetico Water Filters; Judy Faulkner and Terri Leigh Rhody of Epic Systems; Bill Kunkler of Evensong Spa; and Jennifer Bennerotte of the Minnesota Association of Government Communicators for being among my first clients. Thanks also to the management team at House-Autry Breaders, for tracking down Donna and me to restage your brand 17 years after our last successful brand launch, including Rob DePree, Roger Mortenson, Craig Hagood, Keith Vines, Larry Hammond, and James Hall.

A big huge thanks to Joan Gillman, Director of the Special Industry Programs at the University of Wisconsin–Madison and networking genius, for leading me to my teaching, speaking, and Corprov clients, including Theresa Timm, Dave Doetsch, and Jolene Neis of Midwest Family Broadcasting; and Jim Likens and Alison Carr of the Credit Union National Association management schools, who in turn opened the door to teaching marketing and improv classes to many credit unions around the country. Thank you to archetypal marketing master, Fritz Grutzner, of Brandgarten. Thanks to the management and staff of my former advertising agency, Hiebing, for being the only agency in the world to regularly and knowledgably use the PitchPerfect™ process, the naming process, and the positioning process in this book. And thanks for unflagging support as I moved from creative director and employee to independent operator. Specifically, thank you Dave Florin, Sean Mullen, Jeane Kropp, David Schiff, Carl Fritscher, Mike Pratzel, Steve Krumrei, Marion Michaels, and Roman Hiebing. You are all great clients who have taught me a lot.

I dedicate this book to my deceased father, Clifford Callen, who taught me a love of reading and learning and business, and to my very alive mother, Barbara Callen, who taught me a love of creativity, writing, art, and music. Thank you both for demonstrating that it's never too late to have a happy childhood.

Finally, gentle reader, I thank you for buying this book. May it help you end bad advertising, one ad at a time.

—Barry Callen

Manager's Guide to Marketing, Advertising, and Publicity

What Marketing Communications Can Do for You

Many business professionals outside of marketing don't really understand marketing and marketing communications. In this chapter, I want to correct that. Marketing communications is a lot more than "doing ads."

The Importance of Good Marketing Communications

The scarcest resource on the planet is no longer money or diamonds or oil. The scarcest resource is attention. The demand for attention today far exceeds the supply. The resulting scarcity of attention is the greatest problem facing any marketing communicator.

By almost any measure, the noise level or clutter in media has gotten so overwhelming that it is difficult for any one message to stand out and be noticed. Estimates vary depending on the study and the group studied, but the average American is exposed to somewhere between 200 and 5,000 commercial messages a day. We have more demands on our attention in just one day than our great-grandparents had in an entire year. By the time you die, you will have spent years of your life watching commercials and seeing ads.

The vast majority of these messages are ignored, a few are hated, and a tiny percentage are noticed and appreciated. And even if a marketing

1

communication manages to penetrate your consciousness, it must compete with the estimated 45,000 to 50,000 thoughts a day inside your brain.

What Is Marketing Communications?

Marketing communications is anything your organization does that affects the behavior or perception of your customers. The marketing communications process is a conversation between you and your customers that is as much about listening to your customers as it is about sending them messages. It is not a one-way street.

It doesn't matter who your customers are or what you are selling or promoting. Every decision you make and everything you do influences what your customers hear, see, or experience and will affect how they think and feel about your company and your product and/or service. This, in turn, influences what they do. Perception *always* precedes behavior.

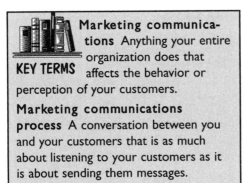

Marketing communications Anything your entire organization does that affects the behavior or perception of your customers.

Marketing communications process A conversation between you and your customers that is as much about listening to your customers as it is about sending them messages.

Be Authentic

"Everything you do" includes product development, price, locations, hours, placement and distribution, hiring, listening, promotion, design, contact points, news quotes, mistakes, and word of mouth, as well as classic advertising media communications. In general, direct experience trumps word of mouth, which trumps sales communications.

If your sales communications are making claims that are not supported by word of mouth or, worse, not supported by direct experience, you are better off adjusting your communications downward to fit reality. Otherwise, you are teaching people not to believe your communications. You are teaching them that your brand is a liar. Unless your product or

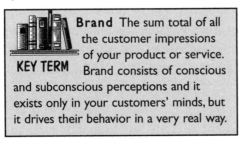

Brand The sum total of all the customer impressions of your product or service. Brand consists of conscious and subconscious perceptions and it exists only in your customers' minds, but it drives their behavior in a very real way.

service is a once-in-a-lifetime purchase (such as a presidential election!), it is always better to underpromise and overdeliver, even if your competition is making exaggerated claims.

Most people distrust corporations, sales, salespeople, and marketing communications. One way to stand out from the competition is to always tell the truth.

Marketing Communications Multiplies Word-of-Mouth

If your marketing communications claims are supported by word-of-mouth and direct experience, your advertising acts as a multiplier. It can actually improve the amount of positive word of mouth (how often and how many people say good things about you), and it can even improve and reinforce your customer's direct experience of your product.

> **Word-of-mouth** The things, good and bad, that people say about your company and its offerings. **KEY TERM**
> This is usually the result of the experience that people have with your product or service and often, even more, a result of the quality of the relationship they have with you as the seller.

Marketing Communications and Your Brand

A brand is perception, and perception is reality for customers.

The total of all the customer impressions of your product or service is your brand. Your brand is not the buildings, equipment, boxes, objects, or people you manage. Your brand is a perception that lives in your customers' minds.

One of the most frustrating experiences for a company is to create a technically superior product that is not perceived as a superior brand by prospective customers. That is one problem that superior marketing communications can help

> **KNOW YOUR BRAND**   **SMART**
> Know how customers, actual or potential, perceive your company and what you sell.
> Know the impressions you're **MANAGING**
> making in the community you serve.
> Know that this is reality.

resolve. In fact, any marketing communications on which you spend time or money that doesn't improve perception is pure non-value-added overhead.

What Is a Target Market?

While it is tempting to try and sell your product or service to everyone in the world, it is not cost effective. You might convince adult men to buy women's makeup, but it's likely that the return on your investment would be negative. You are much better off selling makeup to women or, better still, selling makeup to young adult women who are fashionistas.

To profit from your marketing, you must have a target market—a primary group of people you serve. Your primary market is the group of customers who account for a disproportionate share of your sales and profits. They are the ones you can't afford to do without.

> **KEY TERM**
>
> **Target market** The group of prospective customers to whom your offerings are most likely to appeal. Your *primary* target market consists of customers who account for a disproportionate share of your sales and profits, the customers who keep you in business. Your *secondary* target market consists of customers who are not as important as your primary target—and who may want different things from your brand.

You may also have secondary and tertiary markets, customers who are important, but not as important. For example, in the U.S., women buy most of the men's underwear, usually for their husbands and sons. Wives and mothers are the primary target market for men's underwear. But younger single men and divorced men also purchase their own underwear. They are a secondary target market. This is important to understand because they have different motives and beliefs, they need different messages, and they are reached through different media.

One of the most important marketing decisions you will ever make is to decide which group of people is your primary target market. You can't pursue all markets or even just two markets if they are incompatible. For example, if moms like something, teen boys distrust it; and if amateurs like something, professionals are embarrassed to use it. Sometimes you just have to choose—you can't please everyone. More about this in later chapters.

What About Your Competitors?

We live in an era where customers can instantly find many alternative products and services to meet the same need. Sometimes your competition can even be your otherwise potential customers. For example, for businesses that sell fast oil changes for cars, one competitor is the do-it-yourself oil changer. Sometimes your competition can come from completely different business categories or technologies. To clean my house, do I buy your vacuum cleaner, or do I hire a housekeeper, or do I invest in materials with easy-to-clean surfaces? To get in touch with my friend overseas, do I mail a letter, send an e-mail, call on a cell phone, fax a document, connect face to face via computer, or fly over and meet face to face?

In general, consumers tend to choose from among a small set of products or services and similar brands or suppliers to meet their needs. This is called the *considered set*. It is very telling which of your competitors your customers lump you in with. You may be very surprised at both how customers categorize their choices and who or what your competitors really are. Needless to say, knowing this can have a large effect on your marketing communications.

> **Considered set** The small group of competing alternatives that customers consider when making a purchase. Most customers have several favorites among which they choose. **KEY TERM**

How Marketing Can Benefit Your Business

Increase Sales

Most marketing communications neither dramatically increase nor decrease sales. But there is evidence that the most effective marketing communications help companies outsell the least effective by 600-900 percent! A little-known fact is that the worst marketing communications can even drive sales down by as much as 50 percent every time they run. Part of the purpose of this book is to help you avoid being on the low side of that bell curve and instead move toward that 600 percent elite.

Resist Becoming a Commodity

There is increasing evidence that brands are being driven out of the middle and into two categories: either you are a *discount* brand competing on price or you are a *premium* brand competing on quality and brand loyalty. For example, Wal-Mart competes on price, and Neiman Marcus competes on quality. The big losers are the brands that attempt to stay in the middle of the road, neither premium brand nor discount brand. They become a *commodity*, which means customers will jump if a competitor offers a lower price or a better product. It is a hard place to be. A sure sign is that your salespeople keep requesting lower and lower prices in order to make a sale. Building a brand can help keep you from being a commodity.

Create a Legal Monopoly

A powerful and well-known brand can even create a perfectly legal *perceptual* monopoly. There is evidence that the better a brand is known and the better it's distributed, the more a new competitor must spend just to be noticed, let alone tried. For example, anyone starting a fast food restaurant and trying to compete with McDonald's or Burger King would have to spend a lot of media dollars just to get its name out there. As a result of decades of consistent investment in marketing communications, McDonald's has a strong competitive advantage. This is one legal way to minimize the number of serious competitors.

Improve Customer Intent to Purchase

Marketing communications can affect your target market's *intent to purchase*. That's the degree to

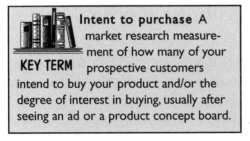

KEY TERM **Intent to purchase** A market research measurement of how many of your prospective customers intend to buy your product and/or the degree of interest in buying, usually after seeing an ad or a product concept board.

which a customer intends to buy your product or service or the number of customers who intend to buy. The greater the intent to purchase, the greater the likelihood of sales.

Make Customers More Loyal

Marketing communications can also inoculate your customers against switching to competitors. If you can create strong brand loyalty, they will even pay less attention to your competitors' ads or price promotions. You create the most powerful loyalty when you create a *badge brand*. A badge brand is a product or name that is so powerful that people define their own identities and social groups around it. No matter how superior motorcycles from Japan may be technically, Harley-Davidson riders view the Harley brand of motorcycle as a symbol of America, freedom, and rebellion. They wear clothing and get tattoos that proudly show off the brand. They are the brand and the brand is them.

Build a Bank of Goodwill for Tough Times

Consistently believable marketing communications can also build goodwill that can help you in the event of a major mistake. A strong brand perception buys some forgiveness. And actions consistent with the character and values of your brand during a crisis can actually improve customer perception. During the Tylenol tampering scare in 1982, Johnson & Johnson, the parent company of McNeil, pulled Tylenol products from store shelves, demonstrating that company officials valued

> **Badge brand** Product or name that is so powerful that people identify with it and its image. **KEY TERM**

>
> **WHEN CUSTOMERS ARE THE COMPANY** **FOR EXAMPLE**
> You know you have created a strong brand when your customers define their very identity with it. I once sat behind one-way mirrors in five cities and listened to product enthusiasts beg the holding company that had just bought their favorite product manufacturer to recognize the power of their feelings. "We are the company," they raged at the mirror. "We believe in it. We keep it alive! Not you!"

> **ADMIT YOUR MISTAKES AND LIMITATIONS** **FOR EXAMPLE**
> A manufacturer of water purification filters sent defective filters to leading department stores. Customers complained and returned them in droves. The manufacturer was able to convince the department store buyers to give it another chance with an advertising campaign that admitted that the company had made a terrible mistake and that proved that its new and improved designs would do a better job. The retailers gave the company a second chance.

customer health over financial health. As a result, the company gained even more trust from current and prospective customers. There may come a time when you have to raise your prices or you receive negative news coverage. When those times come, a bank of goodwill can really pay off.

Get More Retail Distribution

Marketing communications can help a small brand get retail store distribution and provide greater protection against discounting. If retail customers are asking for a product by name, retailers listen. If not, retailers will attempt to discount your price to the maximum. They may even create their own store brand to compete with you. It's a slippery slope between being a brand and being a commodity.

Charge More for the Same Product or Service

A good name alone can increase the perceived value of your product by as much as 20 percent. That's a lot of money to leave on the table due to not understanding marketing communications. Studies show that customers buying products ranging from dog food to automobiles are willing to pay up to 200 percent more for a premium brand than a comparable product. The difference is brand perception and emotional connection. Of course, the quality of the product must justify that connection, so never let quality slip lest you undermine what customers think of your product.

FOR EXAMPLE

MARKETING COMMUNICATIONS MAKES FOOD AND DRINK TASTE BETTER

Marketing communications can actually alter the emotional and physical experience of your product or service, especially if it is an intangible like expertise or something that customers can't evaluate objectively, like gasoline, perfume, or beverages. Studies repeatedly show that even loyal consumers often can't tell the difference among brands of alcoholic or nonalcoholic beverages. Their actual taste experiences are shaped by the design of the bottle, the graphics, the name, and the advertising.

Motivate Employees and Volunteers

Marketing communications can help attract, retain, and motivate better employees or volunteers. For example, to attain some of the best health care performance numbers on the planet, a regional health care provider focused most of its advertising dollars on recruiting the most dedicated and caring types of people. Not only did it communicate to prospective patients that the company provided superior health care, but it also raised the bar and the level of pride among current employees, which improved measurable delivery of health care services directly to patients.

Increase the Value of Your Stock

Marketing communications can help increase the stock value of your company. Brand values can be measured and used to calculate the worth of companies. The owners of a company challenged our agency to revive the sales of a declining retail craft store. We succeeded wildly, enabling the owners to sell the company one year later and become millionaires. The marketing communications demonstrated the growth potential of the brand.

Help Your Sales Staff

Marketing communications can pave the way for your sales staff. First, a well-known brand name can put your company on the short list of vendors. Second, a reputation as a market leader can make you the safe recommendation. There is a famous saying: "Nobody ever got fired for recommending IBM." Wouldn't you like the same to be said about your company? Third, your salesperson is not an unknown person selling an unknown product. Your advertising serves as a kind of introduction, to make a positive impression on the prospect. And fourth, marketing communications can be used to generate leads with interested prospects.

Avoid Nasty Surprises

Customer problems usually appear first as changes in perception. This gives you time to do something about them. If you do ongoing tracking studies of your primary target market or prospects, you can measure changes in things like unaided awareness of your name, intent to purchase, attitudes, trial, and repurchase. Your market research can serve as an early warning system and also help you diagnose the type of problem you are facing.

For example, if prospects don't know your name, you can increase your media reach and frequency. If prospects have an incorrect attitude about your brand, you can adjust the content of your communications. If prospects are not trying your product for the first time, you can look at sampling programs, guarantees, and promotions. If prospects are not purchasing your product after the first time, then you look at customer satisfaction, product design, price, or competitive superiority.

Marketing Results Can Benefit Your Career

High Visibility

One of the blessings (and curses) of marketing communications is that your work is highly visible. Everyone sees your communications: fellow employees, customers, distributors, stockholders, your bosses, people in the trade press, people representing political interests, salespeople, and customers. So your successes (and failures) are noticed.

Marketing typically touches almost all the departments in an organization, and all the departments in an organization affect the target market's perception of your business. This helps you acquire a top-management point of view, because you have to see the big picture to market effectively. The customer-business interface is where the rubber meets the road. Marketing is very different from toiling away invisibly in the backroom operation working on just one tiny dimension of the business.

Brand Championship

One way to succeed in marketing is to take a product or a brand and introduce it or revive it. People can see the sales results of the communications you've created. Championing an early product success is a proven route to a top-management position.

ADJUST INTERNAL EXPECTATIONS

Set reasonable and measurable marketing communications goals, and then track your progress toward those goals from year to year. Most expectations are either too high ("This will save the company!") or too low ("Advertising doesn't work!"). Manage expectations and you'll build credibility for the marketing function within your organization. There's nothing like getting fired because your CEO or Board of Directors was too disappointed or too cynical.

Management Advisor on Customer Behavior

You can also serve as a wise advisor to top management. You should be the resident expert on how prospective customers perceive your company and your competitors. You can provide wise advice in the event of a crisis or an opportunity. You can help reduce the risk of new product introductions through testing with customers. You can find out what is going on through market research or Web monitoring. You can help adjust the spin of news coverage.

Holistic View of the Business

Even if your ultimate goal is to work in another area of your business, marketing is a great way to study all the dimensions of your business and how they come together. It is also a great way to practice looking at your business from the outside in and with more objectivity. You also get a sense of what customers will and will not allow your brand to do. Should Clorox create a soft drink? No. Should Volvo create a sports car? Maybe. Should Apple go into the music business? Yes. Your understanding can help prevent the development and introduction of new products that could harm the credibility of your main brand. Better yet, you can learn to spot unmet needs in your target market and suggest directions for new products.

If you move to another company in that industry or to another industry, what you've learned about the principles, strategies, and psychology of marketing will transfer wherever you go.

Classic Business Situations Where Marketing Can Help

There are some situations where marketing communications can have a greater impact. In these situations, it pays to amp up the marketing budget and take advantage of the opportunity. In general, the marketing budget should be based more on this year's opportunities than on last year's line items.

New Product Introduction

Human beings are wired to pay attention to anything useful or anything new and different. Human beings also tend to form their opinions based on first impressions, and first impressions tend to be lasting impressions. So you generally have only one chance to introduce a new product or company or business and to introduce it correctly. The news value of what you have to say makes it more likely that people will pay attention to your message, which gives you a greater return on investment (ROI) on your marketing communications investment.

In direct mail, headlines that begin with "new," "now," "announcing," and "introducing" tend to get above-average sales response. Make sure, though, that your product has something truly new and different. If you say it is "new" when it's not, you are teaching people not to believe your future communications. Make sure also that what is new is also important and visible to your customers. Sometimes technical breakthroughs are invisible to the consumer or are unimportant. Make sure your customers understand what you are selling, why it's new, and why they should care. Since you only have one chance to launch a new product, it pays to err on the higher side of investment.

Relaunching an Old Brand

Companies make a lot of short-term money by riding on past marketing communications investments in a well-known brand. They invest in the brand, and then they stop investing and reap the short-term profits. Unfortunately, there comes a point where brand awareness drops, and perhaps several years out, sales start to drop suddenly, as customers in the target market age or forget about the product. If competitors are investing heavily in brand communications, this decline accelerates.

However, it's possible to bring a well-known brand back from the dead. To do this, you need to treat it like a new product introduction and invest significant sums to regain brand-name awareness among the new customer groups. Because there is some residual brand-name awareness and a proven market, you get some financial lift.

FOR EXAMPLE

BANK ON THE NATURAL DECLINE

I had one client who used to their advantage the natural tendency of people to lose interest in a product. A number-two competitor was eating their lunch with a powerful campaign year after year. So my client bought the competitor and did only token brand advertising for it. My client reaped tremendous profits from that brand for about four years. But after a few years without exposure of the product in the media, sales dropped 30 percent, then 40 percent at five years, and then practically to zero at six years. My client basically let a competitor die a natural death. Amazingly, many companies cause the same decline for their own brands by cutting back on investments in branding.

Recession

It is counterintuitive, but study after study of every recession since 1949 has shown that companies that advertise during a recession win business from those that don't. Increasing spending during this time can achieve the same net ROI as a cut in spending. A recession is apparently an opportunity to make significant gains in market share at the expense of smaller or less aggressive firms. One study of hundreds of companies showed that companies that advertised achieved 14 times the sales growth of companies that did not. Even more amazing, these gains can last three to five years. Even large and experienced marketers have learned the folly of cutting advertising expenditures during a recession, only to see sales fall even more, for a net loss.

Perhaps one reason recessions are a great time to advertise is that personal consumer spending actually goes up during a recession and is highest at the very bottom of the recession. Companies that cut back on advertising miss their share of this spending spree.

Another reason may be that the overall noise level of advertising goes down as many companies cut back, and so those that advertise stand out more. It's also possible that during a recession consumers get a sense of which companies will survive and which won't, based on cues like whether or not they advertise. Whatever the reason, there is no better time to aggressively invest in marketing communications than during a recession.

Product Quality Better Than Perception

In many categories, products and services are essentially at parity: consumers can perceive no major difference among them. That is because it is easy for a competitor to purchase and duplicate your new technology and hire away your best people and get to market with a reasonable facsimile of your new product fairly quickly. So if your product or service has a genuine and sustainable point of difference, and consumers care about that difference, then marketing communications can make a big difference. You simply concentrate on getting the news out about the important differences and their benefits.

If your company is in the habit of perpetual research and development to create authentically different and superior products, not just me-too knockoffs, then it is in your best interest to make sure your target customers know about them. Just make sure the difference is easy for customers to see, is easy for you to explain, and has an obvious benefit the consumer cares about. That's why companies that sell chunky spaghetti sauce switched to clear glass jars to show the big chunks of tomatoes. The transparency "advertised" the important product difference. If your company actually has a genuinely superior product or service, you are insane not to communicate it.

Low Awareness of a Great Product

If customers who try your product love it enough to buy more again and again, then you can increase sales by making prospective customers aware of your brand name. Get your name out with brand advertising that emphasizes your name to likely prospects and induces more people to try your product, and you're off to the races. The advertising will multiply the positive effect of word of mouth and of trial.

Stumbles by Competitors

When competitors stumble, it's a rare opportunity to seize market share. Perhaps they had a major product recall, or their CEO got caught with his hand in the till, or they had to request a government bailout, or they received a major fine, or they are closing offices or ending products. Maybe they extended their brand into a product area where it doesn't belong. Maybe they are acquired by a company that lets the product or company languish. Maybe they have cut back on sales staff or pulled back on advertising. Whichever way they stumble, be prepared to move in quickly with a marketing campaign that takes advantage of the weakness.

FOR EXAMPLE

FIND THE SILVER LINING IN A COMPETITOR'S CLOUD

One bank client with which I worked knew that a major local competitor had just been purchased by a large national bank. They knew that the competitor would soon revise the signage, the checks, and the service fees, and that some convenient neighborhood locations would be closed down. So they prepared a geographically targeted direct mail, newspaper, and radio campaign so they were ready to take advantage of disgruntled and uncertain customers who lived and worked around their competitor's retail locations. Since people rarely switch checking accounts, this was a rare marketing opportunity—one that really paid off for them as tons of customers switched to my client.

Your Product Sells Itself

If your product or service is clearly superior in ways that are important, and it is selling itself and generating great word of mouth, then that is one of the most lucrative times to advertise. The advertising serves as a multiplier of all the good experiences and word of mouth, generating more and more trials, faster and faster. For the same reasons, avoid advertising a bad or inferior product or service.

Crisis

A crisis is one of those moments of truth when people pay more attention to your product or service or to the situation of people or society. Tylenol is a great example of a brand that grew

> **SMART MANAGING**
>
> ### INVEST IN WINNERS, DON'T SHORE UP LOSERS
>
> Advertising is a multiplier. It multiplies the sales of winning products and damages the sales of bad products. Because you want the highest return on your marketing communications investment, don't try to salvage loser products or increase sales during natural downtimes or pour money into underperforming locations. Back your winners and make more money.

stronger as a result of a crisis. If your company suffers a crisis, it is important to get the word out, especially to the news media. It is imperative to always tell the truth and to hide nothing reporters might uncover.

If there's a crisis elsewhere, you can help out the victims and gain an advantage. Donating your product or service to the victims of a flood, a fire, or any other catastrophe can help build your brand in the eyes of prospective customers. The news coverage that often accompanies a crisis causes people to pay more attention to your company name, products, and advertising and to get a positive impression of your brand because of your generosity.

Don't forget to communicate to your employees if your company is going through a crisis. Their word-of-mouth opinions can have a powerful effect in such times. (See more about crisis management in the chapter on public relations.)

Business Category in a Growth Stage

If your company is part of a new product category that is rapidly growing, such as when the first personal computers hit the market or when pizza delivery started getting hot, it is imperative that you promote the category to grow sales and that you emerge as the perceived market leader. It's more important to be perceived as the market leader or to be the first name to come to mind than it is to be the technical leader.

The best way to do this is to grow sales and market share. That's what made Xerox synonymous with copiers and Kleenex synonymous with tissues and IBM synonymous with computers and i-Pod synonymous with downloadable music. If your name represents the category, you must invest in creating the perception as the first and best-known market leader. You will only have one chance to do this.

Market Shakeout Stage

New business categories typically start out with many competitors. Eventually, a few of them emerge to vie for the top spot, and the rest go out of business. This is known as the *shakeout period*. The brand that is perceived as the market leader at this stage will not only survive, but also likely retain the top spot for a long, long time. So it's worth it to invest in increasing sales and market share and building name recognition at this time. Many

> **KEY TERM** **Shakeout period** The stage in the development of a business category when the number of competitors is significantly reduced. During this critical period, a few market leaders emerge, and the losers go out of business.

of the brands we take for granted today triumphed over many competitors during their shakeout phase, in some cases over a hundred years ago.

Achieve Market Leadership

If your brand is fortunate enough to attain the number-one spot after a shakeout period, or if you have been in a neck-and-neck horse race and you pull ahead, it's a good time to advertise your leadership. Make sure that when you do, you also state a key reason or benefit why people prefer your company over your competitors. This is a chance to solidify your lead.

Competitive Attack

When a competitor, old or new, significantly increases its investment in marketing communications, you must be prepared to match or exceed the competitor's media levels, depending on your share of market. Otherwise, over time, the competitor's brand-name awareness will grow and yours will shrink. Eventually, your low awareness will drive your sales down, especially with new and prospective customers.

If the competitor's advertising is a direct challenge or a direct attack on your brand, think carefully about what your response will say. The competitor may be attempting to bait you into a contest you will lose. The worst scenario here is when competitors start a price war and advertising temporarily drives prices down to unrealistic levels. This tends to benefit the largest and most financially solid players. Wal-Mart has been known to do this when it moves into a town.

New Target Market

If you are taking your same product into a new target market, you must treat it as a new product introduction, with the appropriate level of spending necessary to raise brand awareness if you want to meet the sales goals you set. After all, prospective customers have never heard of you, and they don't know why they should even care about a message from you or about your product or service.

Seasonality or Event Trigger

Many products and services have peak times or peak seasons. It is often best to advertise prior to and during these seasons, when people are considering purchasing. The best time to sell is when people are ready to buy, and that is also the best time to advertise. A hurricane warning is a great time to advertise plywood and duct tape. The Christmas buying season often accounts for up to 80 percent of annual sales for some products. Valentine's Day is big for chocolates. One of my clients, a car repair franchise, maintained a series of localized, ready-to-run advertising and PR campaigns that would be triggered by weather events. At the first sign of freezing temperatures, for example, it ran ads to winterize cars. Some products also have a peak time of day for purchase, such as coffee from a convenience store.

Unanticipated Customer Needs

There are products and services, such as auto glass repair, garage door repair, and cardiac care, that no one wants to think about purchasing.

FOR EXAMPLE

Numbers Slip, Letters Stick

If you advertise on the radio, remember that most people who hear your ads will not be ready with pen and pencil to jot down your number and not many of us can memorize seven or 10 digits that we hear once or twice. Smart marketers try to find a phone number that is more memorable as letters, such as 1-800-FLOWERS or 1-888-COOKIES. Those configurations will stick in the mind better than 1-800-356-9377 or 1-888-266-5437,

But if you provide such products or services, make sure yours is the name that people remember if the time comes. This type of marketing communications is about name recall and phone number recall, and often involves the use of jingles and other memory devices. This usually calls for a year-round communications presence.

Market Gap

Through market research, you can identify product or benefit gaps in the marketplace. If you create and test a product that successfully fills this

KEY TERM
Market gap An opportunity to sell a product or service that prospective customers need and that no other company is providing.

gap, and you have identified a target audience for the product, it pays to get the word out loud and fast. This will give you a head start on me-too competitors.

Sell Across or Up

The most profitable target group to which you can advertise is your current customers. It is almost always a good idea to communicate with them regularly and offer them opportunities to buy other products or services from you. Just make sure you manage their contacts in a database and measure the results. Too much contact or the wrong offers will anger and alienate them. Not enough contact leaves money on the table. Customer relations or customer database management is almost always a good idea.

PERFECT THE PITCH

A friend told me about a marketing letter he'd received that caused him to eliminate that company from his considered list. It began with "We respect your intelligence" and continued with similar flattery. Then, at the bottom of the first page, which ended in the middle of a sentence, it read, "Please turn the page." My friend laughed—and stopped reading. What company would praise a prospect's intelligence and then assume that the prospect was not intelligent enough to turn the page for the rest of the sentence and whatever followed?

That line, "Please turn the page," was no doubt standard on all the marketing letters that company mailed. But it made no sense for that particular letter, which did more harm than good. If you want to market effectively, nothing is standard. If customers have choices, little things can carry big consequences.

Framing Marketing Expectations: Miracle Cure or Money Rathole?

Most businesspeople fall into three categories when it comes to marketing expectations. This is usually based on early personal experience. One group believes that marketing communications can save the company, like a magic wand. The people in this group have personally witnessed the power of marketing communications to drive sales up. One group is largely neutral. Marketing communications may or may not work well, depending on the competitive circumstances, the target market, and the budget available. And one group believes that marketing communications is a creative circus and a total waste of money. Those in this group have seen sales go down when advertising expenditures went up.

The reality is that they are all correct. As we mentioned earlier, studies of advertising results show a classic bell curve. A small group of the best advertisers outsell the worst by 600 percent, a small group of the worst advertisers drive sales down 50 percent, and the majority of advertisers don't move the needle much at all. So all the options are possible.

Why advertise at all then? Unfortunately, if you stop communicating with your target market, your sales eventually will go down (unless your communications and product are awful). Your challenge is to find a way to communicate with your market effectively and achieve the highest return on your marketing communications investment.

The Importance of Measuring Results

There was a time when advertisers could not measure the results of their ads. There is a famous quote by John Wanamaker, millionaire merchant—"Half the money I spend on advertising is wasted. The trouble is, I don't know which half."

Thanks to new mathematics, computers, bar code scanners, industry research firms, and so forth, it is now possible to measure the effects of your marketing communications. Sales, of course, are the result of many factors, not just advertising. A competitor's superior product or stepped-up advertising, bad weather, the aging of a target market, and all sorts of other factors can affect sales. Nevertheless, it is both possible and worthwhile to set measurable marketing communications goals and track results in an ongoing manner.

Marketing prospects vary dramatically from company to company and market to market. If you are an unknown David-sized company competing with long-established Goliaths, and you're selling a me-too product, and you can't spend much on advertising, and your target market is consumers around the world, your chances of success are lower. But if you are an unknown David-sized company in a fast-growing category with other David-sized companies, and you have a clearly superior product, and your target market is 15,000 hydraulic engineers on the East Coast, and you have enough money to get noticed, your chances of success are higher.

It is important as a marketing manager to manage the expectations of the people who approve your marketing budget. Using research and getting help from professionals, you can set realistic goals and expectations, measure your results, and adjust your strategies as you go. You can show the people in power numbers that show what they are getting in return for their marketing investment. This will provide a reality check for those whose expectations are too high and convince those whose expectations are too low.

"That Depends"

A classic marketing answer to any question is "that depends." Because marketing, like any human behavior, depends on a myriad of constantly changing factors, the results always depend on a number of variables.

No one can predict the future with 100 percent certainty. However, it is possible to make reasonable estimates. Most marketers lack the discipline to invest in regular tracking research. You can be the exception.

Manager's Checklist for Chapter 1

☑ Marketing communications is a lot more than "doing ads." Marketing communications is anything your organization does that affects the behavior or perception of your customers.

☑ Marketing communications can benefit both your company and your career in many ways.

☑ There are at least 18 classic business situations where marketing communications can have an above-average impact.

☑ Marketing results vary dramatically among competitors, categories, and campaigns. The best marketing communications outsell the worst by 600%. It pays to frame and manage internal expectations.

☑ Sales depend on many variables, but you can learn to make your marketing communications investments more effective by measuring the results of your efforts.

Don't Make
These Mistakes

The Hippocratic Oath, which is the traditional guide for physicians, contains the promise "to abstain from doing harm," which is commonly expressed as "First, do no harm." Before I continue offering guidance in marketing communications, I should offer a similar warning. First, make sure you're solving the right problem.

Many marketing communication campaigns begin in one of four ways:

- "Our sales are down—we need to (run some advertising, get some PR, offer a price promotion, etc.)."
- "Our competitor just started (going after our customers, advertising more, launching a new product, offering a price promotion), and we need to do what they're doing so we don't fall behind."
- "Our annual budget calls for us to do X amount of advertising. What we've done so far has worked, or at least there are no complaints, so let's do the same thing again."
- "We just hired a new (CEO, marketing director, brand manager, ad agency, graphic designer), and we need to bring some new thinking in here to improve things."

All these approaches are wrong. They are often attempting to solve the wrong problem. In some cases, they can actually make things worse. Let's look at them one at a time.

Our Sales Are Down! Run Some Ads *Now!*

There is good logic here. People won't try your product or service if they have never heard of it or if they have the wrong idea about it. Advertising can increase awareness and improve consumer attitudes if you have enough media dollars to stand out above the clutter and if you have a good product or a good promotional offer.

But the first step is to figure out why your sales are down.

If sales are down because this is a time when customers usually don't buy, you're better off saving your money and then spending more to advertise when they are ready to buy. For example, you can spend a lot of money advertising snow shovels in July and you might even sell some, but you're better off waiting until late fall. Most businesses have peak seasons when it makes sense to increase advertising. It makes sense to advertise more just before peak buying season, when customers are thinking about what they plan to buy later.

If sales are down because you have a problem with your product, you are better off temporarily cutting back on your advertising until you fix the problem. Otherwise, you get more people to try your product and that means more people have a bad experience. This can actually drive sales down and damage your brand reputation long term. You'd be amazed how quickly bad news travels among dissatisfied customers.

If sales are down because you have an inferior advertising campaign, you are better off temporarily cutting back on your advertising until you fix the advertising. Some studies show that the worst ads actually drive sales down as much as 50 percent every time they run!

GREAT ADVERTISING CAN KILL

Great advertising sells more. That's wonderful—if customers react favorably to your products. But if you're selling a product that's going over poorly, great advertising can kill it.

If there's a major problem with a product or service, cut back on your advertising and fix the product. When the problem is resolved, advertise again. Announce that the problem is fixed. Customers will be shocked by your honesty. If you can't fix the problem, drop the product. The more you sell of that product, the more damage you'll do—not only to the product, but also to your brand.

Use research to make sure your ads are working and to make them work even better. You can rapidly test customer responses to your advertising. The problem may be the strategy, the offer, the visuals, the wording, the call to action (what you want them to do), the company or product name, or the tone and manner or personality of the ads. The problem may be that your ads are getting attention but not relevant, or relevant but not unexpected.

> **KEY TERM**
>
> **Call to action** What you want customers to do when they see your ad. Do you want them to be aware of your name, think of your product as the most technologically advanced, find out more information, request a sales visit, order a free sample, try your product, or buy more of it more often? All ads contain the implied call to action of "buy this product." Try to use the call to action that offers the prospect the most benefit for the least risk. Be realistic.

Ads can be tested for positive and negative cues—tiny verbal and visual details that can make or break an ad. Your ads may even be offensive or irritating, and your customers are voting with their wallets.

In rare cases, people may get tired of the same ads over and over again. A poorly managed customer mailing list, for example, can mean mailing key customers the same offers too many times. In cases like this, it pays to control the frequency of contact. You can use research to measure the *wear-out* of a campaign. The best campaigns can run for years without wearing out because they are unexpected or because they are continuously refreshed with new variations on the old theme. But if customers are sick of seeing them, running more ads can actually do damage. (Much more common however, is not running ads long enough, or changing them too soon because you're sick of them.)

> **MISTAKE PROOFING**
>
> **TEST YOUR CUES**
> Cues are what prospects use to draw conclusions about an ad or a product. Cues are how they form perceptions. Before they buy a product, they look for positive cues that it will fulfill their desires and negative cues that it will harm or disappoint them. The most effective products, names, and ads have more positive cues than negative cues. Cues are rarely obvious, except in retrospect. They can be uncovered through testing.

Promotions in which you

SPLIT-RUN COPY TEST

TRICKS OF THE TRADE

One simple method of testing advertising, direct response, has been around for over a hundred years. You use a call to action (e.g., "For more information ..." or "To order ...") and reply cards, phone numbers, or e-mail addresses.

Here's an example. To test one or more variables in a direct mailer, you mail out two versions of the mailer, each version with a different phone number or e-mail address to every other household. Then track the inquiries or orders that come in for each number or address.

If you want to test the results from advertising in several magazines, you place a print ad in each, with different contact information, and track the responses that come from each magazine.

reduce prices, offer a gift, or provide a discount are good when used in moderation, as part of an overall brand-building campaign. A good promotion can usually generate an immediate spike in sales.

But if you run promotions every time sales slack, the promotional offer can become a kind of addiction that destroys

THINK BENEFITS

SMART

To get customers to act, you must promise them a benefit— a positive outcome or feeling. The benefit can be expressed **MANAGING** positively ("Increase your income!") or negatively ("Avoid painful hemorrhoids!"). The benefit can be physical ("Lose weight!") or emotional ("Look and feel great!"). Most ads contain a benefit statement.

the value of your brand. In essence, you are teaching customers to pay less for your brand by waiting to buy until you run a sale. Customers who regularly hunt for bargains are usually quite fickle. They will jump to your com-

BE WARY OF WEAR-OUT

CAUTION

If you advertise in the same way too often and/or for too long, people will pay less and less attention to your ads. In extreme cases of wear-out, your ads will irritate potential customers. Wear-out can be tracked and measured, so you can minimize it.

A far more common error is to change a campaign too soon because you are tired of it. To avoid this *inverse wear-out*, pay more attention to the perspective of potential customers. You know the expression, "The customer is always right." You may agree or not—but nobody ever says, "The marketer is always right."

What's the Frequency?

Make sure you are advertising with the right frequency. You can test this by experimenting with different media levels and watching the results. While it is possible that your advertising is worn out, it is far more likely that you will get sick of it long before your potential customers will. One of the consistently stupidest things marketers do is abandon an advertising campaign that is working because they are tired of it or often because someone else created it.

Promotion Attempt to increase sales through advertising and/or special offers, usually to induce customers to act right away. Benefits include gifts ("Buy one and get a free toaster!"), lower prices ("After-Christmas Sale!"), and discounts ("Save 50%!"). Promotional advertising is very different from brand advertising, which is intended to increase the perceived value of your brand now and in the future.

petitors when your competitors undercut your price. They will not become the profitable long-term customers you want.

Research can tell you if you are attracting fickle customers or first-time customers who will profitably continue to buy from you. In categories where promotions run rampant among competitors, the profitability of all companies in the category declines. Customers come to expect promotional offers and discounts. So, running a lot of promotional advertising can actually damage your long-term brand value and reduce the price customers are willing to pay.

Your advertising budget and market share may be too small to justify increasing advertising media expenditures. There is a minimum threshold of spending for each market and each medium. If you fall below the threshold, you are better off using the money elsewhere, because you will not get enough attention.

If your chief competitor is well known, has twice your product distribution, and spends 1,500 percent more on advertising media than you, it may be smart to invest in another area of your business or concentrate your media dollars to get over the threshold. For example, you could concentrate your dollars on selling your product to dealers (a lot fewer of them than consumers), or concentrate your media on a few key geographies, or concentrate spending on a few key dates or a special event, or concentrate your media dollars on a single medium that you can dominate.

So, it is possible that increasing ad spending may be the answer to your problem of low sales, but it is also possible that it is ill advised.

Our Competitor Is Doing It—Let's Do It Too

There is only one thing more wasteful than imitating your competitor's advertising, and that is imitating the market leader's advertising. The logic goes something like this. "They are the market leader. What they are doing is successful. Therefore, if we do what they are doing, we will be successful too.

Unfortunately, you are not following the leader; you are putting yourself right in the path of the leader. Imitating the market leader is not simply playing a game of follow-the-leader. It's the marketing communications equivalent of choosing to go one on one with the world heavyweight champion.

Here's why imitation or "me too" advertising is a bad idea.

If your advertising is really similar in tone, manner, and content to the market leader's advertising, your target market is likely to attribute your advertising to the leader, not to you. That's because the leader already "owns" that type of advertising inside the customers' heads. If you run a focus group, members may even "remember" your ad as bearing your competitor's logo. You are, in effect, investing dollars in advertising your competitor.

Customers are creatures of habit. Once a brand becomes a market leader, people are very reluctant to change their perceptions.

Once a competitor has more than about one-fifth of the market, you must spend disproportionately more to even be noticed. The larger their distribution and the smaller your distribution, the larger their unaided aware-

KEY TERMS

Unaided awareness Extent to which consumers think of a company, a product, or a service in terms of "top-of-mind." To assess *unaided* awareness, we might ask, "When you think of companies that sell X, which one comes to mind first?"

Aided awareness Extent to which consumers are familiar with a company, a product, or a service. To assess *aided* awareness, we might ask, "How familiar are you with company X— very familiar, somewhat familiar, or unfamiliar?"

ness and the smaller your unaided awareness; and the larger their media budget, the more you will have to outspend them in media dollars just to be noticed.

The only way to be noticed today is to be different, be unexpected, and stand out. So your best strategy is actually to differentiate your advertising as much as possible from what the market leader is emphasizing or doing to advertise. You have to carve out your own niche in the customers' minds and own that niche.

Any major point of difference between what you offer and what your competitors offer that customers care about is worth advertising.

Therefore, don't do something just because your competitors are doing it. Do something because your competitors are *not* doing it. No guts, no glory. Stand out!

SMART MANAGING

OFFER SOMETHING BETTER AND DIFFERENT

In your advertising, say something worth paying attention to, and say it in an interesting way. This includes useful information about new and better products. But make sure it is important to customers and it stands out. To most consumers, there are very few significant differences among products or services or among suppliers. If you offer an important difference, shout it out!

We Do This Every Year—Don't Rock the Boat

A lot of marketing communications strategies are driven more by the annual budget, the past fiscal year, and habit than by current problems or opportunities in the marketplace. The company allocates a certain percentage of sales to a marketing communications budget—and that's that. The problem with this approach is that it fails to take into account changes in the marketplace that may require more spending or allow spending less. It not only misses problems; it also misses opportunities.

For example, if a major competitor dials up its advertising spending or introduces a better product, you are wise to adjust your marketing game plan, including your spending strategy. By the time you feel the effects of the changes in customer perception on your sales, it's too late. The best marketers retain some flexibility.

Perhaps the greatest cost of a fixed budget lies in missed opportuni-

DARE TO DEVIATE

A regional accounting firm approached my ad agency with a request "to stand out from the pack." They showed us a collection of brochures from their competitors. Each had four-color photos of people in business suits shaking hands in mahogany board rooms. Each showed hard-working multiethnic teams staring at a computer screen. Each had computer-generated charts and graphs. Each talked about partnership and integrity and blah blah blah. The brochures were virtually identical. So were the Web sites.

Our agency came up with an approach that was radically different. We created a very unexpected but logical tagline (about black ink—accounting image of profitability) and a visual idea that used only black ink on white paper. Most members of the management team wanted to reject it—it felt unprofessional to them to deviate from the industry norm. But the president prevailed.

The accounting firm then ran with the idea by making all their stationery, bills, business cards, Web site, offices, and even ink pens black and white. They threw out all their four-color materials. One year later, the president attributed their 70 percent increase in income to the campaign. The moral: don't do what everyone else is doing.

ties. If a competitor stumbles, gets bought out, or makes a mistake that harms its reputation or decreases customer satisfaction in some way, it pays to dial up your advertising to its key customers. If there is a major unexpected event that spikes demand for your product, such as a snowfall when you sell snow tires, you are crazy not to take advantage of the opportunity. The smart marketer keeps a war chest ready for such contingencies.

Or what happens if an economic downturn is followed by an upturn, which always happens? Your advertising budget has been set lower because of last year's sales and you are not in a position to take advantage of the better times.

In marketing, so many variables can affect sales, it is impossible to use the past to predict the future. Maintain a flexible strategy and an opportunistic mindset and you will prosper.

Welcome, New Players! Let's Make Some Improvements!

It's human nature to want to make your mark on something. It's human nature to believe your ideas are better than those of others. It's natural, but human nature has destroyed many a proven and effective advertising campaign.

It is extremely difficult to create an advertising campaign that works. On average, across categories, the hardest-working campaigns actually generate about 600 percent more sales than the least effective campaigns. That is one huge competitive advantage. So you would think that businesspeople who inherit a proven advertising campaign would protect it at all costs.

But you would be wrong.

Far more typical is for the new brand manager or advertising agency or creative team to feel saddled with the old campaign. They are sure they can make it better. And so, out with the old and in with the new. The original team members, who know about the brand, the strategy, the consumer, and the research, leave, and their knowledge and commitment to the campaign leave with them.

SMART   **STAY FLEXIBLE**
WITH FINANCES
Keep contingency funds available for unexpected prob-
MANAGING   lems and, even better, for
unexpected opportunities. Or have an understanding with your management that there will be times when significant expenditure is required, such as when you launch a new brand.

This is an extraordinary waste.

All the dollars of research and testing and advertising creation, all the equity built up in the minds of the consumer, all the familiarity with the brand, and all the reduced risk that a proven campaign offers—it is all thrown out the window.

This is not only bad financial management, because effective campaigns have positive effects, both short term—increased sales—and long term—increased brand equity. Customers build a feeling or belief about the brand, much as you build the equity in your home with each payment. Constant advertising change-ups are confusing and potentially damaging to the customers. Companies that change their brand managers, ad agencies, and campaigns will frequently end up with no brand equity and higher creative costs. The effect of these changes is that it causes customers to wonder about the company. What is this brand? Who are these people? What do they stand for?

Smart Marketing Mindset: The Continuous Experiment

Think of your marketing communications as a continuous research experiment with the objective of achieving the highest return on investment. This mindset will prevent you from making the four common mistakes listed above.

Take direct mail marketing as a model. Direct mail has been around for over 100 years. The beauty of direct mail is that the results can be measured, so different strategies and creative packages can be compared.

The best direct marketers are constantly testing new improved versions of the winner against the current winner. They test on a small scale, and only when they find something that performs better than the winner do they make adjustments to the new campaign and roll it out to the entire target market. This is equivalent to sticking your toe in the water to see how cold it is before you dive in. It is just plain smart.

AVOID THE NIH SYNDROME

CAUTION

NIH stands for *not invented here*. Brand managers and creatives tend to throw out advertising campaigns that they did not invent, even if those campaigns are working. But if a campaign has proved effective, the wise manager and the ethical creative (writer or art director) continue the work that others have begun. Don't abandon your winners, whatever their source.

Direct marketers also know that a great campaign can be effective for years, in some cases even decades. And they know that things change in the marketplace and that periodically a campaign needs to be refreshed or reinvented. So they constantly test new approaches on a small scale. If you use research wisely, you can apply this same *ongoing experiment model* to most of your marketing and advertising.

Manager's Checklist for Chapter 2

☑ Don't advertise only when there is a sales slump.

☑ Don't advertise only when a competitor increases its advertising.

☑ Don't base this year's budget on last year's sales. Prepare for current and future threats and opportunities.

☑ Don't throw out a good campaign just because it was developed by other marketers.

☑ Think of your marketing communications as a continuous research experiment with the objective of achieving the highest return on investment.

Planning—
Step by Step

I mentioned earlier that you should think of your marketing communications as a continuous research experiment with the objective of achieving the highest return on investment. One good way to do this is to use the 12-Step Marketing Planning Process presented in this chapter.

But we need to start with the big picture—aligning your marketing with your business.

Define a Realistic Business Communications Objective

Most businesspeople either underestimate or overestimate the benefit of marketing communications. A rare few have a realistic set of expectations for their specific situation. Most people's expectations of marketing are based on early career experience.

All three points of view have a basis in reality. In many business categories, the same bell curve applies. (See Figure 3-1.)

A minority of ad campaigns are the best at generating sales results. They outsell the worst campaigns by up to 600 percent! This is equivalent to the difference between the top of a 110-story building and a pit in the ground 20 stories deep. A minority of ad campaigns are the worst in sales results. They can drive sales down as much as 50 percent every time they run. They live

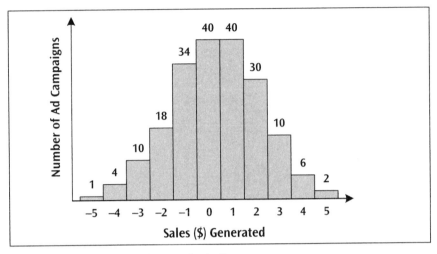

Figure 3-1. Advertising sales results bell curve

at the bottom of the pit. The vast majority of ad campaigns are somewhere in the middle, neither increasing nor decreasing sales significantly. This classic bell-curve distribution of results is why some managers believe advertising doesn't work, some believe it can save the company, and some believe something in between those extremes.

Your business communications objective is to move the results of your brand communications from your current spot on the curve toward the far right end of the curve. Eventually you want your brand to have that competitive advantage of a 600 percent return on advertising. The first step is to reasonably set your expectations and goals should be adjusted to your specific situation. Use the checklist on the next page to set your communications expectations.

When to Advertise: The Best of Times, the Worst of Times

Timing can have a strong effect on the results of your marketing communications. It is tempting to advertise during sales slumps and off-season in order to make your budget numbers. But to get the highest return on your investment, advertise when your customers are considering a purchase or making a purchase. In some industries, 80 percent of sales occur within less than 10 percent of the year.

MARKETING EXPECTATIONS CHECKLIST

TOOLS

What expectations would be reasonable for your particular situation? Pick a marketing communications opportunity, run it through this checklist, and invest accordingly.

For items marked "1-2," award yourself one point for each true answer or an extra point if your answer has been verified by market research. For other items, follow the instructions.

____ 1-2: Overall, the number of customers and the dollar volume of sales are increasing in your business category every year.

____ 1-2: Your product has a clear, easy-to-understand benefit and a simple story.

____ 1-2: Your product benefit is essential to survival. People can't do without it.

____ 1-2: People enjoy thinking about your category and subject area.

____ 1-10: Your brand name is well known by people in the target market. (Score 1 point for every 10 percent of your targets who can recall your brand name unaided; e.g., if 90 percent, score 9 points.)

____ 1-10: Your target prospects have the right attitude toward your product. (Score 1 point for every 10 percent of your targets who have the right attitude; e.g., if 80 percent, score 8 points.)

____ 1-10: Your target prospects have tried your product and would recommend it to their friends or would buy it again. (Score one point for every 10 percent of your targets who have tried and liked it; e.g. if 50 percent, score 5 points.)

____ 1-2: Your product has a genuine positive difference from competitors that people care about.

____ 10: Your product has no significant competitors (or none that are advertising or well known). (Score 10 points.)

____ 1-2: Your product difference will be hard for your competitors to duplicate (i.e., you have a head start).

____ 0-20: Rate your market share or distribution. (Score 2 points for every 10 percent of your share; e.g., if 40 percent, score 8 points.)

____ 0-25: Rate your media spending. (If you are #1, 25 points. If #2, 20 points. If #3, 15 points. If #4, 10 points. If #5, 5 points. If #6 or lower, 0 points.)

____ 1-2: You are advertising at the beginning of the peak buying season

____ 1-2: Your target market is concentrated and easy to reach via media (one region, one town, one neighborhood, one trade association, one advertising medium).

_____ 1-2: Your target market prospects can easily afford your product.

_____ 1-2: Your product costs 10 percent to 30 percent less than the nearest competitor.

_____ 1-2: Your product is important or interesting to the target market.

_____ 1-2: Your brand or company or category already has a good reputation with customers.

_____ 1-2: You are introducing a genuinely new and improved product or technology.

_____ 1-2: Your product name is memorable, with positive emotional associations.

_____ 1-2: Your company has a history of investing in successful marketing communications campaigns.

_____ 1-2: Your marketing communications will be reviewed and approved by no more than two layers of management and no more than five people.

_____ 1-2: Your company culture encourages being innovative and creative, taking risks, and standing out over playing it safe and appearing "professional."

Marketing Expectations Checklist—Scoring

Total your points.

0-38: Lower your expectations. Think twice. You are fighting an uphill battle.

39-79: Expectations of success are reasonable. Proceed with caution.

80-117: Raise your expectations. You have a great shot at success.

Great Times to Advertise

- Just before your peak buying season
- During your peak buying season
- During a recession
- For a relevant holiday (e.g., candy before Valentine's Day and Easter, barbeque grills before July 4)
- When your customer comes into money (e.g., payday, IRS refund check, end of fiscal year)
- When your customer has a life-changing event (e.g., move, new baby, retirement, first job, kids graduate, marriage)
- At a trade show
- At an enthusiast group meeting (e.g., sell muskets at a convention of Civil War re-enactors)
- When a prospect asks for information

- When a customer purchases your product (cross-sell your other products)
- When a prospect begins thinking about a future purchase (before your peak season)
- When your competitors don't have a competitive product
- When weather triggers sales (e.g., windshield wipers during the rainy season, swimsuits during the first warm summer days)
- When people are bored or waiting around
- When a competitor stumbles, goes out of business, gets bought out, raises its prices or fees, changes its name, or pulls out of the area
- When your customer can't afford to have a problem that your product prevents (e.g., machine lubricants during peak manufacturing times)
- When there is extensive news coverage about a problem your product prevents or reduces (e.g., insecticide during a weevil infestation, safe investments during a Wall Street meltdown)

Bad Times to Advertise

- When there is a problem with your product or service
- When demand slumps (off-season)

Use Web Traffic to Spot Peak Advertising Opportunities

TRICKS OF THE TRADE

To the surprise of the prom dress industry, information supplied by data-mining research firms showed that high school girls were doing extensive online searching on prom dresses and related topics in certain winter months— long before the traditional spring/summer prom season.

- When a competitor is significantly outspending you in media (you're more likely to get drowned out)
- When your customers have fewer dollars to spend
- When you are pulling back on products, services, locations, employment
- When customers are not naturally thinking about your product area (e.g., snowshoes in the summer)
- When you are getting a lot of negative publicity that calls into question the honesty of your message or company or makes your promise seem false.

Savvy marketers keep a finger on the pulse of the marketplace and an eye on their competitors, and they advertise at the best time.

What to Advertise: Lead with Your Strong Suit

It is tempting to advertise products that aren't selling as well as hoped. This is a mistake. Advertising will only accelerate the demise of your worst products. Instead, focus ad dollars on winners. This will give you the highest return on your marketing investment. You want to put out the sweetest honey to attract the most bees. There are three kinds of product honey to feature in your advertising:

1. **Your best sellers:** By definition, your best sellers have the strongest appeal for the most people. Advertise and promote your best sellers, and then offer your buyers a chance to purchase other products or services. You can even promote your weaker selling products or services on coupons that you give customers who purchase your best seller(s). But don't lead with your weak seller, fewer people will be interested enough to notice or to act.

2. **Your top-of-the-line dream product.** Even if few people actually buy it, it is possible that many more people will be attracted to it. Your best and perhaps most expensive product or service represents the most compelling dream that people carry in the back of their heads in your market category. The fairy dust of your best offerings rubs off on your other offerings giving them added value and extra cachet. Once again, the best product pulls them in, and then you should make it easy for them to buy your more affordable products. There is an unspoken assumption in advertising that advertisers always put their best foot forward. If you feature a more mediocre variant of your product, you will decrease the selling power of your ads. You will pull fewer people through the door.

SMART MANAGING

DON'T PUSH YOUR LOSERS
For better advertising results, feature your best-sellers, your top-of-the-line dream products, or a promotional offer. Don't flaunt your losers.

3. **A promotional offer.** If you choose to offer a sale, a discount, or a gift with your product or service as an incentive to act now, you are gen-

erally better off featuring the promotional offer over what the consumer will be buying, both visually and in the headline. Once again, the promotional offer entices customers to consider purchasing your other products.

Integrate All Your Products, Services, and Communications

We innately distrust inconsistent chameleons who tell us whatever we want to hear, and we don't like people who say one thing and do another. And yet companies and brands commit this sin all the time. The advertising promises one thing, and the product or services deliver another. Examples are all around us:

- The product provides a caring benefit, but the toll-free customer service number has a surly operator who is anything but helpful and polite.
- The food looks great in the menu and lousy on the plate.
- The corporate vision is to preserve capital for investors, but the news reports that greedy managers lined their own pockets.
- The celebrity spokesperson is hip and trendy, but the package design is dated.
- The brand promise is "personal," but the company name sounds "corporate."
- One division of the company sells baby formula to mothers, and the other sells weapons to developing nations.

DON'T SEND MIXED MESSAGES

Every experience your customers have with your brand—the company, the people, the products or services, the news coverage—sends a message about you. Make sure you don't compete with yourself. Make sure every experience supports your central promise as a company.

This promise is your positioning. To deliver on a positioning, every single aspect of the company must be integrated, working together toward a single powerful promise.

And make sure the personality of your company remains consistent as well. No one likes doing business with a split personality.

- This year's ad campaign is on another planet from last year's campaign.
- The logo on this ad is different from the logo on the Web site.

To a prospective customer, every experience with your company is a message. These messages can all add up to a single powerful message or promise—or they can undercut each other and create confusion.

UNDERPROMISE, OVERDELIVER

If you promise more than you deliver, you are teaching your target customers not to trust your communications. If you deliver on your marketing promises and more, you will delight your target customers and win their loyalty. You are expected to put your best foot forward, but don't put your foot in your mouth.

The same thing is true of your marketing communications. Make sure your brand promise, brand personality, message strategy, and campaign idea are integrated across all media. The cumulative effect of this repetition in different media is greater than the sum of its parts. When customers keep getting the same consistent message about your brand, they notice it more and they believe it more.

The most powerful advertising campaigns are driven by a central idea, the "big idea." A big idea consists of variations on a theme. The variations are usually different executions or examples that support the same conclusion. The theme helps hold it all together, so that you build long-term equity for your brand in the consumers' minds every time you run any of your ads.

The most powerful brands are integrated in all aspects: company mission, vision, values, culture, positioning, branding, messaging, and advertising. Hard to do, but well worth the effort.

Results: You Can't Manage What You Can't Measure

Remember the statement by John Wannamaker, quoted in Chapter 1: "Half the money I spend on advertising is wasted; the trouble is, I don't know which half."

That statement is still true today for most marketers, unfortunately. Fortunately, it doesn't *have* to be true.

Thanks to gigantic leaps in data generation, collection, and processing, and to improvements in mathematical and research techniques, it is now possible to use research to get an accurate picture of most stages of the marketing process, including contributions to the bottom line. Thanks to recent developments in massive database crunching, it is also possible to make behavioral projections with greater accuracy.

The capacity to measure the effect of advertising variables on sales has actually been available since the invention of the *split-run copy test* in direct mail (described in Chapter 2). An ad in a newspaper or in a magazine is printed in two or more slightly different versions, each coded with a different return address (e.g., Box 40, Box 41, Box 42) or a different phone number. Doing this at a sufficient scale (reaching a certain number of people) cancels out the effect of other variables, and you know which version of the ad pulled the most results, which variable was most effective. With new mathematical models, it's possible to test recipes (multiple variables) at the same time.

Amazingly, the vast majority of businesses do very little rigorous market research. They make decisions about price, location, product design, packaging, service, brand strategy, message strategy, and advertising based on history or gut feel, not any objectively measured reality. They could significantly reduce the risk of their marketing investment by testing the waters before they take a plunge. After all, you can't manage what you can't measure.

> **KEY TERM**
>
> **Split-run testing** A marketing technique for comparing two or more variables—versions of an ad, different offers, or separate lists—to determine which is more or most effective. In a split test, two or more versions of an ad are printed, two or more offers are made, or two or more lists are used for the same market target group, each with a call for action. The results for each variation are tabulated and then compared.

We'll talk in more detail about market research in Chapter 15. In the meantime, be the smart marketer who uses research to stay in touch with reality.

12-Step Marketing Planning Process

At the beginning of Chapter 2, we noted that many marketers are reactive. They jump straight to tactics ("Let's run an ad!") as a reaction to a sales decline or a competitor's move. Or they react to last year's sales in designing this year's budget. Or they react to a change in staff by throwing everything out and starting anew.

We also noted that approaching marketing as a continuous measured experiment is a better way to go. The 12-Step Marketing Planning Process outlined below (and shown in Figure 3-2) is a proven method of conducting this continuous experiment. Each step is built on the previous step. Each decision can be informed by market research.

Use this process rigorously every year and you can significantly improve your chances of a successful outcome. Human behavior and competitive behavior are far too complex and ever changing to offer a guarantee of success, but using this process can improve your odds.

We'll sketch out the process briefly here. It helps to assemble a summary of all the information and decisions into a single marketing document.

1. Review Brand, Target Market, Product, and Competitors

A savvy general doesn't begin a campaign until he has studied the lay of the land, the weather, and the size and strength of his own forces and of his enemy. In the same way, a savvy marketer assesses the state of his or her brand, target market, product, and competitors. A partial list of factors to look at includes:

- company strengths and weaknesses
- product strengths and weaknesses
- competitive strengths and weaknesses
- pricing
- distribution
- customer trends (fears, desires, behaviors)
- industry and technology trends
- environmental trends (culture, politics, society)
- media spending by competitors
- target market awareness, attitude, trial, and repeat purchase behaviors.

Data can come from various sources:

- secondary sources like published studies, government reports, books, and news sources
- business financial metrics
- primary research sources like quantitative and qualitative testing, trend reports, and database mining

It's important to look beyond your customer base and even your industry at this stage, to avoid missing huge new opportunities and to avoid being caught unaware and unprepared by changes in technology, society, or business models (e.g., consider Walmart, which left Sears in the dust).

2. Identify Problems and Opportunities

Once the information is collected, a picture begins to form of where challenges and opportunities are today and where they are likely to be in the near future. Often, the 80/20 Rule (Pareto's Law) applies. Twenty percent of the situations you identify will account for 80 percent of the profit opportunities, and another 20 percent will account for 80 percent of the problems you face. The heart of the matter is to identify your greatest strength relative to your competitors in terms of meeting the most important desires of your most important target market. In general, you are better off with strategies that focus on your strengths and take advantage of your opportunities than with strategies that attempt to negate your weaknesses or minimize problems.

3. Set Sales Goals

Based on your assessment of problems and opportunities, you can take a reasonable and realistic stab at setting measurable sales goals. The goal here is to be realistic, based on the data— neither too optimistic nor too pessimistic. You break out sales goals by what is being sold, by market segment, or by region.

4. Set Target Market Goals

Sales result from changes in target market perceptions and behaviors. For example, you may discover that your chief issue with marketing home equity credit lines to homeowners earning over $100,000 a year is their awareness of your brand name. You may decide to set a goal of increasing unaided awareness (that is, how many mention your name as a supplier of home equity credit lines without any prompting) from 23 percent to 26 percent within 12 months. Or you may discover you have adequate name awareness, but you need to increase the percentage of the people in your target market who believe your credit line is "the most affordable." Or the attitude may be just fine, but you need to increase first-time applicants for the credit line from 3 percent to 5 percent. Make sure these goals tie back realistically to your sales goals.

5. Determine Positioning and Branding Strategies

Your *positioning* is the place you occupy in the minds of the target market. Are you the friendly one, the safe one, the advanced one? A positioning statement answers three questions:

- Who is your target market?
- What do you do for your target customers?
- How are you different from your competitors?

Every facet of your business should support your positioning, from personnel to product design to advertising. Your positioning should rarely change over time, because once you stand for something, it is risky to try to stand for something else: people are very resistant to changing their perceptions. Research such as *perceptual mapping* can quantify your greatest area of competitive strength in the consumers' minds.

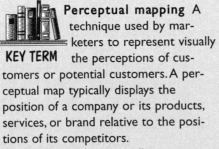

KEY TERM **Perceptual mapping** A technique used by marketers to represent visually the perceptions of customers or potential customers. A perceptual map typically displays the position of a company or its products, services, or brand relative to the positions of its competitors.

A perceptual map usually represents two dimensions by means of two axes crossing and forming four quadrants. For example, a marketer could map a brand in terms of perceived value (from low to high) and perceived price (from low to high).

Your *branding* is your brand character or brand personality. Here, you think of your company as if it were a person you were describing to someone. What personality characteristics does your company, brand, or culture have that make it different from your competitors? Are you fun and friendly? Or serious and safe? Or committed and dedicated? You can't be all things to all people. For some products, the chief difference to customers *is* the brand personality. Your personality should permeate all aspects of the customer experience.

6. Set Communication Goals

What measurable objectives will your marketing communications achieve? Reach 80 percent of your target market with the message six times within one month? Increase name recall 20 percent? Trigger powerful emotional memories of great Southern-fried meals in 40 percent of the TV commercial viewers? Increase Web site visits by 10 percent within the next three weeks? What communications goals do you have to achieve in order to hit your sales goals?

7. Integrate Tactics

There are a remarkable number of marketing and marketing communications tactics. Here is a partial list:

- Product design
- Retail store design and location
- Pricing
- Distribution
- Signage
- Naming
- Public relations
- Cause marketing
- Online marketing
- Direct response (mail, magazine, newspaper, online, infomercials)
- Advertising media (TV, radio, billboards, newspaper, magazine)
- Graphic design and collateral (brochure, menu, point of sale, packaging, corporate identity)
- Co-branding

New media and new marketing disciplines are being added every day. The goal is to take the most appropriate tactics and integrate them into a single plan with just the right mix of investments.

> **Guerrilla marketing** Use of unconventional approaches that require time, energy, and creativity rather than a big budget. The term was first used by Jay Conrad Levinson in *Guerrilla Marketing: Secrets for Making Big Profits from Your Small Business* (Houghton Mifflin, 1984).
>
> **KEY TERM**

8. Develop Marketing Plan (Dollars and Schedule)

Your plan should include a list of tactics, responsible parties, budgets, and timetables. Your marketing team may include people from disciplines and departments throughout your company, as well as a wide range of vendors.

9. Define Message Strategy

Message strategy guides the people who create your ads and the people who buy your advertising media. It is a short, highly focused document, usually on one side of one sheet of paper, that identifies the most powerful emotional message you can convey. A message strategy is the point of one communication to one target market. You usually need many different message strategies for different situations (different products, promotions, targets, etc.) and one overall message strategy that comprises them all. Message strategies can be tested with your target market.

I recommend using the Pitchperfect™ Message Strategy, a process that has been proven with thousands of ads for hundreds of clients since 1993. (This is the subject of Chapter 8.) Pitchperfect™ answers the following questions with provocative insightful one-line answers:

1. Who are we talking to?
2. What is the point of the communication?
3. What is the key word in the point?
4. Why should the target care about the point?
5. Why should the target believe the point?
6. How should the target feel about the message or product?
7. What do you want the target to do?

If you think about it, if you don't know or haven't tested the answers to these seven questions, you have no basis for choosing creative options. You don't really know what you're doing.

10. Do Creative Development

Once you have identified the most powerful message for a target market, you can begin the process of creating the advertising, publicity, or Web site. Rather than a series of individual ads (called "one-offs" in the trade), you want a series of ads unified around a theme or idea. You want an advertising campaign idea that is big enough to work across different media (billboards to radio to Web sites), big enough to work across topics (products, services, recruitment, etc.), and big enough to work over time. This is referred to as a "big idea."

It is not enough for your idea to be relevant. It must also be unexpected enough and engaging enough to break through the noisy clutter of competing ads. It is easy to create small ideas, relevant ideas, and unexpected ideas. But it is very hard to create a single idea that is also big, relevant, and unexpected.

Such ads are made for you by "creatives." Creatives are the copywriters, art directors, graphic designers, web designers, PR writers, directors, actors, musicians, photographers, illustrators, and animators who invent the words, pictures, sounds, and music in your advertising. Some creatives are more skilled at coming up with ideas, and others are more skilled at executing or producing the ideas. A big, well-executed creative idea is worth its weight in gold.

> **Creative** Any person involved in inventing the words, pictures, sounds, and music for advertising. Creatives include copywriters, art directors, graphic designers, web designers, PR writers, directors, actors, musicians, photographers, illustrators, and animators. **KEY TERM**

11. Decide on Media

While the creative team is coming up with the content of your advertising, your media team is identifying the best times and places and advertising media to reach your particular target market with that content. Media people think in terms of touchpoints—or ways in which you can reach your customers, ways for them to experience your brand.

Media is part art and part science. The media team members begin with data on where your customers are located, what they buy, what media they use, and when they use them.

They may look at market penetration and sales opportunities for different geographic areas and adjust the level of media (how much media) accordingly. They will set objectives of GRPs (gross rating

> **Touchpoint** Any interaction that your target has with your brand. (Also known as touch point, contact point, point of contact.) Each touchpoint is an opportunity for a positive experience or a negative experience. **KEY TERM**

points), which are a function of reach (how many people are reached) times frequency (how often). (So, for example, if you can reach 100 people five times, that's a GRP of 500.) They determine the minimum threshold of contact necessary to be noticed at all, given the amount of advertising to which people are exposed. They determine which times offer the greatest opportunities to affect your customers' intent to purchase. They make judgments about whether to provide a continuous flow of contact, or to amp up contact in concentrated bursts, or to do a combination of both.

KEY TERMS

Gross rating point A standard measure of potential advertising impact. It is calculated by multiplying the percent of the target market reached (1 percent equals one point) by the exposure frequency. Media planners use GRPs in developing a media schedule, usually to get the most points at the least cost.

Make-good Compensation for an ad that is not run according to your contract with the newspaper, magazine, direct mail list vendor, or radio or TV station. It is generally either a free run of your ad or a discounted rate for the next ad you run.

They price out the media options, consider different mixtures of media (the *media mix*), and make spending recommendations. Usually, most of your advertising dollars go toward media costs. They negotiate the best prices or the best benefits for you (such as a free live radio event), place the media orders, double-check to make sure every ad ran as planned, and negotiate any make-goods.

Finally, the ads that the creatives have designed are produced and shipped to the various media—and your campaign is off and running.

12. Analyze Results

You have already established your measurable goals in the areas of sales, target market attitudes and behaviors, and communications. Now you collect the data on the results. You then use the data to make adjustments in how you will approach things next year, when you begin again at step one.

Congratulations! Instead of flying by the seat of your pants, you've just used the rigorous step-by-step process for planning your marketing. Instead of reacting, you're treating your marketing communications as an ongoing experiment guided by measurable results. As a result, you can do a better job of managing. You've aligned your business and your marketing.

We'll look at each of these steps in more detail in later chapters. In the meantime, Figure 3-2 summarizes the steps covered in this chapter.

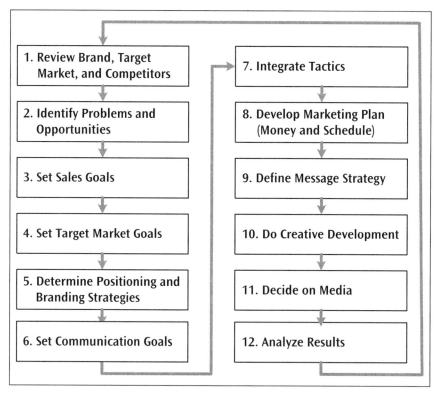

Figure 3-2. 12-Step Marketing Planning Process

Manager's Checklist for Chapter 3

☑ Think of your marketing communications as a continuous research experiment with the objective of achieving the highest return on investment.

☑ Use the 12-Step Marketing Planning Process.

☑ Adjust your expectations to the unique realities of your situation.

☑ Businesspeople tend to either overestimate or underestimate the results to be expected from their advertising.

☑ Know that there are better times to advertise and worse times to advertise.

☑ Measure various dimensions of your advertising, including the effect on sales.

Basic Principles of Marketing Communications Strategy

I f you read no other chapter in this book, read this one. You can have all the marketing tools and knowledge in the world, but if you have the wrong beliefs about how marketing works, how human beings work, or what to expect, you will likely make all the classic errors.

Marketing is an unnatural act.

It is unnatural and painful to suspend your core beliefs about reality and look at the world through the eyes of another with complete acceptance. It is unnatural and disturbing to become conscious of your own and others' deep subconscious motives. It is unnatural to deviate from what is known and professional and considered prudent and safe, especially if it is what your competitors are all doing. It is unnatural and kind of frightening to acknowledge that the target market has more power than your entire corporation. What they want to hear is more important than what you want to say.

But if you develop the capacity to engage in the unnatural act of marketing, you will be rewarded with more success. Paradoxically, by acknowledging the limits of your power and your perspective, you will gain the ability to have greater influence over your target audience.

The following principles are a combination of beliefs and practices

> **CAUTION**
>
> ### DON'T DRINK THE CORPORATE KOOL-AID®
>
> Often, in corporate meetings, especially those involving high-level, highly accomplished, highly educated executives, there is the unspoken assumption that through knowledge, discipline, and prudence you can control the behavior of your customers, much as you control finances or personnel or product engineering. But a mere nanosecond of subconscious decision making from the customers, whoever they may be, can collectively bring a high-powered corporation to its knees. Ultimately, everyone in your company reports to your customers' collective subconscious.

that have been proven to increase your chances of success. It's all about your point of view.

Principle One: Marketing is About Probabilities, Not Predictability

Human behavior is always a percentage, not an absolute. You cannot always count on human beings to do what you expect. This is because people have free will, they behave differently in different situations, and situations change unpredictably. There are even individuals whose primary motive in life is to resist authority and diverge from group expectations.

It is very possible to know what has worked in the past, if you measure results. And it is likely that what has worked in the past will work today or in the future, but there are no guarantees. In general, the larger the group of people studied and the longer the behavior has persisted, the more dependable the prediction.

The smart marketer knows that marketing is always an investment in a future with multiple variables, many of which cannot be controlled. And it is an investment with an

> **TRICKS OF THE TRADE**
>
> ### MARKETING IS AN UNNATURAL ACT
>
> The savviest marketers regularly force themselves to step outside their own nature and look at the world through the eyes and hearts and bodies of their customers. This involves temporarily suspending your fundamental beliefs about the world and accepting uncritically the beliefs and perceptions of your target audience, even if you disagree with them. This is hard to do at first, but you can develop this ability with practice.

uncertain return. It is possible to reduce the degree of uncertainty, but it is never possible to eliminate risk altogether. The smart marketer keeps this risk in mind with each decision.

Principle Two: When You Dance with the Customers, Let Them Lead

If customers want to buy red shoes, but you try to sell them white shoes because you have a lot of white shoes in inventory, you are not likely to succeed. Yet companies consistently try to impose their products and messages on their target markets. Why?

One of the reasons people rise to the top of corporations is because they have an above-average need for power and control. They like to make a dent in the world, and they find it deeply satisfying to see their impact on people and numbers. So it is hard for them to step aside and cede control to the customers. The next time you draw your organizational chart, put your customers at the top, above the president. In a way, everyone reports to the customers.

One way to let your customers lead is through market research. If you think of marketing communications as a conversation with your customers, then research is the part where you listen to what they like and don't like and your product and communications are the part where you get to talk. If you're smart, your product and communications will be strongly influenced by what the people in your target market have to say.

Principle Three: Integrate and Align Everything

Customers love consistency. They love knowing that the promises you made yesterday will be consistently kept today and tomorrow. They love the simplicity of knowing that what you stand for today is what you will stand for tomorrow. They love finding brands they can trust to deliver on what they expect.

Therefore, you should integrate everything. Integrate your product, price, promotion, and locations. Integrate your marketing promises and your product and service delivery. Integrate the messages you send out in every medium from every person in your company. Integrate the type of people that you hire. Integrate your positioning, branding, and messaging.

STRATEGIC ALIGNMENT	STRATEGIC ALIGNMENT
POSITIONING	POSITIONING
BRANDING	BRANDING
MESSAGING	MESSAGING
NAMING	NAMING

Figure 4-1. Out of and in strategic alignment

If you're the safe car brand, don't sell a convertible or sponsor a racecar or make fun of playing it safe. Integrate your design look, your slogan, your imagery, and the tone and manner or personality of your communications. Make sure everyone is singing from the same program. The term for this integration is *strategic alignment* (Figure 4-1).

Do your many strategies compete with each other and confuse the customer? Or do they line up and add up to the same conclusion?

The ideal is *integrated marketing communications*. This is when all aspects of your marketing communications programs are sending and reinforcing a single message. (See Chapter 5.)

> **KEY TERMS**
>
> **Strategic alignment** When mission, vision, values, corporate culture, positioning strategy, product strategy, pricing strategy, hiring strategy, brand strategy, message strategy, and creative strategy are all consistent. That is, they all add up to the same conclusion, and they don't contradict each other. Customers love companies with good strategic alignment. So do employees and stockholders.
>
> **Integrated marketing communications** When all aspects of the marketing communications programs, from product to messaging to creative details, fit together and reinforce a single overarching message in all media. Integrated communications are more effective than diverse or divergent communications, because they reinforce the message through repetition and consistency.

Principle Four: The Heart Trumps the Head

One of the fantasies of academia, economics, and corporate culture is that people behave rationally. But research has consistently shown that human behavior is more psychological than logical, and that, with rare exceptions, the heart trumps the head every time.

> ## TRAIN YOURSELF TO THINK EMOTIONALLY
> **TRICKS OF THE TRADE**
>
> Practice observing the behavior of people around you. Make guesses about their driving subconscious motivations. Then guess what they are likely to do next. Observe how often your guesses are correct, and learn from your mistakes. Keep practicing and you will develop the emotional radar that is essential in marketing.
>
> When you are listening to someone, ignore what he or she is saying and notice the body language. Or close your eyes and listen to the emotional tone of the words. Notice what people are not saying or what they are avoiding.
>
> Notice what you are feeling in any given situation and try to describe it in words or images. The more you know about your own feelings, the more you can recognize the feelings of others. The more you recognize the feelings of others, the more you can influence them.

Even in highly technical business-to-business purchases, before a detailed rational analysis is made of product performance and cost, an emotional decision is made about which suppliers to consider. And when there is engineering or price parity among the finalists, the vendor selection is made on the basis of chemistry or other emotional factors.

> ## BRAND COP
> **SMART**
> **MANAGING**
>
> In order to ensure integration of marketing communications, someone must be the "brand cop" with the authority and responsibility to enforce the rules across divisions and products and departments. The brand cop must have the unflinching support of top management over a long period of time. Otherwise, it's easy for people in an enterprising division to "do their own thing" and confuse your brand.

Your goal as a marketer is to connect the soul of your brand with the heart of your target market. Notice what you are feeling in any given situation, and try to describe it in words or images. The more you know about your own feelings, the more you can recognize the feelings of others. The more you recognize the feelings of others, the more you can influence them. Psychotherapy is a great way to accelerate this learning.

It's bad when your brand lacks emotional connection with your customers. Another way of saying this is that your customers couldn't care less about your brand. They believe you have nothing unique or special. You become a mere commodity to them. (See Figure 4-2.) They believe they can

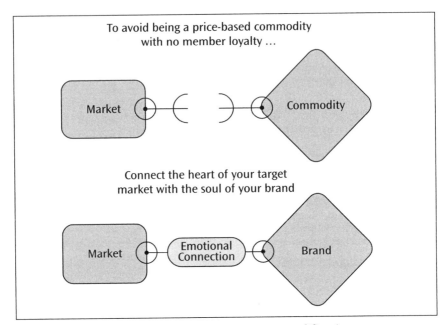

Figure 4-2. Emotional connection prevents commodification

get the same products or services from another supplier, so you're feeling pressure to lower your prices just to stay in the game. When another supplier underbids you, the customers chase the low price elsewhere. You have none of the protection and security that brand loyalty affords.

Marketers who connect their brand to the emotional needs of their targets reap some amazing benefits. When your customers feel a stronger emotional response to your product than to a competitor's comparable product, you will sell more of your product, your customers will be more loyal, and you can charge up to 200 percent more than your competitors.

When it comes to marketing, grab their hearts, and their heads will follow. The main job of our rational minds is to rationalize our emotional choices.

Principle Five: Emotional Truths Are Invisible Truths

Most human beings are incapable of consciously articulating the deep motives for their own behavior. Do you really think the primary reason that people buy an expensive luxury car is because the car is "well engineered"? Or do you think it has something to do with a desire to impress others with their wealth and accomplishment? It is not that people intentionally set out to lie or mislead. It's just that we often need to protect ourselves from our subconscious motives, because our motives are not socially acceptable.

How widespread is this unconscious behavior? Many cognitive scientists operate on the assumption that 95 percent of all human behavior is unconscious. What people can consciously articulate about their own motives has about a 10 percent chance of being accurate.

Many companies spend millions of dollars on focus groups or surveys to ask their customers to consciously articulate their reasons for buying or not buying a particular product. The answers customers give to this kind of literal questioning are almost always misleading, if not downright wrong. "Why, yes," says the customer, "now that you ask, I would rather spend this weekend volunteering to help the poor and the sick, rather than just sitting back and eating a pizza and watching TV." If you believe answers like these, I have some swampland in Florida I'd like to sell you.

You are far better off using actual consumer behavior as an information source, such as information from data mining or direct response tests, or using indirect testing that safely reveals subconscious motives only to the researcher.

Principle Six: Barry Callen's Teeter-Totter Theory of All Human Behavior™

Marketing today is complex. Markets have fragmented into thousands of micro-groups. Competitors can come at you from other countries and from totally unrelated industries. Media are everywhere, from cell phones to restroom walls.

There is a simple tool for dealing with all this complexity. I call it "Barry Callen's Teeter-Totter Theory of All Human Behavior." You can use this theory to reduce the most complex marketing decision to its simplest essence: *Human behavior is a teeter-totter of fear and desire. When desire outweighs fear, we act. When fear outweighs desire, we don't.*

And there is Tipper's Corollary: *Our job as marketers is to add to the desire and take away the fear.* Then the teeter-totter tips and the customer makes a million-dollar purchase ... or calls to find out more.

Figure 4-4. Barry Callen's teeter-totter theory of human behavior: every decision and perception is a balance between desire and fear

Every purchase decision is a balance of fear and desire, usually unspoken. Here are some examples:

- Women's shoes: "I want big comfortable squishy soles, but I'm afraid I'll look like a nurse or an old lady."
- Home loans: "I want my dream house, but I'm afraid I'll end up in the poor house."
- Teenage backpack: "I want to look like an individual, but I'm afraid I won't fit in."
- Diabetic food: "I want something sweet, but I'm afraid this artificial stuff will taste like cardboard."

Your job as marketer is to increase your customers' desire through all

TOOLS

THE FOUR RISKS

Identify which of the following four risks your customers must take in order to purchase your product. Then take steps to reduce their greatest risk through foolproof product design, lower price, demonstrations or free samples, or money-back guarantees.

- *Physical Risk*—"I might lose money, get tired, get sick, die, lose my job, dislike the taste, lose my possessions."
- *Self-Image Risk*—"I'm not the kind of person who does or doesn't do that, or does or doesn't own that, or does or doesn't believe that. That's just not who I think I am."
- *Social Risk*—"I'd be embarrassed if other people knew I did or did not do something or own something or believe something."
- *Risk to Perception of Reality*—"It's not possible. The world doesn't work this way. This can't be real."

MARKETING AROUND THE FOUR RISKS

Physical Risk—Examples of products that help reduce physical risk: FDIC insurance on deposits, power tools, vitamin C, health care, vocational training, restaurants, burglar alarms

Self-Image Risk—Examples of products that help reinforce self-image: luxury car, college diploma, morning-after pill, hair color, gym membership

Social Risk—Examples of products that help prevent embarrassment: adult diapers, hair implants, herpes medication, computer encryption software, expensive watch

Risk to Perception of Reality—Examples of products that help reassure: religion, political parties, education, psychotherapy, New Age healing crystals

It is almost never a good idea for marketers to ask their customers to risk their perception of reality. That's simply too painful for most people to do. It's always better for marketers to build on their customers' current perception of reality.

---

the marketing mix tools at your disposal: product design, price, promotion, messaging, and advertising. And your job is also to reduce their fears through tactics like requesting a low-risk call to action such as "Contact us for more information." Or you can provide powerful concrete reasons for a cynic to believe, such as demonstrations, samples, free trials, testimonials, or a money-back guarantee.

The next time you are faced with a tough marketing decision, ask yourself this: "What do my customers desire? What do they fear? What can I do about it?"

Then use the marketing tools you have to tip the teeter-totter in your direction.

Principle Seven: If You Want to Get Rich, You Have to Niche

If you have all the money and all the time in the world, you do not need to have a strategy. But if you have limits to your budget, you will need a strategy. Which target market will you *not* serve? Which benefit will you *not* offer? It is a difficult and unpopular question, but that is the question market strategy asks.

Be careful of trying to be all things to all people. By casting a wider net and not excluding anyone, you actually *decrease* your chances of success.

Principle Eight: Stand for Something or You'll Fall Down

Don't try to be all things to all people or you'll end up not being anything to anyone. Strategy is sacrifice. Pick something, stand for something, and stick with it.

Principle Nine: Zig When Others Zag, and Vice Versa

The human brain is hard-wired to notice anything new or different. To make sure your ads stand out in a sea of clutter, make them different from everyone else's. This takes guts.

It also takes a different approach. To make sure your advertising stands out in any form (TV commercial, print ad, Web site, brochure, etc.), do a zig-zag analysis (see sidebar on next page).

ZIG	ZIG	ZIG	ZIG	ZIG	ZIG	ZIG
ZIG	ZIG	ZIG	ZIG	ZIG	ZIG	ZIG
ZIG	ZIG	ZIG	ZIG	ZIG	ZIG	ZIG
ZIG	ZIG	ZIG	ZIG	ZIG	ZIG	ZIG
ZIG	ZIG	ZIG	ZIG	ZIG	ZIG	ZIG
ZIG	ZIG	ZIG	ZIG	**ZAG**	ZIG	ZIG
ZIG	ZIG	ZIG	ZIG	ZIG	ZIG	ZIG
ZIG	ZIG	ZIG	ZIG	ZIG	ZIG	ZIG

Figure 4-5. Which word did you notice first?

There are four things you can do to help your marketing communications stand out more:

- Offer something relevant or useful that is worth paying attention to.
- Create an unusual ad or idea that is new and unexpected.
- Narrow your target market and your media, and tailor your message to them.
- Use permission marketing.

KEY TERM

Permission marketing Technique of obtaining the prospect's permission before advancing to the next step in the selling process, usually beginning by offering information on the subject or brand. That way the advertising is not an intrusion, not interrupting what the prospect is thinking about already.

ZIG-ZAG ANALYSIS

TOOLS

Step 1. Gather together all the brochures, home pages, commercials, ads, etc., from all your major competitors.

Step 2. Stick them up on a wall or a large piece of cardboard or matt board.

Step 3. List all the elements those materials have in common. For example:

Zig-Zag Analysis of Trade Magazine Ads

1. Four-color photo of the computer exterior
2. Obviously staged photo of multiethnic business team members shaking hands around a mahogany conference table
3. The color blue in the logo
4. These words in the headline or tagline: partnership, quality, solutions, professional, scientific, leader
5. Long list of dealer locations
6. Company name and logo at least 12 times per ad
7. Small legal type taking up the bottom quarter of ad
8. Helvetica type

Step 4: In designing your new marketing communications, do *not* make an ad with any of the characteristics listed. Create something different, unique, and your ad is far more likely to stand out.

SWIM IN UNCHARTED WATERS

FOR EXAMPLE

Our ad agency did a zig-zag analysis of the ads in the enthusiast publications for scuba diving. All the ads, including our client's ad, were virtually identical. There was a blue underwater shot of a scuba diver floating by, observing an undersea terrain or creature. (Even the editorial in the magazines largely used the same type of shot.) There were very few words: only a list of technical specifications. Nothing stood out.

So we created ads that used unusual background colors: red, yellow, pink, orange, and purple. We inset a small photo of an unusual or dramatic undersea detail into a long adventure story with a provocative headline. The stories were all true and all demonstrated the lifesaving benefits of the scuba equipment under extreme conditions, such as exploring the world's longest underwater cave. The ads got noticed because they zagged where all the others zigged.

Principle Ten: One Ad, One Idea

The average person will take less than half a second to decide whether or not to pay any attention to your ad. This means that you must pick your most attractive point and make it the first thing people see or hear.

People no longer read. They skim. Think about how you open your mail. Change the channels on your TV. or read a magazine.

Studies show that even after you decide to pay attention to an ad, you still actually only skim it for points of interest—first the headline or main visual, then subsidiary photos and photo captions, then the logo or tagline. Only then do you actually read the body copy in the ad.

Because of the way people now skim information and skip large chunks to save time and energy, it is ill-advised to present the readers or viewers with a long list of points. Make sure every ad has one main idea.

Principle Eleven: Be Both Relevant and Unique

Your goal as a company and as a marketer is to create an important difference that will cause your target market to choose you over your competitors. That's what the customer takes for granted. For example, we expect every car to have an engine, a chassis, brakes, an accelerator, and a steering wheel. But if you're the first carmaker to include lots of useful cup holders, you just might attract some new customers, as one Japanese carmaker discovered. And it's not enough to do something different that is not important to the customer. So what if your gasoline has a chemical additive that no competitor offers? Why is it important to the customer? How will the customer benefit? But if you tell the customer about your chemical additive that cleans the engine, you might have a difference that is important to them.

The same thing is true of your ads. They must be both relevant to the audience and unexpected. The relevance makes them useful. The unexpected makes them get noticed. Very few ads are both relevant and unexpected.

You must do both.

Principle Twelve: Don't Swim Upstream

Trout make lousy marketers because they are always trying to swim upstream, which requires a far greater investment of time and energy. It is no accident that many trout die along the journey. So do many marketers who spend considerable sums trying to impose their views on their target market.

Your job as a marketer is to go with the flow of your customers' natural tendencies as much as possible. You don't want to change their minds; you want to build on their current perceptions. You want to require the least possible change on their part—the least change of perception, the least change of behavior. The less you ask of them, the more you lower their risk and the more likely they are to act in ways that benefit you.

Don't try to make water run uphill. A sure sign you are doing this is when you use the word "should." "Well, gosh darn it! Diabetics should want to give up sweets! They should want to eat our vegetables." Instead, say, "Diabetics want sweets. Therefore we'll develop a sweet-tasting low-glycemic dinner dessert for them." The less change you ask of them, the more likely you are to succeed.

Go with the flow. Ride the market horse in the direction it's going.

Principle Thirteen: First, Pick the Low-Hanging Fruit

The single most profitable target market you will ever have is your current customers. They know your name, they believe your reputation, they've had a good experience, they've developed some loyalty toward you, and they perceive purchasing from you as less risky. You often know their names and have their contact information, which enables you to bypass expensive mass media and use less expensive, more targeted media, such as in-store signage, e-mail, or snail mail. They are often more receptive to information about your category or product or brand.

They are also most likely to generate the most profit and make the most purchases each year—and most likely to persuade the people they know to try your product. It almost always costs far more money to attract a first-time customer than it does to get a current or past customer to buy more or buy again. So before you reach out to prospective customers, make sure you have maximized your return on your current customers.

In many businesses, developing a customer profile and database enables companies to identify which customers have the highest lifetime value. For example, mortgage customers are more profitable to a bank than ATM customers, because they are likely to have a relationship with the bank for decades. Checking customers are more profitable than auto loan customers, because they tend to stay with the bank longer.

You can even create databases that are capable of predicting which of your customers will respond best to particular cross-selling opportunities. You can also use databases to identify types of people who are most likely to buy your product. There are lifestyle databases that can be combined with your actual customer sales to determine the degree of market penetration and the likely total market potential of a particular city or zip code or media broadcast area. Wise marketers first concentrate on maximizing awareness and sales among people who match the profiles of their heavy users. Only when they have worked that group or geographic area to the max do they move to the next group or area. They pick the low-hanging fruit first.

Principle Fourteen: Avoid B.S.

Almost all adults in America believe that they can see through advertising B.S. That is, until they become advertisers. Then they start generating advertising B.S. and believing in their own corporate B.S. It feels disloyal not to believe.

But it doesn't matter what they believe. Because, in test after test of advertising, their customers see right through the vague wording, the bragging, the exaggerated claims, and the staged photos. Today, words that are too "addy" or "selly" or "commercial" or "corporate" are actually cues to consumers not to believe the advertiser. The marketers who use such words generate a backlash of skepticism that can destroy the credibility of their brand. The use of B.S. words has become so prevalent that there is now a piece of software that analyzes the words in a communication for its percentage of B.S.

These days it is almost impossible to surmount the skepticism of the public. People need powerful reasons to believe your message, not B.S. words to make them disbelieve.

The first and best way to avoid B.S. is not to exaggerate. I repeat: underpromise and overdeliver. Advertising sets expectations by making promises. Set them too high and you're actually disappointing your customer and damaging the credibility of future communications. Always check your advertising claims against your ability to deliver.

Manager's Checklist for Chapter 4

☑ Marketing is an unnatural act. You must train yourself not to fall into your own natural human tendencies.

☑ Understand, remember, and apply these 16 principles:

1. No one knows for sure what will work.
2. When you dance with the customers, let them lead.
3. Integrate and align everything.
4. The heart trumps the head.
5. People lie, especially to themselves
6. Barry Callen's teeter-totter theory of all human behavior™: "Human behavior is a teeter-totter of fear and desire. When desire outweighs fear, we act. When fear outweighs desire, we don't."
7. If you want to get rich, you have to niche.
8. Stand for something or you'll fall down.
9. Zig when others zag, and vice versa.
10. One ad, one idea.
11. Be both relevant and unique.
12. Don't swim upstream.
13. First, pick the low-hanging fruit.
14. Avoid B.S.

Chapter
5

Types of Marketing Communications and Expertise

As a marketer, you have many tools in your toolbox. And new tools are being developed all the time. Each of these types of marketing involves different knowledge, skill sets, assumptions, experts, processes, and technology. It helps to be aware of all the options and understand what they can and cannot do. It is also imperative to integrate the various approaches you use, so that your brand makes sense.

Direct Response Marketing

Direct response marketing has been around for over 100 years. Today it accounts for over half of all ad spending in the U.S. Any medium where the ad calls directly for the sale and where the sales response can be measured is a direct response ad.

The most common direct response medium is mail, called "direct mail" by the industry and "junk mail" by irritated consumers. In addition, direct response advertising is on TV, on the radio, in newspapers and magazines, in the classifieds, on billboards, in catalogs, in telephone directories, and on the Internet. TV commercials in the form of news or entertainment programs, called *infomercials*, are a highly specialized form of direct response advertising. There are even channels completely devoted to perpetual live infomercials, such as the QVC Network. Catalogs (also called *mail order*) are collections of large numbers of individual direct response ads, each one tested to justify taking up "real estate" in the catalog, much as products take up real estate in a store.

> **Direct response marketing** Any form of marketing that is designed to cause the prospect to contact the company directly. The response is usually specific: e.g., to request more information about the product or service being marketed or to order the product or service. Responses can be tracked.
>
> **KEY TERM**

Direct response prospects may be asked to call a toll-free number, to return an envelope, to fill out an order form, or to stop by with a coupon or promotional offer. The ad triggers the sale, and the result is captured by coding.

The heart and soul of direct response advertising is comparative testing of results. At least two variations of an ad are created (called variables), and the difference in results is measured. (We briefly explained *split-run testing* in Chapter 3.) Variables are usually tested on a small scale; the more or most successful version is then rolled out to the entire market.

There are two types of testing. A/B testing is the direct comparison of one variable against another. For example, a newspaper ad might alternate between version A and version B. Usually only one difference is tested at a time. These A and B versions are randomly distributed among newspaper readers, and results are measured. If the sample size is sufficient, it is possible to predict the improved financial result or *lift*. The other type of testing uses advanced mathematical techniques and large sample sizes to test "recipes" (combinations of variables) to see which combination "pulls harder." It is often discovered that one combination can outpull another by a significant margin, spelling the difference between profit and loss. The most important variables to test are, in order:

- the list of prospects
- the offer (the main promise of the ad)
- the creative

The *creative* can include everything from the number of elements in a mailer (coupon, promotional flyer, letter, fact sheet, etc.) to the writing, design, and photography of the elements.

Most direct response ads also include a promotional offer to encourage prospects to "act now." Formats can range from a simple black-and-white

Lift Improvement in response between or among two or more alternatives. It can be the difference in volume of responses:

KEY TERM

- when using two or more variations of the same ad
- when running one ad, in comparison with the *baseline*, the volume of sales that would have come without running any ad
- when running the same ad in two or more newspapers or magazines or on two or more radio or TV stations
- when sending the same ad to two or more mailing lists

letter in an envelope to a 10-piece, four-color, computer-personalized mailer with clever perforations and return elements.

The people involved in direct response marketing include copywriters, art directors and designers, list suppliers, printers, production artists, print buyers, account managers, broadcast producers and directors and actors and voice talent, staff at toll-free call centers, staff at fulfillment houses (warehouses that send out the merchandise ordered), database analysts, and direct response agency staff, who are like the main contractors who supply and/or coordinate all the pieces.

Database Marketing

Database marketing applies relatively recent computer technology to the mailing list management side of direct response marketing. It collects, stores, sorts, and retrieves information about customers and prospects. Individual customer records are combined to create large databases. Using either simple matching criteria or complex mathematical calculations (algorithms), marketers can use the customer database to personalize marketing communications to maximize return on investment.

The more data collected on a group of customers and the larger the group studied, the more accurately the computer can be used to model or predict their future buying behavior. Individual human behavior is difficult to predict, but collective human behavior is much more predictable. A classic example of this is the Labor Day Weekend traffic fatality predictions. The predictions can't predict who will die in a traffic accident, but they can predict with surprising accuracy how many people will die in a given time period. The larger the group, the more predictable the behavior, so the primary users of database marketing are large organizations with many customers, such as the government, retail stores, and consumer financial institutions. Thanks to the computerization of business transactions and the Internet's computerization of communication, extraordinarily large amounts of data can be collected and "crunched" to make remarkably accurate predictions in real time.

The collection of retrieveable data, called a *data warehouse*, is organized differently from daily customer transaction data. Clever analysis of the data in a data warehouse, called *data mining*, can be used to create metadata (data about the data), such as behavioral predictions, correlations, and other observations that can guide business decisions and strategies. For example, a bank might learn that customers who secure a home equity credit line will stay with the bank for more years, purchase more financial products, and have greater lifetime value than, say, ATM

> ### USE DATA TO FIND THE BEST CUSTOMERS
>
> **FOR EXAMPLE**
>
> A bank I worked with purchased a set of research data that could predict with 95 percent accuracy which customers were most likely to purchase which financial products, based on only five variables: household income, age, marital status, and number and age of children. Instead of mailing offers to all its customers all the time, which many customers find irritating and which costs a lot of money, it was able to target only the customers most likely to respond.

customers. The bank may then decide to invest more marketing dollars in attracting these more profitable customers.

> ### LIFESTYLE DATABASE
>
> **TOOLS**
>
> Use lifestyle databases to find and segment your customers. Lifestyle databases, such as Claritas's PRIZM®, break every household mailing address in the United States into market segments. The people in each market segment share geographic, demographic, and lifestyle tendencies that make their attitudes, income, and purchasing and media behavior statistically predictable. By running your heavy user customers through such a database, you can identify pockets of similar folks who are likely to become good customers. You can use this information to develop creative and messaging strategies, measure market penetration, identify promising store locations, make media decisions, or target households for mailings.

LIFESTYLE DATABASE

FOR EXAMPLE

I once worked with a lifestyle database and research firm that specialized in teenagers. The firm enabled us to identify and characterize the age and social group of teenagers who were at greatest risk for date rape, either as victims or as perpetrators. Their predictions were so accurate that we had to have a therapist ready at the focus groups, to counsel girls who had been recently raped.

One variant of database marketing is CRM, *customer relationship marketing*. At its simplest, it is computer software that helps you mine data and manage contacts with your customers to maximize your sales yield from each one. At its best, CRM is designed to enable you to improve overall service to the customer through better understanding and by coordinating all points of customer contact with your company: ordering, delivery, service, complaints, manufacturing, and so on.

CRM revolves around a central individual customer record that automatically collects and updates every transaction with the customer and is accessible to anyone in your company who might need the information to serve the customer. A common use of CRM is to create special benefits and loyalty programs for the most profitable customers and to identify opportunities to up-sell or cross-sell to your current customers. In general, as mentioned earlier, your most profitable target markets are your current customers, and CRM helps you manage your relationship with them. It is not unusual for 20 percent of your customers to account for 80 percent of your profits. So it is just good business to give them special treatment.

Cause Marketing

Studies show that everything being equal (price and quality), people are predisposed to buy from companies that they believe support their values and that are making the world a better place. Since most products and services today are at parity, supporting a good cause can tip the balance in favor of your company. Over the last 100 years, consumers have developed a strong amount of cynicism regarding the motivation of corporations, salespeople, and marketers. Supporting a good cause is one way to help defuse this cynicism.

SUPPORT YOUR LOCAL NEIGHBORHOOD

FOR EXAMPLE

In my neighborhood is a building that has housed three restaurants. The first two failed after two years. The third restaurant owner reached out to people and causes in the neighborhood, donating free dinners to local school fundraisers, offering seniors and the indigent a free or discounted spaghetti dinner every Wednesday night, and sponsoring a local community center and a neighborhood girls soccer team. The owner even provided a free place to meet for a group of volunteers concerned about pollution from a nearby factory.

As a result, her neighbors view her restaurant as a key part of the community, and now she is in her fifth year of business and regularly has lines out the door for dinner. The goodwill she's created through her donations, sponsorships, and volunteer efforts has helped build her brand.

CAUSE MARKETING IS VERY DEMANDING

CAUTION

Once you start publicly supporting a good cause, it requires a high standard of behavior. If you support causes that benefit children, you cannot be caught using goods made with child labor in Third-World countries. In your marketing communications, you must put the cause first and your brand sponsorship second. Otherwise, it seems as if you consider your company more important than the cause.

Once you take on a cause, you appear hypocritical if you stop your support. If you always put the cause before your marketing, you will do alright. Otherwise, you will be judged even more harshly than if you had never supported the cause.

Event Marketing

Instead of investing in traditional advertising media, you can consider creating or sponsoring an event. Make sure the event appeals to your target market and is a natural fit with your brand.

For example, if you are a pharmaceutical company specializing in neurochemical drugs, sponsor an annual research meeting that attracts the most influential minds in your category. Make sure your company name and logo are prominently featured everywhere: signage, invitations, booth displays, badges, schedules, and parties. Underwrite or name chairs, scholarships, awards. Find ways to put your employees in touch with your customers.

In some business-to-business categories, these annual events are the primary method of reaching customers. Perhaps the most common examples of event marketing are in the sports marketing area. Some brand names are even part of the name of a tennis or golf tournament or car race.

You will likely need to assign a staff member full time to developing and running this annual event, coordinating everyone from event planners to public relations specialists.

Permission Marketing

Permission marketing is a term coined by Seth Godin. Advertising is usually uninvited, an intruder whose job is to interrupt what you are doing or thinking and get your attention. When the advertising is annoying or irrelevant to them, people dislike being interrupted. With the extraordinary quantities of advertising today, many audiences seek to shield themselves from interruption.

Godin calls this kind of marketing "interruptive" and proposes a model that asks the prospects for permission to communicate with them on a particular subject. This gives the prospects control over what they see and hear, reduces the amount of unwanted interruption, and gives them access to more relevant information. It also makes them more receptive to the message.

Promotional Advertising

Promotional advertising seeks to get prospects to act now, by offering a discount or a perk in addition to the product or service being sold. For example, a standard ad about a hamburger might talk about taste and ingredients. But a promotional ad about that hamburger might offer the opportunity to buy one and get one free, but only for a limited time.

Promotional advertising can usually generate a short-term spike in sales, but often at the long-term expense of the brand. Constantly trying to discount or give away your product cheapens its perceived value. Usually the best approach is to do a mixture of promotional advertising and brand advertising (next section).

Promotional tactics include contests, sales, discounts, everyday low-price offers, coupons, savings clubs (like frequent flier programs), guarantees, BOGOs (buy one, get one free), freebies, gifts, trips, bonuses, and premium items. There is an entire industry just devoted to providing personalized or branded premium items such as pens, balloons, plaques, steak knives, thumb drives, etc. Typical promotional media include in-store signage and display, direct mail, newspaper, radio, and TV, because these media are good for limited-time offers.

Brand Advertising

As explained in Chapter 1, a brand is the sum total of all the feelings and perceptions your customers have about your product. Brand awareness, interest, and attitude always precede purchase. In contrast to direct response, promotional, or product feature/benefit advertising, brand advertising seeks to build a favorable feeling and perception about your brand and tie it to your brand name or brand image. There is no rational reason to buy vegetables because your brand is represented by a green giant, or to buy cigarettes because your brand is represented by a cowboy, but human behavior is driven more by emotion than by reason. Today, even presidential candidates are marketed as brand images.

Classic brand advertising elements include an image or character (Energizer Bunny), a pithy memorable catchphrase (What happens in Vegas, stays in Vegas.), or music ("Like a Rock" for Chevy trucks). With repetition and consistency, a brand can even become part of popular culture. Procter & Gamble is a company that has consistently created some of America's most successful brands. It is worth studying.

Most people think of brand advertising as national TV, radio, magazine, and outdoor ads for packaged goods

KEY TERM

Brand positioning What you stand for to your customers and how you're different from your competitors. For example, there is a toothpaste that "whitens" and another that "brightens."

Brand image The mental or physical visual associated with your product.

Brand personality A description of your brand as if it were a person or a character.

Brand DNA The twin strands of reason and emotion that make up your brand in your customers' minds.

Brand story How all these brand elements fit together in a story to mean something to the customer.

aimed at mass markets. But this does not have to be the case. Even the tiniest neighborhood store or nonprofit cause can brand itself.

Employee Branding

If you are in a service business, such as health care or credit unions, your employee represents your entire brand to the customer. If your positioning or advertising claims that you are friendly but a nurse or call-center employee is rude or negligent, then your brand perception suffers. In fact, negative word of mouth has proven to travel farther and faster than positive word of mouth.

Recognizing that their employees are their brand to their customers, some companies have begun carefully recruiting, training, measuring, and rewarding employees for living the brand promise every day. This involves everything from on-brand recruitment advertising, personality profiling when hiring, and extensive employee communication and training programs, to hiring, firing, promoting, and rewarding employees based on measurable brand promise delivery.

TRICKS OF THE TRADE

EMPLOYEES: YOUR MOST POWERFUL MARKETING TOOL

One large health care client I worked with used employee branding to successfully deliver better patient care, create competitive superiority, and send a powerful brand message to patients, their families, and their employers. We used research with model employees and their patients to identify the most powerful brand promise and the employee behaviors that were essential to communicating that promise. We identified 10 key behaviors and a personality profile of the ideal employee at any level (including beliefs and actions). We created recruitment ads to attract applicants matching the profile. These ads used actual employees to demonstrate to the public the kind of care they could expect. They also served as the basis of a strong internal employee communications campaign through newsletters, posters, and contests. The training department built the characteristics into its training programs. The personnel department developed a test to identify recruits who matched the profile and built measurements of the key characteristics into the performance reviews of every department. A year later, employees who met the performance standards were rewarded, and employees who did not were let go (including doctors). This organization has now achieved some of the highest performance numbers in the world in delivering quality health care, in all areas.

Public Relations

Paid advertising gives you complete control over when, where, and what you say and show, but the level of credibility is usually very low. Public relations (PR) offers you very little control, but it gives you outstanding third-party credibility. A TV news report or newspaper or magazine article is far more credible than a paid advertisement, because a third-party expert screens and therefore endorses the information.

Public relations is not free, as you must do a lot of work and you may want to hire a PR firm or expert, but it is considerably less expensive than most paid advertising media. The only catch is that there is no guarantee you will get media coverage.

One measure of the productivity of public relations is the number of inches of or minutes of coverage you get in the press and the dollars it would cost to purchase an equivalent amount of space or time.

An equally important but opposite dimension of public relations is *crisis management.* When negative events and news coverage happen, a skilled PR person can help you minimize the damage and manage or "spin" how the story is covered in the media. Some companies pay PR experts to keep them out of the news. A standard tactic is to send press releases and press kits to publications and news reporters. But public relations can also help you create news, by creating events that are worthy of news coverage.

A large public relations firm may employ almost all types of marketing communications strategies and tactics. All the same elements are needed: a clear business objective and target market, a message strategy, media tactics, unexpected and relevant creative ideas, budgets, timetables, and performance measurements. For more detail, see Chapter 13 on public relations.

Graphic Design

Long before any prospects read a single word of your marketing communications and long before customers use your product or service, they see visual images and register feelings and draw conclusions based on those images. Visuals are usually the first part of the impression made by an ad, and human beings have an instant visceral reaction to shapes, colors, photos, materials, typography, and style. If your product is intangible, such as software or a service, it pays to give people a visual handle to grab onto. Most of the human brain is devoted to visual thinking, and visual communications transcend language, which is great if you have a global target market.

Most businesspeople, scientists, engineers, accountants, and doctors are unskilled and insensitive to the effects of their visual style, and view design as mere ornamentation rather than an element critical to functionality. But your software product is not very functional if the graphical interface is hard to use. And it's hard to claim a premium price for your cutting-edge service if your offices and brochures and logo look like they were designed by a Soviet planning committee in 1930.

Design and visuals also enable you to communicate messages indirectly that would sound silly if said out loud: e.g., "This car makes me look rich and successful" or "This dress makes me look young and feel sexy." As product parity becomes the rule and as customers start seeking experiences over products, design can become a critical element in your marketing plan. If you are in a style-driven business—such as fashion, perfume, entertainment, hospitality, travel, adult beverages, or teenage products—great design is a must. If your business is large and complex, with many different products in markets in many countries, or if you market a system of franchises, you may need a graphic standards manual for your troops to use. This will ensure that your brand looks and feels the same at all times. But it is only as good as your ability to enforce it.

You'll generally work with three types of designers or design firms:

- *graphic* designers who create marketing communications, usually in print and Web media
- *product* designers who integrate form and function
- *space* designers, such as retail store designers, interior designers, display designers, and architects

Typical elements that clients will have designed are logos, brochures, letterhead, business cards, Web sites, signage, packages, annual reports, PowerPoint presentations, trucks and vans, uniforms, in-store displays, store interiors, and products and product interfaces and controls. The best marketers choose their designs based on market testing, rather than personal opinion. But make sure you use indirect methods of testing or you will get false opinions as people play "creative director."

Online Marketing

What once was a world of computers talking to other computers has evolved into a vast network of people, communications, and devices including video, text messaging, cell phones, and PDAs such as the iPhone and the BlackBerry. And the opportunities for targeting consumers with marketing messages have become as vast.

E-marketing (aka Internet marketing, i-marketing, Web marketing, and online marketing) is now the fastest-growing marketing communications area and likely to be the dominant marketing medium in the near future.

Low Cost, Highly Targeted, Global, Interactive

The Internet has brought many unique benefits to marketing, one of which being lower costs for the distribution of information and media to a global audience. The interactive nature of Internet marketing, in terms both of providing instant response and of eliciting responses, also makes the medium highly effective, as does the ability to target users based on behavior, history, interests, and geography.

Internet marketing also refers to the placement of media along different stages of the *customer engagement cycle* through search engine marketing, search engine optimization, banner ads on specific Web sites, e-mail marketing, and Web 2.0 strategies.

Internet presence is often the first point of contact: The first place a news reporter goes when writing a story about your company is the Internet; consumers often research online before purchasing, or they locate retail outlets, and prospects often look to see what others are saying about a company or product before considering it. Rather than being present on the Web only

Customer engagement cycle A series of four broad stages through which prospects/customers **KEY TERM** typically pass as a relationship develops with a company. The terms vary, but generally the stages are labeled as awareness, consideration, inquiry, and purchase. Some marketers add a fifth stage, expansion.

in maintaining and promoting their Web sites as destinations, companies are finding that their Web presence is ubiquitous—in online news channels, YouTube videos, blogs, Flickr images, Facebook pages, and other social networking venues. Managing a brand online is much more complex than ever before.

The Internet has successfully broken the tyranny of the two-mile radius of retail store selling and made it possible for even companies consisting of a single individual to sell their wares globally. This has also ended the dominance of the mass market blockbuster and opened the door for products that appeal to tiny percentages of the giant global population.

Micro-Marketing

Rather than reaching their target markets simply by blasting out a mass message or building a brand in the historical way, companies are finding it increasingly difficult to reach their targets. Relationships have become ever more important, as has the concept of niche marketing. Users are in control of what they see, which products they interact with, and by whom they want to be contacted. They are often the ones to initiate a contact, whether through search engines, direct load, or referral.

Top online tactics for businesses are those mentioned a little earlier in terms of the customer engagement cycle—search engine marketing, search engine optimization, banner ads on specific Web sites, and e-mail marketing, all resting on a bed of social networking and based on relationships between trusted people. Companies need to understand the potential of these tactics and the concept of one-to-one marketing in the online space.

For more detailed information, see Chapter 14 on Internet Marketing.

Guerrilla Marketing

Guerrilla marketing is the use of nontraditional tactics to reach a target market. Often, this involves inventing your own media or turning common daily objects and occurrences into media and events to sell your message.

The two chief advantages of guerrilla marketing are that the methods are unexpected (and therefore more likely to garner attention) and the tactics are often cheaper than traditional advertising media. Examples include writing your message in sidewalk chalk outside a key location where your target market gathers, putting up Post-it® note graffiti in a public restroom, having actors ride in elevators of key office buildings and have conversations about your product that other people "accidentally" overhear, and paying beautiful young women to go from bar to bar ordering your new brand of liquor. One gambling casino even paid a young man to have its logo tattooed on his forehead for a year, in order to gain publicity as the first brand to do so. Using a specific location to dramatize your message is another powerful guerrilla tactic. Here's an example: painting a sign on the side of a barn that points to cows grazing out in front and says, "If our hamburgers were any fresher, they'd look like this."

DAY-IN-THE-LIFE EXERCISE

Use this exercise to create guerrilla advertising tactics.

TOOLS

- Write a rough description of a day in the life of the people in your ideal target market: list where they are and what they are doing from minute to minute.
- Make a list of every detail: what they need, what objects are in their environment, what they are wearing, whom they are around, how they get from one place to another. Include all five senses.
- Take that detailed list, and find a way to put a message in it or on it or to create a dramatic and unexpected event. For example, "8:00 am, they pull into their parking stall. Put a sign on it. 8:15, they enter the front door and wipe their feet on the welcome mat. Have mats printed with a new message" ... and so on.
- Choose the least expensive and most effective tactic(s).

GUERRILLA MARKETING FOR MUSIC CREATION SOFTWARE

FOR EXAMPLE

A small, unknown software company invented music creation software for the personal computer. The company needed to introduce it to the buyers of large retail electronics stores at the world's largest trade show (over 10,000 products featured), but the company's budget was limited. We used the "Day in the Life" exercise to identify that most of the trade show participants would be arriving there through one airport. (to be continued)

GUERRILLA MARKETING, CONTINUED—IN ACTION

FOR
EXAMPLE

We spray-painted messages on luggage that went around and around the airport luggage carousels. We hired out-of-work actors to dress like rock stars and walk through the airport with guitar cases with messages painted on the side. We hired more out-of-work actors to dress as limo drivers and hold up signs with the brand name. Within 10 minutes of arrival, we had hit our targets with a message three times.

When they got to the trade show, we staged a protest of the product and passed out flyers asking participants to boycott the booth. Human nature being what it is, the booth received so much traffic that vendors at adjacent booths complained. At the booth we passed out pads of printed Post-it® notes with provocative messages that participants stuck on bathroom walls and even on competitors' ads. (to be continued)

GUERRILLA MARKETING, END—THE RESULTS

FOR
EXAMPLE

The campaign received an award for generating the most buzz, international media wrote stories on the guerrilla tactics, the company stock went through the roof, and the product successfully sold into the retailers. Within one year, the product had the largest market share in the category—more than double that of the nearest (and much better funded) competitor.

Integrated Marketing

As you can see, there are many types of marketing and many types of media. Integrated marketing is what pulls them all together for maximum effect on your target market.

Integrated marketing is about strategic alignment. Your price, product, placement, and promotion strategy (the 4 P's) should line up and work together. Your position, brand, messaging, and communications should sing the same tune. Your traditional and online and guerrilla messages should work together to reach the same conclusion.

The purpose of integrated marketing is to create a single powerful brand that is consistently reinforced over time in every way that your brand touches your consumer (touchpoints). The secret of integrated marketing is:

- strategic alignment
- consistency over time and across all touchpoints

▪ consistent enforcement

The critical tool to achieve integrated marketing is a marketing plan. Without support from the top management of the company, it is almost impossible to achieve full marketing integration, because every department touches your customer in some way.

Manager's Checklist for Chapter 5

☑ Managers have a variety of types of marketing they can use:
  ▪ Direct response
  ▪ Database marketing
  ▪ Cause marketing
  ▪ Event marketing
  ▪ Permission marketing
  ▪ Promotional advertising
  ▪ Brand advertising
  ▪ Employee branding
  ▪ Public relations
  ▪ Graphic design
  ▪ Online marketing
  ▪ Guerrilla marketing

☑ The most effective marketing is *integrated marketing*, which aligns all the ways you touch your customer.

☑ The best way to integrate is to use a marketing plan.

Positioning and Brand Personality

Picture your target market's heart and mind as a map. The map has continents, countries, states, cities, zip codes, streets, and addresses. The continent might be "things to eat." The country might be "eat at home." The state might be "dinner." The city might be "meal for the whole family." The zip code might be "chicken." The street might be "something new and different, not boring." And the addresses on that street might be your brand of boxed dinner and your competitors' brands. Each of you occupies a location or "position" in the customer's mind. In marketing speak, that current customer perception is the positioning that you "own." Positioning is the battle for territory in your customers' hearts and minds. Think of it as a mind map. This is a graphical way to capture the relationship amoug ideas.

What Is Positioning and Why Is It Important?

Positioning is what you stand for in the mind of the market. A good positioning answers at least one of three questions:

- Whom do you serve?
- What do you do for them?
- How are you different from their other choices? Or what are you good at?

Here are some simple, straightforward positioning statements for different companies:

- Light and crispy Southern-fried chicken breading for experienced Southern cooks
- Pure, great-tasting water for families
- The most aggressive divorce lawyers money can buy
- The not-for-profit venture capital fund for new developments in public education
- The friendly local bank for homeowners
- The rowdy fruit-flavored drink for young adult males
- The health care system that puts patients first

Position or Be Positioned

The question is not *whether* you have a position in the minds of your target market. The question is whether it is the *right* position.

Unless people have never heard of your business category or never heard of your business, they will place you at some spot on their perceptual map in relation to competitors. People tend to form their opinions early and hold them for a long time, so it pays to clearly establish the best position you can early in the development of your category or early in the introduction of your company. First impressions are lasting impressions.

However, it is not the first company with a product that gets to be the market leader; it is the first company that is perceived by the most people to be the market leader. This is the reason for "first mover" advantage. You can probably name the first two men to walk on the moon. But can you name the third? The sixth? The 12th? You can probably

> **TRY NOT TO CHANGE POSITIONS**
>
> **CAUTION**
>
> It is extremely risky to change your market position. Target markets tend to hold onto their perceptions of your company for years, so it takes time and money to change. The change often creates confusion, which opens the door for competitors to take advantage. And the new position may not be believable for your brand because of your old position or the position of a competitor that already owns the position you want to take. In general, you are better off building on or refreshing or updating or tweaking your positioning, than you are changing it.

RESEARCH PREVENTS BAD MOVE

As the new creative director and managing partner of an ad agency, I wanted the agency to be repositioned as a creatively led shop, producing original and award-winning world-class ideas. But the agency already had 10 years of reputation as a market-led shop, using research to guide all advertising decisions. Research with current and prospective clients showed that it was believable for us to create great creative work that was market-led, but not to create great creative work for its own sake. So I relented and sought to build a better creative department that built on our previous positioning.

---

name the first American president. But can you name the fifth? The 11th? The 27th? The same mental principle applies to brands. First one into the most hearts and minds wins. If you're lucky or smart, you can eventually become such a leader that you stand for your entire category. That's why Kleenex means facial tissue and Xerox means photocopy.

Figure 6-1 shows a perceptual map for three fast-food establishments (A, C, and M). Note that different brands are rated as being good at different things by the customers. These advantages can serve as the basis for choosing a position.

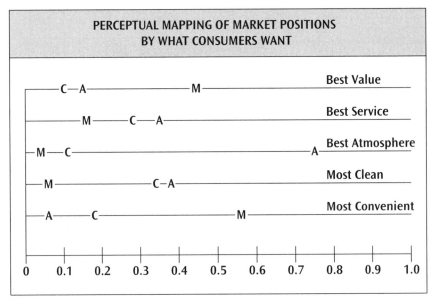

Figure 6-1. Position mapping: Perceptual mapping for three fast-food establishments

Whom Do You Serve? Market Segmentation

If you try to be all things to all people, you will end up being nothing to anyone.

Unless you are selling air or water, every product and service appeals to a specific subgroup of people. And today even water has different market segments, from industrial users who buy by the truckload to individuals buying water by the bottle of upscale brands. Because these groups are different, you cannot reach them in the same media with the same messages.

A subgroup is referred to in marketing as a *niche* or *market segment.* You can even run mathematical programs to break your target market naturally into *affinity groups*, groups of individuals who share a common set of beliefs and behaviors.

All subgroups are not of equal value to you. You have to prioritize your markets. At most, you can have a primary

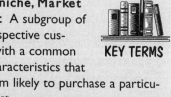

Market niche, Market segment A subgroup of total prospective customers with a common set of characteristics that make them likely to purchase a particular product.

KEY TERMS

Affinity group A group of people who share a common bond, such as interest, background, goal, or membership in the same organization.

SMART

MANAGING

OWN YOUR PRIMARY MARKET SEGMENT

Every business and every nonprofit organization considers one group of people more important than any other—its primary target market. Without this group the organization could not survive. These people account for more of the profits and they remain loyal customers longer.

The smart marketer knows who these people are, what they fear and desire, and how to communicate with them regularly. When faced with a tough decision, the smart marketer makes the decision in favor of the retaining and growing the primary market segment, rather than reaching out to many market segments. Typically, one competitor is stronger in one market segment than other competitors. You are generally better off growing the market segment you own than trying to take market share from a market segment owned by a competitor.

SMART

MANAGING

THE ONE-RABBIT RULE

If you are a hunter and you come across two rabbits running in opposite directions, don't try to chase them both, or you'll end up with nothing. Instead, choose one rabbit and stick with that one. You're far more likely to have rabbit stew for dinner that night. The same rule applies to target markets. Pick one primary market and stick with it.

market, a secondary market, and a tertiary market, as explained in Chapter 1. The most important subgroup is your primary target market. The people who constitute this market are most likely to use your product. They account for a disproportionate share of your sales volume and profits. They are the group of people you cannot afford to do without.

There are countless ways to segment your target market, including these:

- by *geography*: neighborhood, city, county, state, country
- by *demographics*: income, age, sex, kids or no kids, home ownership, marital status
- by *psychographics* or *lifestyle*: believes in God, likes to drink beer, seeks new experiences and sensations, seeks safety and comfort, lives in the 53704 ZIP code, etc.
- by *product use*: heavy user, occasional user, light user, uses one brand exclusively, likes four different brands, etc.

- by *emotional dilemma*: wants high earnings but fears risking capital, wants to eat cake but fears gaining weight, and so on
- by *experiential occasion*: e.g., dinner, breakfast, lunch, brunch, midnight snack, on the go

The best way to segment your market depends on which market segments you own and which segments your competitors own, which segments are the most profitable, which segments are growing, which segments respond strongly to a particular message, and which segments are reachable by media.

USEFUL TYPES OF MARKET SEGMENTATION

TOOLS

- Geography
- Demographics (statistical characteristics): e.g., gender, age, income, marital status, children
- Psychographics (psychological variables): e.g., attitudes, beliefs, values, fears
- Product Use: volume and/or frequency of purchases
- Emotions
- Experiential/Occasion: events, such as holidays and birthdays, or special occasions, such as a romantic dinner

---

DIFFERENT STROKES FOR DIFFERENT FOLKS

CAUTION

Sometimes what appeals to one market segment turns off another market segment. For example, both mothers and teenage boys buy a lot of backpacks, but for completely different reasons. Research showed the teenage boys liked images of death, a vibe of coolness, and a mocking sense of humor. Moms hated all of that. Moms were drawn to stories about self-sacrifice, hard work, and responsibility. Teen boys hated that. How do you create ads for these two audiences?

The solution is to create one ad campaign for moms and another for teenage boys and put each campaign in completely separate media. Attempts to create one campaign to reach both markets would have simply resulted in an unemotional, commoditized listing of product features and benefits that would not have made either group care about the brand.

Write an Emotional "Who Statement" for Your Positioning

The most powerful positioning statements are emotional as well as rational. When describing your targets, describe them (A) as people types, (B) as seeking or avoiding, and (C) as being in a particular situation, occasion, or mindset (Figure 6-2).

People type ... seeking or avoiding ... situation/occasion/mindset

Nervous head secretaries seeking foolproof office furniture recommendations to the management committee

Sleep-deprived long-haul truck drivers who are facing an all-nighter

Groggy working stiffs who shave daily for work because it's their duty

First-time cardiac patients who fear death and disability and hospitals

Millionaires past their prime earning years who now dream of relaxing and having fun

---

Figure 6-2. Examples of who statements for your positioning

What Job Do You Do for Them? Drill Bits, Holes, and Happiness

For-profit or nonprofit, product or service, everything has a job to do for someone. Sometimes that job can be literal and physical: "I want to make more money." Sometimes that job can be more emotional: "I want to feel like I'm rich." Essentially your product or service is an employee of the people in your target market. It does a job for them. The heart of any positioning is in the job it does or the promise it makes to the customers (Figure 6-3).

Product	Feature	Benefit	Emotion/Belief
Drill bit	Unbreakable	Hole	Job well done
Donation	Tax-deductible	Help the poor	I'm a good person
Sports car	0–120 in 15 seconds	Speed	Thrills
Plastic surgery	Safe	Look younger	Feel beautiful

Figure 6-3. What are people really buying?

The heart of your positioning statement about the job you do for your customers should be an active verb, not a passive verb. To most customers, it's not as much about *who* you *are* to them as it is about *what* you *do* for them.

EXAMPLES OF GOOD AND BAD VERBS FOR POSITIONING STATEMENTS

Good	Bad
Teflon's your recommendation	*Is* the safe choice
Refuels your energy	*Is* the premiere energy drink
Lets you *autopilot* through shaving	*Is* the Cadillac of shavers
Surrounds you with caring experts	*Are* the caring experts
Guides you to the right investment	*Are* your prudent investment guides

---

How Are You Different? USPs and Reasons to Believe

Today it is so easy to copy competitors' products or hire away their best people that it is difficult to achieve a genuine point of difference. In advertising, this difference is called your *unique selling proposition* (USP). Your USP is the main promise you offer that makes you different from your competition. To create a USP, ask yourself, "What does our product or service offer that our competitors' products or services don't offer, and what is the specific benefit for our customers?"

Unique selling proposition What sets one company's products and/or services apart from those of its competitors and offers prospects a specific benefit that they consider worth purchasing.

KEY TERM

The USP is a simple statement about your product, service, or brand that tells prospects that it is the only choice for them. It is a concise, memorable statement that answers the question, "Why should I buy from you and not somebody else?"

Own a Key Word

People take your entire company, in all its complexity, and reduce it to one or two words or images to store in their brains. It is the difference between the bull and the bullion. Many companies try to stand for too many things, and they end up standing for nothing. Pick one promise to stand for and stick with it, year in and year out. You can freshen it with new advertising, but stick with the same basic promise. Stand for the same thing over and over again. You will be bored with it long before it seeps into the brains of your target market.

For example, Las Vegas stands for wild adult times and gambling. Disneyland stands for good clean family fun. Las Vegas shouldn't try to attract families and children. Disneyland shouldn't offer gambling.

EXERCISE: "THE _____ ONE"

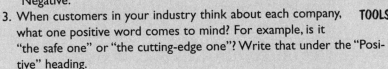

TOOLS

1. List the names of your company and your top competitors.
2. To the right of each name, write two headings: "Positive" and "Negative."
3. When customers in your industry think about each company, what one positive word comes to mind? For example, is it "the safe one" or "the cutting-edge one"? Write that under the "Positive" heading.
4. When customers in your industry talk about each company, what one negative word comes to mind? For example, is it "the risky one" or "the expensive one"? Write that under the "Negative" heading.
5. Study the words for each company. They probably show how your customers have positioned you and your competitors in their minds. Rather than inventing a new position or trying to take the position of a competitor, you are better off identifying the strengths of your current position and owning and reinforcing your strengths. Accept your strengths and weaknesses and take a stand.

FOR EXAMPLE

"THE _____ ONE"—SOME TYPICAL PAIRINGS:

Top Competitors	Positive	Negative
Company A	best-quality	expensive
Company B	low-cost	bad service
Company C	innovative	risky
Company D	big leader	arrogant
Our Company	safe	dated

There is increasing evidence that all brands now are being driven to one of three positions:

- price leader
- quality leader
- specialty leader

For example, Wal-Mart is a price leader, Mercedes is a quality leader, and Robitussin® is a specialty product.

The brands that are suffering today are those that try to stake out a position in the middle of the road. They face price competition from the price leader, quality competition from the quality leader, and specialty competition from the specialist. They cease to stand for anything. Brands in the middle of the road get run over.

What if You Don't Have a USP?

Maybe what you do for customers is not unique. So what is something you do really well as a product, company, or organization? Perhaps you offer a product feature, a cultural difference, a location, or a core strength. That's what your positioning statement should reflect—something special that you offer, even if it is not unique.

Prove Your USP or Core Strength with a Strong Reason to Believe

Just as you have something you do really well, you have a reason why you do it really well. It might be a technology, a patent, a process, a skill, a focus, or an investment. Or you might have proof that you do it really well: a measurement, a

Proof point A fact that provides evidence in support of the marketing claim of a USP or a core strength.

KEY TERM

certification, a demonstration, a cue, a client list, a testimonial, or a behavior. This is your *proof point.*

Examples USPs or Core Strengths and Proof Points

USP/Core Strength	Proof Point
Most popular choice	Made from titanium
Without an energy crash	Doesn't use caffeine or sugar
Won't cut you	Contour blade-buffer
Caring experts	Psychologically tested
Investment team	Triple-reviewed recommendation

Avoid B.S. Words

Today, as a result of advertising, the following words are virtually meaningless: "convenient," "friendly," "professional," "quality," "partnership," "affordable," "solutions." B.S. words tend to be empty claims, abstract, and overused. The best words are concrete, specific, conversational, unusual, and emotionally charged.

"Convenient" is a B.S. word in part because it can mean so many things. In contrast, consider "Next door. Instant. Effortless. One-step. Intuitive. Open 24/7." All these words are more specific about the convenience being offered. "Bulletproof" is more unusual and specific and emotional than "safe"—although "bulletproof" is losing its strength through excessive use. Perhaps the ultimate B.S. word is "solutions." It should come as no surprise that a company is in business to provide solutions for its customers' problems. That's not much of a claim.

CUT DOWN ON JARGON WITH A JARGON GENERATOR

Before the next meeting to review advertising copy, have the group of writers and reviewers create a jargon generator. It's easy and fun, and it will sensitize contributors to B.S. words in your own advertising.

1. Divide a pad or board into three columns: (A) verbs, (B) adjectives, and (C) nouns.
2. Ask the group to suggest for each column five or 10 words that are overused, jargon, or B.S. in advertising in your business category.
3. When the three columns are filled, combine one word from column A, one word from column B, and one word from column C to create a phrase such as "Enjoy Extraordinary Amenities" or "Celebrate Superb Cuisine." Try random ABC combinations to generate tons of meaningless phrases, and read them aloud. It is hard for participants not to laugh, because these very phrases often appear in competitive advertising.

JARGON GENERATOR: SPA INDUSTRY

FOR EXAMPLE This jargon generator was created using common advertising words in the spa industry.

Spa Jargon Generator		
A	**B**	**C**
Enjoy	Exquisite	Accommodations
Celebrate	Exceptional	Services
Experience	Extraordinary	Ambience
Be rejuvenated by	Superb	Amenities
Savor	Beauiful	Cuisine
Luxuriate in	Luxurious	Luxury

Brand Personality: Hitler vs. Mother Teresa

Both Hitler and Mother Teresa were famous leaders in history, influenced millions, had a strong set of beliefs, and inspired others with their beliefs. In addition to the great difference between the things they did and the results they produced, they were very different from each other in their personalities, styles, and beliefs.

Think of your product or service or company as a person with a personality. Sometimes, what truly differentiates companies that provide roughly the same product is the style of their culture or the reputation of their brand. This style is known as their *brand personality*.

Brand personality, as defined in Chapter 5, is a key part of your positioning statement. Basically, think of your company or your product as a person, not a thing, and just list either names of people or adjectives that are very descriptive of your brand. Try not to list more than four. Avoid B.S. words and generic words. Avoid contradictory combinations like "calm yet exciting." Above all, avoid meaningless words like "exciting," "curious," "intriguing," "interesting," "compelling." Use these criteria:

1. If you described a person this way, would it help me pick the person out in a crowd?
2. Would it help a writer, art director, musician, or actor choose a different word, design or photo, musical instrument, or character to play?
3. Does it conjure up a specific image?
4. Is it loaded with feeling?

BRAND PERSONALITY DESCRIPTORS

Good	Not as Good
Bulletproof	Safe
Revved	Enhanced
Airplane pilot	Easy
Mother Teresa	Caring
Guide dog	Trustworthy

FOR EXAMPLE

Put It All Together in an Emotional Positioning Statement

Your product and services have both rational and emotional attributes. Your positioning statement will contain both attributes, but the strongest positioning statements are emotional. They are written in emotional language and consist of the following parts organized into a formula:

1. Title: Usually states what you do (E) and whom you serve (A)
2. Who: "For (A) type of person who wants/fears (B) benefit/loss when facing (C) situation …"
3. What product/service does: "… product (D) active verb (E) …"
4. (Optional) Why care: "… so that reason to care (F) …"
5. Why best: "… product does main strength (G) best, because of reason to believe (H)."
6. Brand personality adjectives: List up to four personality characteristics (I).

Here's an example, labeled to show the various parts of the formula:

(E) **Teflon Furniture Recommendations for** (A) **Office Secretaries**

For (A) nervous head secretaries seeking (B) foolproof office furniture recommendations (C) for the management committee, (D) Brand X (E) Teflon's your recommendation so (F) you don't have to worry about being questioned or fired.

Brand X is (G) the most popular choice because (H) it's made from titanium.

(I) Bulletproof. (I) Solid. (I) Unquestioned.

Emotional Positioning Statement #1

Refueling Truck Drivers
For sleep-deprived long-haul truck drivers who are facing an all-nighter, Brand X *refuels* your energy without a crash (so you don't have to worry about crashing your truck), because it doesn't use caffeine or sugar.
Personality: Revved, Pony Express, Alert

Emotional Positioning Statement #2

Shave on Autopilot

Groggy working stiffs who shave daily for work because it's their duty to look clean-cut and not offend others. Brand X lets you autopilot through shaving. You don't have to worry that it will cut you, because of its contour blade-buffer.

Personality: Airplane pilot, Guardian, Dutiful, Uncomplaining

Emotional Positioning Statement #3

Surround Cardiac Patients with Compassion

For first-time cardiac patients who fear death and disability and hospitalization, Brand X *surrounds* you with caring experts who have been psychologically tested for their heartfelt compassion.

Personality: Mother Teresa, Attentive, Empathetic, Respectful

Emotional Positioning Statement #4

Investment Guides for Millionaires

For millionaires past their prime earning years who now dream of relaxing and having fun, Brand X *guides* you to the right investment. Every investment recommendation from our crack investment team is triple-reviewed.

Personality: Wise, Thorough, Meticulous, Guide Dog

How to Use an Emotional Positioning Statement

Now that you've developed a positioning statement, how can you get the greatest benefit from it?

- Create internal communications to employees to guide them in their daily choices.
- Guide employee recruitment, training, performance, and rewards.
- Guide or evaluate marketing message strategies and creative campaigns.
- Guide or evaluate product, price, and distribution decisions.

Manager's Checklist for Chapter 6

✓ Know that positioning is the territory you own in the hearts and minds of your target market. You either position or get positioned.

✓ Positioning answers one or more of these questions:

- What do you do?
- Whom do you serve?

- How are you different?
- What are you good at?

☑ Positioning tools include position mapping, market segmentation, a jargon generator, and an emotional positioning statement.

☑ Both brands and people have personalities or styles.

Chapter 7

PitchPerfect™ Message Strategy for More Powerful Persuasion

W hat you want to say and how you say it are two different problems to solve. It pays to create a message strategy before you create a message. Otherwise, you are aiming your arrows without a bull's-eye. It's possible you'll hit your target, but unlikely. You might even cause some damage. Without a message strategy first, creating marketing communications is "Fire, aim, ready!"

> **Message strategy** The point of one communication to one target market. If you change the target or **KEY TERM** you change the point, you need a new message strategy.

PitchPerfect™ Message Strategy
Corprov™ Corporate Improvisation Training Class
"Don't bore your employees."

1. **Who are we talking to?** Passionate corporate trainers with tightfisted cynical CFOs and jaded employees.*

2. **What is our point?** Don't waste money trying to *bore* your employees into learning, caring, and changing.

3. **What is the key word in the point?** Bore.

4. **Why should the target care about the point?** Morale is in the tank and budgets are tight. I can't just offer the same old speakers.

*On a normal typed page, none of these answers would exceed one line.

---

5. Why should the target believe the point?

- No boring PowerPoint lectures. Just fun training games everyone can play together.
- Learn useful business skills like leadership, collaboration, creativity, and flexibility.
- Trained thousands of corporate employees across the U.S. since 1993.
- Testimonials from leading U.S. corporations and graduate business schools.

6. How should the target feel? Fun and smart. Games with a serious business purpose.

7. What do we want the target to do? Contact Barry Callen at 608.347.8396 or corprov.com or barry.callen@gmail.com.

LETTER INSPIRED BY MESSAGE STRATEGY

To: Corporate Training Officer
From: Barry Callen, Cofounder, Instructor
    Nell Weatherwax, Cofounder, Instructor
    Corprov™ Corporate Improvisational Training

Dear X,

Nothing wastes more training dollars than boredom. The speaker drones on to the next PowerPoint slide, and 15 minutes into your training day, everyone's eyes have glazed over and everyone looks at the clock to figure out how long it will be until lunch. In this era of tight budgets and low morale, we can offer you a more effective and fun training alternative.

That's why I started Corprov™, corporate improvisation training.

I was the creative director and vice president at an advertising agency. All my people were burning out under the relentless pressure of deadlines and rejections.

I had taken classes at Second City in Chicago, the improv theater that spawned many of the Saturday Night Live players. I simplified the games we learned there so that anyone who could walk or talk could play them, and we started playing them at lunch to boost morale and creativity.

I never expected my staff to also learn how to lead and follow, how to listen and collaborate, how to think on their feet under pressure, and how to present ideas and deal with change, but that's exactly what happened. In our pressure-cooker business, we had to account for the profitability of every person for every 15-minute increment, so devoting any amount of time to the games had to be worth it.

Over the next few years, demand for the classes spread to other departments, then the entire agency, then to our clients, and finally to organizations like yours. This stuff works.

Since our founding in 1993, we have gone on to teach these games to thousands of employees at leading corporations and graduate schools of business across the U.S., including University of Wisconsin Graduate School of Business Executive Education students and faculty, Credit Union National Association Management Schools, Famous Footwear, Fiskars, Minnesota Association of Government Communicators, and Walker Broadcast Management Institute. We've even trained hundreds of veteran trainers at places like Experience Learning Live in Arizona and The Hoffman Institute in California.

Here are a few of our favorite comments about our classes:

"… superstar ratings. You two nailed it the first time. Bravo." Western Management School

"… the highest praise and the highest marks ever recorded for a Superstar Sellers Training Session, since we began in 1993." Midwest Family Broadcasting

"I liked the fact that I didn't have to sit down and listen to New Age psycho-babble while trapped in a stuffy room." Student Verbatim 2008

Students learn by doing, so their learning translates quickly to the work they are doing, and tends to stick. While the exercises are fun (which also helps with motivation and retention), the objectives are deadly serious. It is impossible to reinvent or improve your business if your employees are burned out, unmotivated, poor listeners, subversive power-mongers, timid order-takers, and unable to innovate in the moment under pressure. These Business Improvisation Exercises keep your employees nimble.

All you need to supply for these classes is a private space to move around in, employees in comfortable clothing, and your sense of humor.

To find out more, contact Barry at 608.347.8396 or corprov.com or barry.callen@gmail.com.

Thanks!

The first example is a message strategy.

The second is a cover letter inspired by the message strategy.

The strategy and the execution are two different things.

To improve the power of your communications, separate *what* you want to say from *how* you say it. What you want to say is your message strategy. How you say it is the unexpected creative idea that drives your ad campaign. What you want to say is the emotional bull's-eye. How you want to say it is the arrows of specific communications that you aim, such as ads, Web sites, and press releases.

The Purpose of Message Strategy

Message strategy helps you find the most powerful thing to communicate to your audience—*the reason for customers to care.* Clear message strategy inspires the creatives who invent your ads, press releases, Web sites, brochures, etc. It provides focus. Taking the time to create a message strategy is one of the best ways a company can prevent wasting time and money on activities that are unfocused and won't grab the attention of the market.

SMART MANAGING

STRATEGY BEFORE MESSAGE

Create a message strategy before you create a message. Otherwise, you are aiming your arrows without a bull's-eye. It's possible you'll hit your target, but unlikely. You might even cause some damage. Without a message strategy first, creating marketing communications is "Fire, aim, ready!"

What Is PitchPerfect™ Message Strategy?

PitchPerfect™ Message Strategy is a simple, seven-question method for finding the most powerful thing to say. It is the point of one communication to one audience about one subject. It is called "PitchPerfect™" because it helps you sound just the right note to resonate in the heart of your audience. If you have ever been hit by a sales pitch or advertisement that was off-key, you know just how irritating an imperfect pitch can be.

As you begin, you must know who you are selling to (target audience) and what you are selling (product or service). There is a preferred order to the Pitchperfect™ Message Strategy questions. It is best to start with the "who." Then do the "point," then the "key word," and then the "reason to care." After that the order doesn't matter. Some answers will align more easily with others. Some answers may cause you to go back and start over with new understanding. None of the answers may exceed one typed line, except for "reasons to believe": you get as many as four lines. (Fig 7-1 summarizes the creation of a message strategy.)

1. Pick the right people to brainstorm
   Approvers
   Creators
   Outsiders
   Market Representatives
   Wildcard Know-nothings
2. Do a brief set-up
   Explain the process and benefits
   Provide a brief background on the marketing problem
3. Use traditional brainstorming techniques
   Moderator
   Scribe with big Post-it® pad and easel
   Set the rules (no arguing or evaluation)
   Go for quantity of ideas in sound bites
4. Start with "who"
   Develop an individual profile
   Look at individuals as a whole person, not a target market
   Explore their joys and sorrows and hidden desires and fears
5. Generate a list of options per question
   Go in any order
   Get stuck? Move to another question and come back
   Try the same answer in different questions
   Pursue fresh insights
6. Cluster the options in two to five groups
7. Assemble the clusters into two to five rough message strategies
8. Refine the language
   Write in sound bites (one line, about 12 words)
   Write in the market's language
   Write in Martian, the language of the heart
   Don't perfect, get the ideas down
9. Do an elevator story for each one
10. Evaluate the strategies against criteria
11. Test the stories with the target

Figure 7-1. The process of creating a great message strategy

THE SEVEN PITCHPERFECT™ MESSAGE STRATEGY QUESTIONS

1. *Whom* are we talking to? (defined emotionally in terms of fear and desire)
2. What is our *point*? (emotional conclusion we want target to draw)
3. What is the *key word* in the point? (unusual, concrete, specific, powerful)
4. *Why* should the target *care* about the point?
5. *Why* should the target *believe* the point? (four lines maximum, in order of importance)
6. *How* should the target *feel* about the message, brand, or product?
7. *What* do we want the target to *do*?

TOOLS

The process involves going back and forth: for each question, you brainstorm options and then choose one option for each answer. When all the questions are answered, you have a rough message strategy. Then, in a second step, you perfect the wording. Once the strategic language is perfected, then the different message strategies can be analyzed and compared. The finished message strategies can be put into a creative brief, handed out when evaluating creative work, or used to create "elevator stories"—audio recordings of the message strategies to test in focus groups.

This message strategy process has been proven to work in hundreds of message strategy sessions, creating thousands of ads worth millions of dollars for hundreds of clients since 1993. It has been used to help major national consumer brands sell millions of dollars worth of products and services, to help nonprofit organizations generate donations and volunteers, to help small start-ups triumph over larger competitors, and to help business-to-business companies increase sales and press coverage.

THE STRATEGY IS NOT THE MESSAGE

CAUTION

Do not confuse strategy and message. They are two different things. In fact, not a single word of the message strategy *must* appear in the message. The message strategy is the emotional takeaway or conclusion of your target audience. This conclusion (this message strategy) is not the words. But it guides and inspires the words and pictures you create for your message.

Here's another example of using the PitchPerfect™ Message Strategy. Notice how this gets to the heart of potential consumer concerns, problems, and desires:

PITCHPERFECT™ MESSAGE STRATEGY
Lubey-Dooby-Do
"Self-Reliance for Do-It-Yourself Oil Changers"

1. **Whom are we talking to?** Aging but proud DIY'ers embarrassed when they repeatedly spill oil on their engine.*
2. **Point?** No smelly engine oil spills proves you are still competent, independent, and self-reliant.
3. **Key word?** Self-reliant.

*On a normal typed page, none of these answers would exceed one line.

> **4. Why care?** "I can't stand not being able to take care of myself or my car just because I'm older."
> **5. Why believe?**
> - No-Spill Easy-Pour Spout™ virtually eliminates spills, even with shaky hands.
> - No embarrassing burning oil smell or oil puddles on floor.
> **6. How they feel?** Proud. Independent. Self-reliant. "I've still got it. I can still take care of my own car."
> **7. What to do?** Prove to yourself you've still got it.

Can you feel the difference in emotional power and creative inspiration that comes from using this formula and answerig these questions? Notice that no answer exceeds one typed line. In fact, the entire strategy fits on one side of one piece of paper. This helps the message strategy get to the point.

> ### AD CREATED BY PITCHPERFECT™ MESSAGE STRATEGY
>
>
> **Photo:** Two cars, one old and one new, and in front, an old man smiling holding a grease rag and a young man frowning and looking clueless.
>
> **Headline:** "95-year-old Buster Kelmer can change his own oil. His 21-year-old great grandson, Ted, can't."
>
> **Body Copy:** Buster has kept his car in top running shape for decades thanks to frequent oil changes—and Ted doesn't even know how to find the latch to release the hood of his new car. Thanks to our patented No-Spill Easy-Pour Spout, even Ted could change the oil during an earthquake and not spill a drop, if he knew how.
>
> **Inset Photo of Oil Can with Logo and Spout Feature**
>
> **Tagline:** The no-spill easy-pour oil.

Pitchperfect™ Message Strategy Requires Forced Choice to Be Effective

Physically, a message strategy is simply seven answers to seven simple questions on one side of one piece of paper. No answer (except one—reasons to believe) may exceed one typed line.

This limit forces choice. It is essential to force choice because the average American will take less than half a second to decide whether to pay attention to your ad. The forced choice of the message strategy process helps you focus your message so you can communicate it in less than half a second.

Tips for Finding Better Answers to Each Question

To get the best results using the Pitchperfect™ Message Strategy process, you'll want to follow some underlying rules when trying to answer the questions. First, make sure each answer is defined emotionally, rather than rationally, subconsciously, rather than consciously. Second, make sure the answers are defined from the point of view of the receiver of the communication, not the sender. And finally, reduce every answer to one typed line to force choice. Remember, you cannot make a list of answers that will please all of the people involved in the process. What follows are tips for each step.

FOR EXAMPLE

INCREASE RESPONSE RATES 41 PERCENT

A bank offered a home equity line of credit that most customers used to fix up their kitchens and bathrooms. Because of heavy government regulation, prices and products were virtually identical among competitors.

The client used direct response and measured every response down to the penny. Two ads were used: the message strategy for one was "fix up your dream home at a competitive rate," and the message strategy for the other was "fix the things around the house that are bugging you." The resulting newspaper and direct mail campaign showed a kitchen with an avocado-colored refrigerator from 1970, torn tile, pliers on the stove dial, and other problems.

The "bugging" message strategy—with no major change in product, price, or media—sold 41 percent more than the "dream home" message. It was a great demonstration of the use of message strategy to find the most powerful thing to say.

Question One: Whom Are We Talking to?

This is the single most important question. It frames all the other answers. As much as half the time of a message strategy session can be spent on this question. The trick is to go beyond simple demographic categories (e.g., women 18-40, men 50-65) and beyond buying behaviors (e.g., drivers who buy premium tires) and define your target as a charac-

---

FIND AN EMOTIONAL COMMONALITY

TRICKS OF THE TRADE

If you don't have the marketing dollars to target each market segment, you can try to find a common emotional message strategy. That will enable you to invest in a single ad for all markets. Here's an example from health care:

Due to budget limitations, a health care provider needed to reach both moms and business CFOs with a single mailing. Those market segments seemed worlds apart, but message strategy enabled us to discover an emotional commonality and craft a single "whom" statement for the message strategy: Chief Health Officers burdened with the responsibility of making tough trade-off health care decisions for people they care about.

---

ter in a story, full of hopes and fears (e.g., middle-class professional fashionistas who crave the comfort of squishy-soled shoes but fear looking dowdy and old). This enables you to identify your target customers' greatest emotional needs and dilemmas and attract their attention by solving their problem. It inspires better creative work.

Question Two: What Is Our Point?

When choosing a point, I often ask people to use this criterion. If a genie gathered all your target prospects in one place and magically made them believe one sentence from you, what would that sentence be? I tell them that the genie will also give their competitors the same opportunity. What point would you make?

So how do you pick the right point? Go back to your "Whom?" question, and identify which emotional drivers are the most powerful. Is it more powerful to feel confident or to not be afraid? The two promises are very different.

Look for the best balance of power and believability. "We cure cancer free" is a powerful statement, but hard to believe. "Eat noodles if you like them" is easy to believe, but not very powerful. This balance is not easy.

Question Three: What Is the Key Word in the Point?

The human brain tends to turn bulls into bouillon cubes. We take complex information and simplify it. You can either let your target customers (or your competitors) do that for you, or you can do it yourself by choosing a powerful key word. Think of the key word as the point of the arrow. Without one, it won't stick.

SMART   **FORBIDDEN MESSAGE STRATEGY WORDS**

MANAGING

Here are some examples of BS words that are *forbidden* to be used in message strategy: *solutions, partnership, quality, scientific, engineered, stylish, convenient, trusted, service, best of breed, leader, advanced, intelligent,* etc. These words often create the opposite effect. If a car dealership is called "Quality Cars," it sends up a flag that these cars are not very high quality.

Here are some examples of key words that were used in actual message strategies and have power: *bulletproof, bugging, screw, crave, ritual, speedseeker.*

It is worth spending some time on finding the most powerful key word. Often, a single point contains several good possibilities.

It is worth spending some time on finding the most powerful key word. Often, a single point contains several good possibilities.

In general, choose the key word that:

- is the most unusual
- makes you feel something
- creates a concrete image: you can see it or draw a picture of it
- highlights the chief brand difference
- is believable
- is ownable
- makes people laugh at the truth of it
- is forbidden: it would be really bad to say it out loud to the target customers

One rule: your key word must appear in the point of your message strategy. For example, if your point is "Avoid even feeling the slightest panic before you speak," you can choose your one key word from among "avoid," "slightest," "panic," and "speak." Those are the most powerful words in that sentence. You must choose one.

Even something as complex as a Web site will end up owning one word in the customers' minds. What is your word?

Question Four: Why Should the Target Care About the Point?

With the exception of genuine news, such as a hurricane or an unprecedented technology (Introducing ... the telephone!), you will not be able to *make* a reason to care about and *insert* it in their brains. Instead, you must find something they already care about and build on it. Their reason to care already exists; you don't have to create it. You just have to find an underlying emotional commonality or desire that all target customers share.

Question Five: Why Should the Target Believe the Point?

You are allowed to list up to four reasons to believe. You should rank the reasons, put-

GUILTY OR NOBLE?
In a United Way campaign, the main message was "No matter what you believe, you can act on your beliefs by giving to United Way." In that message there were several potential reasons to care: "You'll feel guilty if you don't," "You'll feel like a good and noble person if you do," and "You were raised to believe giving back is what you should do." The most powerful reason to care turned out to be #3.

FOR EXAMPLE

ting the most powerful first, the second most powerful second, and so on. You need not have more than one. Your goal is to have the most powerful and most believable answers. Don't try to list four for the sake of having four. A weak reason is a negative communication cue. The target customers assume, "If you think that reason is good, you must be desperate."

A great question to explore is "What do people need to believe in order to justify their view of reality or their perception of themselves?" Since they have already made a commitment to believe certain things, if you can tie your point to their current beliefs, you are one step ahead of the game.

Question Six: How Should the Target Feel About the Message?

There are several places you can go to look for guidance in choosing the answers to "how should the target feel?" Positioning and branding usually dictate a set of adjectives around a brand personality. What you use in your message strategy should be that or, at the very least, be congruent with that. Cue testing of words, pictures, ward-robe, music, style choices, etc. can provide strong guidance in defining feeling as a zone. The style choices of the type of individual you profile as representative of the target market can also provide clues: the magazines they read, the music they listen to, the way they decorate their homes, the cars they drive, etc.

Question Seven: What Do We Want the Target to Do?

Why are you sending your target customers this message? Here are a few examples of actions you may want from your target market:

- Trade up, upgrade, or make an expanded purchase from your product line.
- Become aware of our name
- Become an advocate or ambassador for your product
- Believe you are worth checking out: change their attitude or belief about you, find out more information (Web, phone, free booklet, etc.).
- Put you in the considered set for purchase (i.e., put us on the short list)
- Pay ahead of time and save

Avoid the temptation to have a list of calls to action. To the target customers, getting several calls to action feels very demanding and very confusing. Pick one and emphasize it.

FOR EXAMPLE

BE CREATIVE IN YOUR CALL TO ACTION

A major boat manufacturer invented a new hull material that was virtually indestructible. The company wanted to get lots of trade press coverage at the annual boating trade show. So it invited boating magazine editors to come to the show by sending them a baseball bat and encouraging them to whack away at the hull of a sample boat and write about the result.

A typical call to action for the press release would have been "Write about our interesting new technological breakthrough." But editors get tons of such requests. Instead the call to action was "Beat the living daylights out of our new boat hull and write about whatever happens." This resulted in a publicity bonanza for the new boat.

Put It All Together

Check your answers for alignment. Usually you have multiple answers to each question to choose from. Some answers tend to fit better together than other answers.

Experiment with using an answer for one question as the answer to another. In essence you are changing the function of the information. It is common for the main point and the reason to care to be easily exchanged to achieve a different meaning.

Replace weak words (abstract, unemotional, general) with powerful words (concrete, emotional, specific).

Make sure that no single answer exceeds one typed line and that the one-word point is in fact one word.

Use evaluation criteria to compare and select the best message strategies to test (Figure 7-2). Then create an "elevator story" from each strategy to test (Figure 7-3). Make sure you write the elevator stories in an equally interesting way, so that your clever, creative writing doesn't interfere with the way in which the focus group participants react to the story.

Put the final message strategy into the creative brief for creatives to use to make new ads (Figure 7-4).

	Weight	Strategy A	Strategy B	Strategy C
Compelling				
Ownable—different from competition				
Believable				
Works across products				
Works across markets				
Long life				
Motivates employees				
Consistent with positioning, brand personality, culture				
TOTAL				

Figure 7-2. Tool for evaluating message strategies

Enhance the Experience (High, Zen, Therapy, Escape)
I can lose myself for hours in the simple joy of gardening. It's not just a chore; it's almost my form of meditation or therapy. I'm a million miles away from ringing phones and urgent messages, getting my hands dirty, using my muscles, smelling the earth and the flowers. I get into a rhythm, and before I know it, hours pass by like minutes. The right tool adds to the pleasure. If it feels good in my hand, if it cuts effortlessly, if it doesn't punish me physically, or break on me, then I can stay in the flow of gardening almost without thinking. I recently found this fine line of garden tools that are so ergonomically designed and so
(continued on next page)

Figure 7-3. Message strategies can be tested as audio recordings called "elevator stories."

(continued)

lightweight and strong, they f.eel like an extension of my own hand. They really enhance the experience of gardening for me.

Less Effort, More Productive (Pride of Accomplishment)
Gardening doesn't have to be hard and brutal work. With the right tools, it can be a rewarding labor of love. I garden because I like to keep busy. I enjoy getting outside and getting things done and seeing the results of my efforts. I recently found a new line of gardening tools that help me get more done in less time. They have a lighter weight, an easier grip, and an ergonomic design that's easier on my body. I can use less effort and keep going longer. They are strong and durable so I don't have to waste my time racing to the store to replace a broken tool. It's a great feeling when you're done, if you can stand back and feel proud of what you've accomplished in a day. With these gardening tools, it takes a lot less effort to feel more productive.

Revolutionary Performance (Creative Self-Expression, Beauty)
I recently came across these garden tools that were so revolutionary in their design. I'd never seen anything like them. They certainly didn't look like those old heavy tools in my grandfather's shed. When I picked one up, I immediately felt the difference. Their lightweight metal was a lot stronger and tougher than it looked. They were precision-engineered to give more power in less effort. They were ergonomically designed to fit my natural hand and body movements. Using them in my garden, I felt like an artist creating different compositions with different paintbrushes. I often forgot how hard I was working and concentrated more on what kind of effect I wanted to achieve. The way these garden tools perform is truly revolutionary.

My Favorite Tools (Simple, Honest, Physical Labor)
I have my favorite garden tools … the ones I use the most. We're as comfortable as old friends. In this age of speed and quantity over quality, there's just something simple, honest, and noble about a well-crafted hand tool. I choose garden tools with my hands. I feel the balance, the heft, the weight, the precision action, the durability, and the strength. Many of my favorite tools are from the same line. They tend to be very well made. You can tell that somebody who actually works in a garden put some real thought into their design. Whether I'm busting up sod all day, or down on my knees pruning, they help get a lot more done with a lot less pain. Gardening keeps me grounded. And it's way more fun when I can use my favorite tools.

Multiple Message Strategies

Most brands need multiple message strategies because they change the target audience or what they are selling. For example, they may need to

Before Message Strategy	After Pitchperfect™ Message Strategy
Target: Meeting planners and CEOs who want to have a good meeting	**Target:** Businesspeople who want to inspire coworkers who hate meetings
Target: Big-box music software retailer buyers	**Target:** The teenage boy inside the adult retail buyer who always wanted to be a rock star
Promise: #1 leader in mobile storage for institutions	**Promise:** A bulletproof shelving recommendation for secretaries afraid of losing their job
Promise: Great loan rate to fix up your dream home	**Promise:** Fix the things around your house that are bugging you
Promise: X Life Insurance offers a wide choice of payments, premiums, benefits, and riders.	**Promise:** With X Life Insurance, I can feel good about being indecisive today because I can be decisive tomorrow.
Reason to Care: Save 50% on any second purchase of name-brand shoes.	**Reason to Care:** Finding the right shoe at the right price is better than sex.
Reason to Believe: Cool contemporary famous musicians use this backpack.	**Reason to Believe:** If you have to wear a backpack to be cool, you're not cool.
Call to Action (PR): Write trade journal articles about our revolutionary patented new damage-resistant boat hull.	**Call to Action (PR):** Use this baseball bat to repeatedly beat our new damage-resistant boat hull as hard as you can—and then write about what happens in your trade journal.

Figure 7-4. Before and after application of the PitchPerfect™ message strategy

communicate their positioning or their brand, and then to advertise a promotional sale, and then to recruit or motivate staff, and then to introduce a new product, and so on.

To have a single coherent brand, these various strategies must support each other, instead of contradicting. For them, you need a Meta-Message Strategy (MMS). The MMS is the roof that all the other messages support. The MMS can be used as a filter to determine whether a particular message strategy is on-brand and on-positioning.

TRICKS OF THE TRADE

MAINTAIN CONFIDENTIALITY ABOUT HARD TRUTHS

Keep your creative brief and message strategy notes confidential. You would not want any hard truths to leak into the press or get out to your target customers. And, of course, sometimes you must be extra careful that the things you discuss in a message strategy session will not wind up in the actual message.

For example, people may choose cardiac care because they are afraid of death, but they don't want to think about death. A headline or a visual about death would scare them away. Understanding this deep-seated fear would help guide the creative team to make the ads more powerful and honest. However, you would not want this message strategy to become public.

Sometimes it helps to think of all your messages as a house you are building (Figure 7-5). The Meta-Message is the roof supported by all the messages. All the messages are built on the same foundation of *positioning* and *brand personality*.

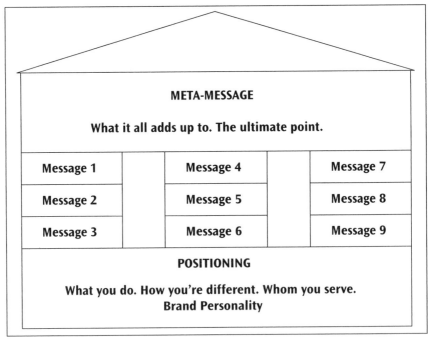

META-MESSAGE

What it all adds up to. The ultimate point.

Message 1	Message 4	Message 7
Message 2	Message 5	Message 8
Message 3	Message 6	Message 9

POSITIONING

**What you do. How you're different. Whom you serve.
Brand Personality**

Figure 7-5. House of multiple message strategies

Differentiating Message Strategy from Messaging, Positioning, and Branding

There is a lot of confusion about *message strategy, creative, positioning,* and *branding*. It helps to understand the difference.

Message strategy is *not* the message. It is *not* the ad, press release, speech, Web site, brochure, billboard, or TV spot. It is *not* the headline or the visual. Those are *executions* of the message strategy.

Message strategy is *not* positioning. Positioning should precede message strategy. The message strategy should be congruent with the positioning. What makes this confusing is that sometimes you may want to communicate your positioning and nothing else. In that case, you need a message strategy about your positioning.

Message strategy is *not* branding. The brand personality should precede the message strategy. If necessary, you can add a question to the message strategy to guide the creation of the communications: "How should the brand feel?" What makes this confusing is that sometimes your message strategy should be about communicating your brand.

Think of ideation as a conveyor belt (Figure 7-6). Each piece is built upon the previous piece. Note that message strategy is the critical bridge between the business process and the creative process. It's a hybrid of both.

1. **Business problem:** Define the job that communication is to do. The client brings symptoms, like "sales are down." Our job is to figure out the cause and find the solution that offers the highest ROI.

2. **Positioning strategy:** Define who the client's true customers are, what job the client does for them, what the client is best at doing, and …

3. **Brand strategy:** … What is the brand personality or style of the client or product?

4. **Message strategy:** What is the most powerful point we can make to the target market in the communication? What objective do we want the communication to achieve? Awareness? Attitude? Action?

5. **Concept creative message:** Using the media designated, conceive a driving campaign idea in rough form.

6. **Execute creative message:** Using various crafts (e.g., writing, pho-

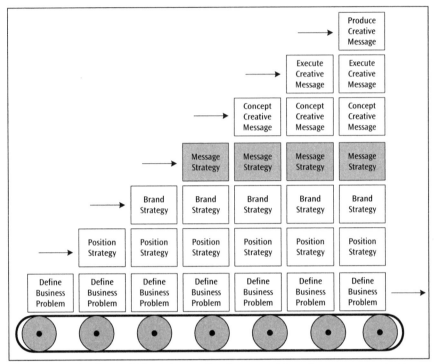

Figure 7-6. The flow of ideas: how a business problem becomes marketing communications

tography, design, music, etc.), improve the quality of the execution. Finesse, tweak, finish. Adjust positive and negative cues.

7. **Produce creative message:** Prepare final files, and send them to the printer, dub house (video duplication service), server, etc.

Manager's Checklist for Chapter 7

☑ Message strategy is the point of one communication to one target market. Change the point or the target and you need a different strategy.

☑ Message strategy can make your marketing communications more effective at a lower cost.

☑ The message strategy is not the ad itself. It is the emotional conclusion you want the target market to draw.

☑ Message strategy can be used to get everyone on the same page, to guide and inspire your creative team, and also to evaluate their creative ideas.

☑ The PitchPerfect™ Message Strategy consists of one-line emotional answers to seven questions, from the target's point of view:

1. *Whom* are we talking to? (defined emotionally in terms of fear and desire)
2. What is our *point?* (emotional conclusion we want target to draw)
3. What is the *key word* in the point? (unusual, concrete, specific, powerful)
4. *Why* should the target *care* about the point?
5. *Why* should the target *believe* the point? (four lines maximum, in order of importance)
6. *How* should the target *feel* about the message, brand, or product?
7. *What* do we want the target to *do?*

Creating Breakthrough Advertising Campaign Ideas

T he average American is now exposed to somewhere between 200 and 6,000 selling messages a day, depending on lifestyle and who is doing the estimating. The vast majority of these selling messages are ignored, a few are hated, and a tiny, tiny portion of the total are noticed. If a message manages to get our attention and get into our heads, it must still compete with an average of 50,000 thoughts per day, most of which are about ourselves.

A part of our brain constantly and subconsciously scans our environment for anything new or different and anything useful or important. (In advertising parlance, anything "unexpected" and "relevant.") If this part of the brain notices something new or useful, it tugs on another part of our brain, and a half second later, we believe we are consciously paying attention to something. But the decision has actually already been made subconsciously. This process is continuous and virtually instantaneous. It is a hard-wired human behavior.

Stand Out in the Clutter

What this means is that your communication must stand out immediately in a sea of clutter. It must be new and different. That is the purpose of a *campaign idea*.

PLAYING IT SAFE IS PLAYING TO LOSE

If you have something important to say, but you fail to get noticed because you say it in a way that doesn't stand out, you have wasted your advertising dollars. Ads that don't get noticed are a big waste of money. Playing it safe creatively is one of the consistently stupidest mistakes that companies make. Consequently, most ads are ignored or hated, a terrible waste of money.

HAVE THE GUTS TO STAND OUT

Here are a few examples of how brands have used creativity to stand out among competitors using conventional ads and achieved a better return on their advertising investments.

Breading Product
Conventional Marketing: Show food preparation. Use actors. Emphasize ease of preparation.
Creative Marketing: Show authentic documentary photos of families enjoying traditional Southern meals, set to a traditional Southern blues song.
Results: Sales up 20 percent.

Introduction of Music Software Product
Conventional Marketing: Use trade show booths to reach retailers with the message that they can make more money because this new product will sell well.
Creative Marketing: Reach retailers at airport with graffitied luggage, fake limo drivers, and fake rock stars carrying the message. Stage protest at trade show to encourage retailers to boycott booth.
Results: Successful sell-in. Record booth traffic. International publicity. Stock value increase. Forty percent market share within one year (nearest competitor 21 percent).

Home Equity Credit Line
Conventional Marketing: Emphasize great rate and creating your dream home. Show a large amount of money and a picture of a luxurious home.
Creative Marketing: Fix what's bugging you, like the avocado-colored refrigerator from the 1970s or the pliers on the broken stove dial.
Results: Sales up 40 percent.

Accounting Firm
Conventional Marketing: Partnership, professionalism, and technology. Images of multiethnic teams working hard at computers, handshakes between silver-haired executives, and mahogany boardrooms.
Creative Marketing: Use black ink (a metaphor for financial success) on white on everything from ads to walls to business cards. Show Rorschach ink blots to emphasize ability to spot data patterns.

Results: Sales up 70 percent within one year.

Business Meeting and Convention Center

Conventional Marketing: Show rows of chairs neatly arranged inside meeting rooms, speakers doing PowerPoint and executives sitting, catered lunches. Talk about architecture, amenities, and service.

Creative Marketing: Show beautiful picture of lakeside view at sunrise, make fun of how much people hate being cooped up in business meetings, and talk about how inspiring this setting is.

Results: Highest reader attention ratings in trade pub, second only to back cover ad. One out of three phone prospects ask for more information.

Prevention of Teenage Date Rape

Conventional Marketing: Parent-pleasing "Just say no" posters with scary statistics about rape, warning teens not to be "bad."

Creative Marketing: Use mirrored posters showing a teen's face as a mug shot, stating, "Force her to have sex and you're screwed."

Results: 14 pre- and post-measurements of teen attitudes and behavior shift for the better. Posters torn down regularly, not ignored.

Automotive Repair

Conventional Marketing: Show clean-scrubbed neatly pressed mechanics using computers to repair engines and handing back bags of used parts as proof of "no rip-offs." Show brand-sponsored race car.

Creative Marketing: Show customers with extreme stories that prove how good the dealer is (driving 100 miles, keeping a vintage car running for 450,000 miles). Dare people to call a phone number that proves the commercial is true.

Results: Sales up 11 percent. 10,000 phone calls. Free publicity.

What Is a Campaign Idea, and Why Do You Need One?

An idea is a new way of looking at an old thing. Most of the points you will want to make in your ads are old things that humans have wanted for centuries: quality, convenience, technical superiority, great taste, fun, less effort, saving money, improved performance, dependability, security, etc. Your challenge as a marketing communicator is to find a new way to communicate them, a way that no one has yet seen.

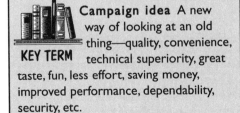

Campaign idea A new way of looking at an old thing—quality, convenience, **KEY TERM** technical superiority, great taste, fun, less effort, saving money, improved performance, dependability, security, etc.

But as hard as it is to come up with a new idea, you must go a step further and create a new idea that will remain new over and over again, no matter what product or topic you tackle. The Holy Grail is an idea that can remain the same, so that it builds equity through consistency, and yet can be constantly refreshed and updated so that it is always unexpected. You need a theme big enough to have variations. In advertising speak, this is known as the "big idea." Like algebraic formulas that stay the same but the variables change in values, big ideas always have two elements: something that always stays the same and something that changes. This gives the advertiser two important business advantages: it builds equity in the brand through repetition, and it stands out from a sea of advertising and attracts attention.

> **Big idea** A new way of looking at an old thing that has elements that stay the same and elements that change, so that it builds brand equity and stays continually fresh enough to capture attention.
>
> **KEY TERM**

Relevant and Unexpected—You Have to Do Both

It is easy to be relevant and expected. Just look at the ads in your business category. They are probably all making similar points about the same relevant topics. In food, taste is relevant. In vacations, fun is relevant. In investments, safety is relevant. In discount retail, savings is relevant.

It's not enough for an ad to be relevant. Your customers expect to hear about the relevant benefits of your business category, so they don't pay attention to your ads. They've seen it and heard it before.

Your Competitors Are Remarkably Predictable . . . and So Are You

There is tremendous pressure in American business culture to take no chances. Employees are rewarded for eliminating surprises, creating predictability, fitting in, getting along, not rocking the boat, and not calling attention to themselves. Humor, silliness, sexiness, childishness, forbidden truths, entertainment, provocation, and passion are considered unprofessional and bad for businesses. Anyone who stands out or offers a different point of view is labeled "not a team player."

ANATOMY OF A BIG IDEA: SOMETHING OLD, SOMETHING NEW

FOR EXAMPLE

Here are some big ideas from the past. The big ideas are so powerful and ran for so many years that you may recognize the brands.

Something Old—What Stayed the Same in Every Ad	Something New—What Changed in Every Ad
A repairman who never has any work to do because the machine he repairs is made so well.	Improvements in the dependability of the product that make him even less needed. Ways he tries to cope with boredom.
Humorously exaggerated situations in which someone runs out of milk at a critical time and bad things happen.	Different people in different situations with different exaggerated bad outcomes.
Black-and-white fashion photography of a celebrity wearing a brand of sunglasses. A question that invites the reader to see who is hiding behind the glasses.	Change the celebrities. Change the glasses.
Ordinary people returning to their ordinary lives from vacations in a city renowned for wild behavior. They are attempting to hide what they did while on vacation. A tagline emphasizes the importance of keeping the details of a trip to this city a secret.	Different ordinary people at different moments of return to ordinary life. Different wild behavior they are trying to hide. Different people they are trying to hide it from. Different extreme methods of keeping their recent behavior secret.
A backpack so durable that it outlives its adventurous owners. An image of a skeleton being discovered wearing a perfectly preserved backpack after a lot of time has passed. A line that draws the conclusion that the product will have a longer life than the owner.	Different humorous and dramatic ways for a person to die while his or her backpack survives, such as starved to death on a raft and discovered by a helicopter, eaten by a dinosaur and discovered during an archeological dig, skiing into a tree and discovered when snow melts.

Companies mostly just look at the advertising their competitors are doing and try to keep up by creating their own versions of what the others are doing. This is not fiscally prudent behavior. The only ads that get noticed are the ads that stand out because they are different. For the smart businessperson, the predictable similarity of most advertisers is a golden opportunity to stand out from the crowd and get a higher return on advertising investment.

DON'T BE A COWARD: INSIST THAT YOUR BRAND STAND OUT — **SMART MANAGING**

As a brand manager, you have a fiduciary responsibility to your company to insist that your advertising stand out or be different in some significant way. Otherwise, you are wasting the company's money.

Try doing a zig-zag analysis, as presented in Chapter 4, to come up with a radical new idea. When it's time to present your idea, show your zig-zag board, point out that ads must stand out to be effective (this is hard to argue with), and then unveil your new ads.

How to Spot an Idea

Finding great ideas is not as easy. Ideas almost always start out in rough form, sometimes even as rough as a spoken phrase or a doodle. Like newborn babies, new ad ideas are kind of small and squishy and messy and they require love and cleaning to grow into their full potential. On the flip side, there are executions that are worked out perfectly in every detail—great writing, great photography, great layout—but that contain no extendable idea at all. In the course of looking at thousands of ads in every medium for over a decade, I developed a set of criteria to help marketers spot potential big ideas. The

Extendability The ability of an idea to be continuously refreshed with new twists or variations on the main theme. The idea can extend into the future, across media, across target markets, across subjects. The greater its extendability, the bigger the idea. — **KEY TERM**

checklist on the next page summarizes these criteria and provides a tool for evaluating big ideas.

BIG IDEA EVALUATION CHECKLIST

Rate each campaign idea from 0 (lowest) to 10 (highest) for each criterion.

Criteria	Campaigns		
	A	B	C
Unexpected	____	____	____
Relevant (strong reason to care, compelling)	____	____	____
Extendable across media	____	____	____
Extendable across markets	____	____	____
Extendable across products	____	____	____
Extendable over time (long life)	____	____	____
Simple and clear	____	____	____
Has an unchanging element for brand equity	____	____	____
Has a changing element for freshness	____	____	____
Can be described in one sentence or image	____	____	____
Halo effect (says less, means more)	____	____	____
On strategy (on positioning, brand personality, Pitchperfect™ Message Strategy)	____	____	____

Let's examine these idea evaluation criteria and why they are important.

Unexpected: This means something new, different, shocking, surprising, fresh. The unexpected compels attention. Most people do not like to be surprised. Tell your creative staff you want to be surprised by the ideas they bring you.

Relevant: It does no good to catch the attention of prospects if the topic is of no use or no interest to them or to your business. They must find your message useful, even if the use is to be entertained and amused. If your idea is inspired by a good Pitchperfect™ Message Strategy, then it will have a relevant main point and a powerful reason to care. Who needs brilliance if it's irrelevant?

Extendable across media: Your idea transcends the limitations of any particular advertising medium. It can be done on radio without visual images.

It can be done on a billboard without sound or music. It can be done in a stationary medium like print without relying on a sequence of images or stories revealed over time. Your idea is not limited to one advertising medium.

Extendable across markets: Your idea has consistent themes and elements that are so strong that you can use it to reach different target markets.

Extendable across products: Your idea has consistent themes and elements that are so strong that you can use it for different products.

Extendable over time: Your idea can have a long life and be used well into the future without becoming dated. This is one of the truest tests of a big idea. Some advertising campaigns have lasted over 50 years.

Simple and clear: An idea can be stated in one simple sentence. As a creative director, I used to require my creative teams to give each campaign a name and a one-line description of the idea before they presented it. If the idea was indescribable or fuzzy, then it was a sign I was not looking at a true idea, but rather at an executional tactic, which could not be extended.

> ### LONG-RUNNING CAMPAIGN
>
> **FOR EXAMPLE**
>
> The longest-running campaign I ever personally helped create has lasted for over 17 years: the "Jazz It Up" campaign with the silhouetted clarinet player for Zatarain's New Orleans dinners. But the client gets the most credit for continuing to stick with it, instead of changing for the sake of change. If you are fortunate enough to have a campaign idea that works, you're crazy not to stick with it.

> ### STICK WITH YOUR WINNERS
>
> **CAUTION**
>
> A great campaign idea can have a long life. Research can measure wear-out with consumers. And a marketing idea will wear out with you long before it wears out with consumers.
>
> There is a story, perhaps apocryphal, that Henry Ford called in his advertising director and told him he was tired of the latest ad campaign—and the director had to tell Ford the campaign had not yet started running. On the flip side, there is research that indicates that if your campaign does not generate results in the short term, it is unlikely to generate results in the long term. The moral? If you have a loser, change it. If you have a winner, stick with it.

ONE-SENTENCE CAMPAIGN IDEAS

Here are some one-sentence idea descriptions from famous ad campaigns that you may recognize.

- Visual puns in the shape of an alcohol bottle based on wordplay using the word "absolute."
- Exaggerated scenarios in which running out of milk has bad consequences.
- An appliance so well made that the repairman is bored and lonely.
- A rabbit that tries and fails to steal a sugar cereal from kids.
- An overnight delivery service so fast that everyone in the commercial talks at lightning speed constantly.
- An athletic drink that shows famous athletes sweating the juice from the product.
- Two very different people representing two different computer brands discuss their respective abilities to accomplish tasks.

Has an unchanging element for brand equity: There are several continuous and unchanging elements about the ad, no matter how it is new and different. In the sugar cereal commercial, the animated rabbit looked and sounded and moved the same, always went silly over the cereal, always concocted a scheme to steal the cereal, and was foiled every time by the kids, who shouted a tagline at the end that the cereal was for them, not for rabbits.

Has a changing element for freshness: In the sugar cereal commercial, the settings, the schemes, and the disguises were always different. Everything else was the same. Yet this campaign has continued for over 40 years.

Can be described in one sentence or image: The list in the sidebar above gives examples of one-sentence ideas. It is also sometimes possible to express an idea in a single image or a single piece of music. Most great TV commercials can be reduced to one key frame or snapshot.

Halo effect: A big idea always says more with less. I once created a TV commercial for a breading used in frying Southern foods like chicken and fish. In communications tests, the target market played back a long list of copy points that were never mentioned in the commercial: tastes good, easy to make, made from the finest ingredients, premium quality, affordable, and so on. What happened is that we successfully made the point that this was authentic Southern breading in a way that triggered happy childhood memories. Once the memories were triggered, a whole host of positive thoughts and emotions came forth. There was a halo effect from the ad.

Make one key emotional point well and you won't have to list product selling points. The associations in your customers' brains and hearts will do all the writing for you.

On strategy: Any marketing communication you do should be built on the foundation of your relatively unchanging position in the market. It should be true to your brand personality. And it should be inspired by your Pitch-perfect™ Message Strategy. Your message strategy will tell you what the key emotional takeaway should be and provide an important reason to care. Staying on strategy helps keep your communication relevant and build a clear, strong brand equity. Remember this: A message strategy is *what* you want to say. A campaign idea is *how* you want to say it.

MESSAGE STRATEGY AND CAMPAIGN IDEA

TRICKS OF THE TRADE

Know the difference between message strategy and campaign idea. A message strategy is *what* you want to say. A campaign idea is *how* you want to say it.

Message Strategy: A technologically advanced dairy show.

Campaign Idea: A dairy show so good your cows will want to sneak in. Extensions include cow disguise kits, cows hijacking truck, letter addressed to **dairy farmer's cow.**

Message Strategy: Our doctors are really good.

Campaign Idea: The person with the most to lose is not the patient, but the person who loves the patient. Extensions include a son talking about his father with brain cancer, twin sisters talking about each other's hospitalization, a daughter talking about her father's stroke.

Message Strategy: A really durable long-lasting backpack.

Campaign Idea: Your backpack will have a longer life than you. Extensions of skeletons discovered wearing perfectly good backpacks after owner starved to death, owner was eaten by a dinosaur, owner skied into a tree, etc.

Message Strategy: Financial success for your business through smart accounting.

Campaign Idea: Accounting is about staying in the black ink and avoiding red ink. Extensions include printing everything in black ink on white paper, Rohrschachk inkblot test, black-and-white ink pen drawings, fingerprints in ink.

Message Strategy: Our bankers understand you and you can understand them.

> **Campaign Idea:** Mortgage bankers speak a language no one understands. Extensions include banker speaking pig Latin, using semaphore, being a mime, using smoke signals, speaking a foreign language.

CAUTION

Don't Confuse a Glittering Execution with a Big Idea

Sometimes ads have no extendable idea. There is only provocative language—"super" and "awesome" and "inspiring" and "razzamatazz"—and jazzy computer graphics of happy people. Often it is not possible to describe the idea in one line because there is no idea. There is nothing to extend or refresh. There is nothing unexpected or original. Ads of this type are like a bright shiny piece of fake jewelry, a triumph of execution over idea. Don't be suckered by glitz.

How to Create Ideas

Creativity requires the ability to conceptualize while ignoring the practical limitations of time, money, and people. Creativity requires the ability to make mistakes often and well and to be imperfect at first. Ideas can be very rough when they first appear. Creativity requires that we turn off our judgmental critical mind and just play and have fun. Creativity requires not knowing the answer in advance, not following a formula or rules, and being open to happy accidents. Creativity can even require redefining the problem to be solved or solving an entirely different problem. All these characteristics of creativity are punished by the rewards and control culture of our schools and businesses.

TOOLS

Improv Comedy Training

Use improv comedy training to stop your business culture from killing creativity.

Through Corprov™, Nell Weatherwax and I teach improvisational comedy games to people in corporations around the country, specifically for the purpose of enabling them to reclaim their creativity, flexibility, innovation, leadership, teamwork, and communication skills. It's amazing how serious professionals can reclaim their sense of fun, play, and creativity in a business setting. Improv comedy training not only makes companies more open to change and competitive, but also builds morale.

How to Create Ideas: Five-Step Process

To create original ideas, it helps to follow a five-step process:

1. Separate
2. Preparate
3. Incubate
4. Generate
5. Evaluate

Paradoxically, it is important that you take each creative step in order, one step at a time. For example, don't attempt to evaluate your ideas as you are generating them, and don't start generating ideas until your brain has had an opportunity to incubate your thoughts on the subject.

Step One—Separate. When I was a creative director at an advertising agency, I used to tell my creative teams to get out of the office, turn off their phones, and find a fun place to hide in order to conceptualize ad ideas. For some reason, sitting in a bar on a pier overlooking a beautiful lake on a sunny day as pleasure boats come and go leads to bigger and better ideas than sitting in a dark office cubicle being continuously interrupted by phone calls, irritating people, and deadlines.

It is not enough to separate from the grim daily grind physically; you must also separate emotionally. This requires some decompression time. I've known members of creative teams to tell jokes, play pool, eat pie, visit art museums, play practical jokes, or talk about romance as a way to separate from the grind of business deadlines and problems. The most productive teams usually spend most of their time lounging and laughing until a great idea comes. It may appear that they are being lazy, but they are not. Once you find the right headspace and attitude, the quality and quantity of your ideas increase dramatically. The best ideas often come when you least expect them: in the middle of the night, in the shower, or while washing dishes, exercising, or driving a car.

Above all, it is important to separate yourself from the creative killers: the individuals you work with whose very attitudes and styles work against creativity. You must avoid the naysayers, the devil's advocates, the people panicked by deadlines and consequences, the pragmatics, the logical, the critical thinkers, the literal, the controlling, the political, the angry and burned out, the creative wannabes, the committees, the reviewers, the envious, and the pessimists. And you must avoid those voices in your head that have the same effect as those people. We all have an internal critical judge. Tell those voices to get lost. Keep them from destroying your joy and inspiration.

One advantage of separation is that you open yourself up to new inspiration. Maybe a walk in the woods, a song, a comedy show, a magazine story, or a conversation will inspire a new idea. Get out of your grind and get new stimuli. One consistent way to build this skill is to do one new thing a day, even if it is just driving to work a different way. Separate yourself from your routines.

Step Two—Preparate. Prepare your mind to create. We all have a creative zone, and we all have unique ways of getting into that zone. Maybe you have a lucky pencil or you like to sit by the fire with a glass of wine or you like to look at advertising awards books for inspiration. Do whatever it takes to put yourself into a creative mood. One of my creative mantras was to simply tell myself, "Have fun!" I have also found the following mental preparation techniques helpful.

> **PREPARATE—YES!**
>
> "Preparate" is a made-up word that means "Prepare your mind to create." If you balk at using this word, you may not be ready to use this process. If you're a stickler on language, consider this linguistic logic: separation, separate; incubation, incubate; generation, generate; evaluation, evaluate; and … preparation, preparate.

- Get exposure to art, nature, or kids.
- Gag your inner judge. Don't evaluate quality while creating. Go for quantity.
- Make yourself laugh. Forget the consequences. Play.
- Redefine the problem to solve by asking stupid questions.
- Do a rough mental flyover of potential areas of exploration before you dig in and start conceptualizing.
- Dare to look foolish. Set your pride and ego aside in order to try bold new things.
- Dare to be imperfect and to create ideas that are "quick and dirty." Work rough.

- Surround yourself with creative and inspiring people, especially a concepting partner.
- Study the best for inspiration.

Step Three—Incubate. Your subconscious is a creative powerhouse. When it comes to generating new ideas, your subconscious mind can run circles around your conscious willpower. But you must feed your subconscious first and give it time to work offline. This is known as "incubating" an idea. Eventually, with time and care and feeding, your subconscious will hatch a new idea or many ideas.

GAG YOUR INNER JUDGE   *TRICKS OF THE TRADE*

We all have an inner voice that judges us, our creativity, and our ideas harshly. The judge often works subconsciously, just below the surface, to sabotage our motivation and inspiration. This self-talk is very damaging to the creative process: "You'll look stupid," "You're not creative," "That's a dumb idea," "We tried that and it didn't work," "You're running out of time." To be productive, you must gag your inner judge while you create. This gets easier with practice. Psychotherapy can also help.

To put your subconscious to work, you must first define the problem you want to solve. You must define it with as much focus as possible. Message strategy is a great way to do this. Then do a brain dump of your most obvious ideas, to clear the path for the arrival of newer, more original ideas. Divide your concepting into at least two sessions—an early rough one, to prime the pump, and a later one, after incubation.

Before you begin conceptualizing, feed your mind as much inspiration as possible. Look at past ads or successful competitive ads or awards books. Read books, look at pictures, watch films and TV, listen to music, or go where the target prospects live to "get the scent" of your target market. Hold the problem to solve in the back of your mind as you go about your daily business. Give yourself a break from working on the problem.

The solution will often appear when you least expect it. Thanks to your incubation period, your new ideas will hatch. Make sure you carry a notepad and pencil or a tape recorder with you at all times to capture the ideas when they hatch.

Step Four—Generate. Set aside a time and place to generate ideas. If the assignment is complex, involving multiple media, pick one simple medium to conceptualize in, such as a billboard with headlines and visuals. Don't worry about writing the entire ad; just go for the headline and main visual scrawled or doodled with a black marker on a white piece of paper. Later, when you have selected a rough idea to "blow out," you can create more finished versions of that idea in other media. But first, though, concept as many different rough ideas to choose from as possible.

TRICKS OF THE TRADE

Concept Rough and Fast

When you conceptualize ads, work rough and fast. Just do enough to get the idea down on paper. Usually this means a headline and a visual. Here's an example:

Here are some other tactics that might help:

- Get the idea on paper fast. Go for quantity over quality. Paper the walls with ideas.
- Conceptualize with a partner. Say, "Yes, and ..." to automatically build on each other's ideas.
- Work rough. Don't perfect. Don't fill in details.
- Think in pictures instead of words. Free-associate images instead of thinking logically.

BOOST GROUP CREATIVITY THROUGH BUILDING ON IDEAS

TRICKS OF THE TRADE

Organizations can no longer afford to depend on the solitary genius who comes down from the mountain with the amazing new solution. Today's creativity is group creativity.

The secret to group creativity is to automatically build on the ideas of others without critical evaluation. A good way is to use "Yes, and ...," a Corprov™ exercise.

USE "YES, AND ..." TO BOOST GROUP CREATIVITY

TOOLS

You can develop creativity with an improv comedy game called "Yes, and ..." Each person in the group contributes to building a story, one sentence at a time. Each sentence must refer to one thing in the previous sentence and begin with "Yes, and ...."

So, for example, if I say, "Once upon a time there was a blue rhinoceros," you might say, "Yes, and the blue rhinoceros liked to read *People Magazine*" or "Yes, and the blue rhinoceros was promoted to vice president." The next person in line then refers to one item in your sentence (e.g., "Yes, and the vice president declared war on all hippopotami") and so on around the room.

No arguments or questions are allowed. "Yes, and it wasn't a blue rhinoceros, it was a purple monkey" or "Yes, but what kind of rhinoceros was it?" would both be mistakes. As team members learn to build on each other's ideas, their ability to innovate under pressure improves. For added fun, you can ask the group to "buzz" anyone who forgets to say "Yes, and ..." or argues or asks a question. Eventually, "Yes, and ..." can become part of your business culture. This Corprov™ exercise can be used to warm people up before a brainstorming session or at the beginning of a corporate retreat.

- Change your perspective. Look at the problem through the eyes of a kid, a Martian, a customer, a dog, a molecule.
- Find an unusual metaphor. For example, "The scented candle is like a cup of coffee, because it smells good but it can burn you."
- Do the opposite of everyone else. "Everyone else shows a picture of the hardware in their ad, so we won't."
- Conceptualize against random stimuli. Flip through a dictionary or encyclopedia or picture book as you hold the main message in your mind. See if any new combinations result. Unexpected juxtaposition is a great source of new ideas.
- Follow your joy and your fear. Notice which concepting directions delight you or scare you. Chase those directions rather than options that feel safer.
- Exaggerate to ridiculous levels. Is the customer problem bad? Make it worse. Is the product solution surprising? Make it shocking. Push your idea too far. You can always pull it back later.
- Think like a comedian. What is it about this situation that makes you laugh? What are the obvious human truths? Don't be afraid to use dark humor to find fresh insights.
- Take breaks. Generate ideas. Then evaluate them. Then take a break. Then do it again. This gives your subconscious the opportunity to incubate on the problem.
- Use the Idea Generator (sidebar) to stimulate a variety of creative approaches to the problem.

Step Five—Evaluate. The important point here is not to evaluate while you are generating ideas. It is the mental equivalent of hitting the brakes and the gas at the same time. Instead, keep the two phases separate. Generate ideas. Then evaluate those ideas. Which ones do you like? Why? Why are certain ideas stronger than others? Look for useful principles to guide further areas of exploration.

Then, take a break. Then, start generating ideas again. At some point, you decide when you have enough good ideas (perhaps because the time has run out) and you choose which ideas to develop further for presentation.

IDEA GENERATOR

TOOLS

Take the creative problem you're working on, and try to create rough ad ideas using these different proven approaches or techniques.

- Demonstration
- Dramatization
- Testimonial
- Expert
- Celebrity
- Exaggeration
- Humor
- Question
- Music/jingle/sound/rhyme
- Advertorial
- Character
- Shocking statement/image
- Animation/cartoon
- Involvement device (e.g., mirror, game, sound chip, paper airplane)
- Slice of life
- News
- Promotional offer
- Borrow another genre (e.g., TV commercial as a newscast)
- Personalization/localization trigger
- Helpful hints
- Three-dimensional gift
- Free sample
- Consecutive series (e.g., Burma Shave)
- Teaser
- Flag the prospect
- Cause marketing
- Sponsorship
- Premium item
- Anti-advertising
- Guerrilla tactics

How to Evaluate Ideas

There are four kinds of genius in advertising:

- The genius to *create* a great idea
- The genius to *recognize* a great idea
- The genius to *improve* a great idea
- The genius to *execute* a great idea

Very rarely does any one person have all four kinds of genius. Most creatives have the ability to create and execute a great idea. They can invent the idea and write the words and design the images as part of their craft. However, creatives are notorious for being unable to recognize the quality of their own ideas. They tend to think their work is either complete trash or complete genius. The line for the most famous Super Bowl TV spot in history, Apple's 1984 introduction of the personal computer, was allegedly discovered in a writer's trash can by a desperate creative director after everyone had gone home. The writer had discarded it as worthless.

Creatives are also notoriously resistant to suggestions for improvements in their work. As with a mother and her newborn baby, it is impossible for a creative person to be objective about the ideas to which he or she has given birth. It is a part of that person, who cannot accept that his or her baby is less than perfect. This is true of anyone who creates something, not just artistic personalities.

That is why creative reviewers and creatives must always be two different people. Reviewers should never try to create, and creatives should never try to review.

As a creative director or as a client, your skill set must include the ability to review creative work, identify the best ideas, and articulate the kinds of changes and improvements you want to see. Saying "I'll know it when I see it" is a waste of money and time—and proof that you don't know what you're doing. It is the creative equivalent of playing the game "Battleship." You are requiring your creative team to be telepathic in order to hit the battleship of your expectations.

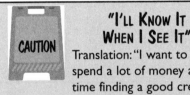

"I'll Know It When I See It"
Translation: "I want to spend a lot of money and time finding a good creative idea." If that's how you feel about what you expect from creatives, master the art of reviewing creative work.

Creative review is about the genius to recognize a good idea and the genius to improve it. The great challenge is how to do this without demotivating the creative team.

The Two Schools of Creative Review

There are two general approaches to reviewing creative work. The Sculpture School of Creative Review is about cutting away all the parts of an idea that are bad, leaving the good stuff. This is very demotivating to creatives. The Gem School of Creative Review is about finding the gem of an idea and polishing it to perfection. This motivates creatives.

The purpose of creative review is not to cut away all the bad stuff, like carving a sculpture. The purpose is to find the gem of an idea and polish it.

So as you undertake your review, remember the following:

- Find the best idea.
- Make it even better.
- Inspire the creative team.
- Discover useful principles about what works creatively and what does not, to guide future creative development.

The "gem" approach to creative review has six steps:

- Control your expectations.
- Get into a receptive frame of mind.
- Experience the ideas without judgment.
- Choose the best idea(s).
- Inspire the creatives to improve the idea(s).
- Agree on clear next steps (who, what, when).

Let's take a look at each one in a little more detail. Note that the "choosing best ideas" step is the only one that involves critical judgment. Note also that the focus is on what works, not on what does not.

Ad Evaluation Checklist

The criteria listed in this checklist are proven to make ads more effective. You may want to add a few criteria specific to your category, brand, or product.

TOOLS

- ___ On strategy?
- ___ Unexpected?
- ___ Made me notice?
- ___ Made me feel?
- ___ Made me care?
- ___ Stand out from competitors?
- ___ Ownable? (only my logo may go there)
- ___ Believable?
- ___ Compelling promise?
- ___ Has a big idea?
- ___ Extendable idea (over time)?

___ Extendable idea (over products, markets)?
___ Extendable idea (over different media)?
___ Simple, clear point?
___ Consistent with positioning and brand personality?
___ Does it work in rough form?
___ What are its limitations/problems?

Just as physicians use differential diagnosis, tapping here and there and getting different combinations of reactions, so you can diagnose what areas of an ad need improvement by isolating the four chief dimensions of any ad:

- **Is it on *strategy*?** (Pitchperfect™ Message Strategy, Chapter 7)
- **Does it have a strong campaign *idea*?** Is the idea unexpected, relevant, extendable? Or is it merely an execution?
- **Is the *execution* of the ad well crafted?** For example, how well executed are the words, graphic design, photography, illustration, Web design, music, acting? Where is the emotional power in the ad? Can the power be exaggerated even more? Is there clear dominance and simplicity? Does everything work together? Is something missing? Is something unnecessary? Do the words have the right content, voice, and brevity? Do the visuals have story appeal, the right personality, and usefulness?
- **Can *production* of the ad take place in the real world?** For example, can the ad be produced within the limitations of cost, politics, turnaround time, technology, and graphic standards?

Manager's Checklist for Chapter 8

☑ The average American is exposed to 200-6,000 selling messages a day. You usually have less than half a second to capture their attention.

☑ To capture attention, you must find a way to be unexpected. If your ad fails to stand out, you have wasted your money.

☑ A message strategy is *what* you want to say. A campaign idea is *how* you want to say it. Message strategy makes it relevant. A campaign idea makes it unexpected.

☑ An idea is a new way of looking at an old thing. A *big idea* is a campaign idea with a consistent theme and new variables that keep it fresh. A big idea is extendable in many directions: customers, products, media, and time.

☑ Most business cultures kill off creativity, so you are generally better off going outside for unexpected creative ideas.

☑ To create ideas, use the five "ates": separate, preparate, incubate, generate, and evaluate.

☑ To evaluate ideas and motivate creatives:
- Control your expectations.
- Get into a receptive frame of mind.
- Experience the ideas without judgment.
- Choose the best ideas.
- Inspire the creatives to improve the ideas.
- Agree on next steps.

☑ Any ad can be diagnosed by looking at the strategy, idea, execution, and production issues.

Chapter

9

The Most Important Creative Elements of an Ad

Most ads in most advertising media contain common parts. This chapter explains the basic parts of an ad. As a marketing communicator, you must understand the role of each part in order to evaluate an ad properly. Ads that lack most of these parts are called *teaser ads*, because they use the missing information to tease your curiosity to find out more. Common parts of an ad include:

- Name
- Logo
- Headline
- Tagline
- Reasons to believe
- Call to action
- Visual

> **Teaser ad** An ad that purposely withholds information to pique curiosity. It usually raises more questions than it answers because it is designed to provoke, not inform. A teaser ad is often done in two steps. The first step raises a question, "What is this?" The second step reveals the answer. This is called the *reveal*. This strategy can be the basis for a *teaser campaign*.
>
> **KEY TERM**

Name

The name of your company, product, service, technology, program, or flavor is the single most powerful piece of creative communication you will ever invest in. It appears in every marketing communication you do, from answering the phone to running an ad. It is the first thing prospects see in the Yellow Pages or on Google.

The bold HEADLINE grabs your attention

The
The MAIN
The MAIN VISUAL
MAIN VISUAL grabs
your attention. The MAIN VISUAL
grabs your attention. The MAIN VISUAL
grabs your attention. The MAIN VISUAL grabs
your attention. The MAIN VISUAL grabs your attention.
The MAIN VISUAL GRABS your attention. The MAIN VISUAL
grabs your attention. The MAIN VISUAL grabs your attention.
The MAIN VISUAL grabs your attention.The MAIN VISUAL grabs your
attention. The MAIN VISUAL grabs
attention. The MAIN VISUAL grabs
attention. The MAIN VISUAL grabs
attention. The MAIN VISUAL grabs
attention. The MAIN VISUAL grabs
attention. The MAIN VISUAL grabs
attention. The MAIN VISUAL grabs
attention. The MAIN VISUAL grabs
attention. The MAIN VISUAL grabs
attention. The MAIN VISUAL grabs
attention. The MAIN VISUAL grabs
attention. The MAIN VISUAL grabs
attention. The MAIN VISUAL grabs
attention. The MAIN VISUAL grabs

The *reasons to believe* explain why you should believe the headline. The *reasons to believe* explain why you should believe the headline. The *reasons to believe* explain why you should believe the headline. The *reasons to believe*

The Call to Action asks you to buy something, change your mind, or make contact.

Any product or name

The tagline states the main benefit, position, or brand.

Figure 9-1. Common parts of an ad

It will appear in every communication, on every sign, and in every conversation about you. It will enable people and search engines to find you even if they've never heard of you. A great name can increase the perceived value of your brand. Here's an industry secret: intent-to-purchase research suggests that a great name alone can enable your company to charge as much as 10 percent more or, in the area of hard goods, perhaps up to 20 percent more—just because the prospective customers perceive that you offer more value.

Unfortunately, we've run out of words. An estimated 94 percent of the words in the *American Heritage Dictionary* are owned by someone. The words that are not owned are not words you want to own (Diarrhea Foods™, anyone?).

So, in order to have a name you can own and use without getting sued for copyright or trademark infringement, you must invent a word or phrase to use as your name. Unless you have millions of dollars to spend in media to make a meaningless word mean something (e.g., Xerox), you need to be clever about combining existing words to create the meaning you want. This is both an art and a science. And a surprising number of created words are already taken. In some categories, such as beverages and pharmaceutical products, it is not unusual that eight out of every 10 names a company creates are already legally owned. So don't just create one or two names for consideration. Create 10, 20, 100, or 500.

It is extremely difficult to create an unusual (new and not owned) word that actually means something good. Consequently, there are creative firms that specialize in nothing but naming. They name companies, categories, products, services, processes, and technology. Some have on-staff linguistic experts, foreign language divisions (to prevent your lovely sounding product name from meaning something awful in another language), online word searches (for creative inspiration and emotional power), and graphic design capabilities, so you can test the name and then the logo or look. Most advertising agencies also do naming as a subspecialty.

CHANGING A SIMPLE FLAVOR NAME MADE MILLIONS

FOR EXAMPLE An internationally famous beverage brand once asked my agency to change the name of the little flavor descriptor on the side of its bottle. Nothing else changed—not the product name, not the flavor, price, distribution, package, or promotion dollars. (Confidentiality prevents sharing the actual name change, but it was the equivalent of changing "Watermelon Strawberry" to "Strawmelon Madness.") The flavor went from being its worst seller to one of its best sellers. This one little change in two words made the company millions and millions of dollars. The name was so popular the company eventually created a special logo for it.

Both naming agencies and ad agencies also offer name testing. Research into finding the right names is almost always an excellent investment. No single communications decision is more important than choosing your name.

Shakespeare gave Juliet this famous line to say of Romeo, "What's in a name? That which we call a rose by any other name would smell as sweet." Figure 9-2 shows four roses. Which would you like to smell? We form impressions of the smell of the rose according to the name. Shakespeare was wrong. Names matter.

Sweaty Gym Socks Rose   Road Kill on a Sunny Day Rose

La Parfum Heirloom Rose   Bus Station Restroom Rose

Figure 9-2. Which rose would you like to smell?

Time-Tested Characteristics of Great Names

A great name is easy to say and pronounce (Sprite), is short and sweet (Tide), and has concrete imagery (Apple). It answers one or more positioning questions. Who is it for? (*Playboy*) What does it do? (TurboTax) How is it different? (Southwest Airlines) It creates a strong, distinct feeling (Yahoo!). It has more positive than negative associations (Bud Lite, Golden Books). It is unusual (Amazon). It uses rhyme (Piggly-Wiggly) or opposition (Stop-N-Go).

No one really knows why, but these naming approaches resonate deeply with the way our human brains are wired. You'll find the same principles at work in great poetry, music, and speeches.

Classic Naming Mistakes

Don't imitate the conventions of your category (First Affiliated United Federal Bank & Trust of Wisconsin). Don't use initials (C.R.P.T.M. Corporation). Only your customers can shorten your name. IBM was International Business Machines for years before it gained its acronym. Don't use numbers by themselves (The 1000 Series). And don't use abstractions in the name (Solutions, Quality, Professional, Technology).

Names like these are leaky buckets into which you pour your marketing communication dollars. These names are easy to ignore and even easier to forget. Be smart and test your name for positive and negative cues before you use it.

NAME GENERATOR

TOOLS

Use these 24 proven approaches to generate your company or product name. (For more detail, see my book *Perfect Phrases for Sales and Marketing Copy*.)

1. Combination (Combine two words from your business area or consumer benefits.)
   - Taxpro Accounting
   - Foodbreak Restaurants
   - Weldrite Fabricators

2. Soundalike (Spell your name phonetically.)
   - Klipt Hair Salon
   - Softwhere Programming
   - Art-kitecture

3. Phrase (State your name as a phrase your customer might say.)
   - Cute Shoes
   - I'm Ready for My Close-up Children's Photography
   - I Need to Rent a New Tool

4. Benefit (Build your chief customer benefit into your name.)
   - Compumatch Dating Service
   - Speedy Remodeling
   - Likemom's Restaurant

5. Visual image (Create a concrete visual picture using an object.)
   - Gavel Legal Services

- Paintbrush Graphic Design
- Gardenia Gift Shop

6. Oxymoron (Combine opposites.)
   - Stronglite Welding
   - Freshtorn Blue Jeans
   - Richpour Molasses

7. Alliteration (Join two or more words that begin with the same letter or sound.)
   - Capital Cabinets
   - Eddy's Eatery
   - Ready Rentals

8. Rhyme
   - The Finer Diner
   - Sweet Treats Bakery
   - The Ancient Merchant Antiques

9. Foreign (Words from other cultures evoke sophistication or fun.)
   - Parthenon Builders
   - Oui Café
   - Mañana Bed and Breakfast

10. Place (Pick a place that evokes appropriate associations.)
    - Niagara Home Water Systems
    - Sahara Dehumidifiers
    - Prairie Software Design

11. Wordplay (Play on words to convey fun or friendliness.)
    - Hair Studio 54
    - Nice Buns Bakery
    - Pros & Concrete

12. Mythology (Pick appropriate gods, mythical creatures, or fictional or historical characters.)
    - Sherlock Diagnostics
    - Phoenix Remodeling
    - Zeus Electrical Contracting

13. Animals (Find animals, insects, or plants with the right characteristics.)
    - Fox Modeling Agency
    - Rhino Industrial Equipment
    - Dragonfly Delivery Service

14. Colors
    - Orange Optical Shop
    - Viridian Landscaping
    - Blue Sky Consulting

15. Personal names (Find a relevant person.)
    - Mbutu's Imports
    - Rembrandt Housepainting
    - Jones/O'Hallaron Investments

16. Letters
    - H.A.H.A. Comedy Club
    - I-8 Roadside Diner
    - W.G.P. (We Grow Profits)

17. Unrelated borrowing (Borrow a word from an unrelated area and combine with your business.)
    - Mr. Furniture
    - Snaptastic Photography
    - 101 Donations

18. Sound effect (Use sounds that show how people feel or what happens when your product is used.)
    - Flush Plumbing
    - Holy Cow! Ice Cream Shop
    - Whoosh Delivery Service

19. Verbs
    - Harden Concrete
    - Blossom Nursery
    - Zap Pest Control

20. Personification
    - Grandma Anna's Toy Shop
    - Two Roofers and a Ladder
    - Aunt Leah's Frozen Custard

21. Target market (Make your customers part of your name.)
    - Homeowners Interior Design
    - Visitors' Guide to Duluth
    - Moms Deserve Chocolates

22. Slang
    - Honest-to-Goodness Car Repair
    - Far-Out Computer Games
    - Stone-Cold Ice Delivery

23. Category label (Literally describe your product, service, or business category.)
    - The Plumber's Plumber
    - Corporate Improvisational Training
    - Kilnfire Ceramics

24. Odd punctuation or phrases for the Internet
- Beau.Ti.Ful.com (cosmetics)
- CleanUpYourMesses.com
- AEIOUandsometimesYou.org

NAME EVALUATOR

Use these proven naming criteria to evaluate the names you're considering. Add criteria specific to your product. For example, should it sound like it tastes good? Better yet, test the names with your customers.

TOOLS

NAME	A	B
Short		
Easy to say, conversational		
Easy to remember		
Relevant to category		
Relevant to benefit		
Creates strong feeling		
Likable		
Believable		
Rhyme		
Alliteration		
Oxymoron		
Consistent with brand		
Consistent with name family		
Concrete visual image		
Stands out, unusual, different		
Ownable		
TOTALS		

There's a word for people who choose great company names—rich.

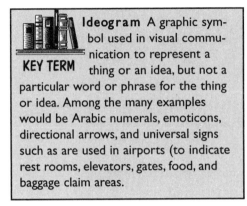

Ideogram A graphic symbol used in visual communication to represent a thing or an idea, but not a **KEY TERM** particular word or phrase for the thing or idea. Among the many examples would be Arabic numerals, emoticons, directional arrows, and universal signs such as are used in airports (to indicate rest rooms, elevators, gates, food, and baggage claim areas.

Logo

A logo is a consistent visual shape and color that helps people recognize your brand. Examples include Apple's apple with a bite out of it or Shell Oil's yellow seashell. But logos can also be abstract shapes (Figure 9-3). The logo can be made of a symbol, a sign, an emblem, or an ideogram. Emoticons (the little symbols used online to convey emotions, such as a smiley face like this: ☺ are ideograms. So are universally recognized airport signs.

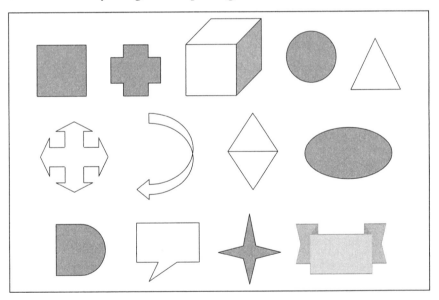

Figure 9-3. Abstract shapes

Logotypes use consistent typography (type styles) to spell out your name (Figure 9-4). Notice how different typography can give different feelings and messages about the exact same company. Typography is like the voice of a word.

CorProv™ **CorProv™ CorProv™**
CorProv™ CorProv™ **CorProv™**
CorProv™ CorProv™ **CorProv™**
CorProv™ CorProv™ CorProv™
CorProv™ *CorProv™* CorProv™
CorProv™ CORPROV™

Figure 9-4. Logotypes

The logo, the logotype, a tagline, and a set of visual rules about what colors and designs to use can be combined to create your *brand identity* (also known as your *brand ID* or *visual identity*). (See Figure 9-5.) These elements make up a core set of visual communications that are usually found in every communication you do. Their purpose is to provide consistent recognition and to communicate your brand identity and positioning.

CorPROV™

Corporate Improvisational
Training

Contact Barry Callen or Nell Weatherwax at 608.347.8396,
barry.callen@gmail.com, or corprov.com

Figure 9-5. Brand identity

By being consistent in your visual identity, you create a visual equity. The equity is similar to building equity in your home. With each additional exposure, people begin to recognize your images, shapes, colors, design, and typography instantly and at a distance. With designs as powerful and distinctive as a box of Tide, it is even possible for customers to recognize the brand name when the front of the box is cut into pieces and rearranged. Brands like UPS that own recognizable images and colors (e.g., brown) have built entire advertising campaigns around their visual identity.

Paradoxically, it is important to both maintain a consistent visual identity in all your communications and periodically update or refresh your identity. To do this, you need to know what your visual equity is. For example, if UPS changed its color to green, it would lose its visual equity. But Apple could change its apple color to green and still retain some visual equity, because the equity lies more in the image of an apple with a bite out of it than in the color of that apple. Research can reveal where your visual equity lies. There are firms that specialize in visual identity or corporate identity work.

Because times, tastes, and visual styles change, it is necessary periodically to update or refresh your visual identity. The trick is to maintain the core visual identity and make only incremental equity changes over time that don't cause unacceptable equity loss. So, for example, if you look at Betty Crocker 50 years ago, 25 years ago, and today, she still looks like Betty Crocker, even though she has a more modern hairstyle and makeup. These incremental makeovers keep a brand from appearing dated and help attract new generations of customers.

The hardest part about maintaining a visual identity is policing and enforcing consistency across many products, divisions, media, and people over time. Someone must be assigned the job of being "brand cop" and must have the power of approval and the support of top management. In addition to reducing the potential for customer confusion, maintaining a consistent brand identity can actually save you money in printing costs, sometimes even a significant amount of money.

The key to visual consistency is to have a short and simple set of guidelines or rules for all graphic designers to follow, with visual exam-

---

CREATE A SIMPLE BRAND STANDARDS MANUAL AND ENFORCE IT

Avoid confusing your customers with inconsistent logos, colors, and designs across your various media, divisions, products, designers, and vendors. Create a simple brand standards manual. The shorter the better. Show examples of what to do and what not to do. And make sure you have final approval over all designs and the power to enforce your approval. It's a dirty, frustrating political job, but someone must play brand cop. As an added bonus, consistent enforcement could save significant dollars in printing and supply costs.

ples of what to do and not to do. The rules should cover placement and size of the logo, relationship to other logos and visual images, page layout and design, color use, and trademark requirements. This document goes by many names: e.g., brand standards manual, brand identity guidebook, and visual identity guidelines.

Headline

Your headline is the single most important point you want to make. It is your hook, your grabber. It must work in under half a second to capture the attention of your audience. If it fails to attract attention, then the rest of your communication is wasted. The vast majority of readers will only read your headline and look at your main visual, so it better be good. Your headline is the 20 percent of the words in your communication that account for 80 percent of the results.

Even in nonprint media, you must have a headline or a most important point to make. On TV or radio, it might be your opening statement or the conclusion you build up to. On a Web site, it might be the slogan or category descriptor just under your name. In direct mail, it might be the sentence or phrase on the outer envelope.

Headline/Main Visual Combinations

Your headline must work in combination with the main visual. This affords you the opportunity to create unexpected and therefore attention-getting juxtapositions.

For example, I once wrote an ad with a large headline, "Why should I give money to some homeless guy I don't know who's just going to use it to buy a bottle?" The visual answered the question. It was a photo of a small baby drinking milk from a bottle.

I've seen TV commercials for luxurious beach vacations that used "news reporter speak" to talk about "oil spills in the Gulf" while showing a beautiful model squirting suntan oil on her bronzed bikinied body.

Sometimes, the purpose of the headline is to provide literal relevant information and the purpose of the visual is to provide the unexpected juxtaposition. For example, picture an ad in a computer software magazine that shows a snarling Doberman Pinscher guard dog and a headline that says, "This is how fiercely our new security software will protect your data."

So important are the headline and the main visual that when ad agency creative teams conceptualize ideas, they usually just draw up rough headlines and visuals without additional explanation. If the "marker rough" can communicate powerfully without additional explanation or details, then it is likely the ad will work when readers are flipping pages a half second at a time. Detailed writing explanations or design finesse cannot save a bad headline or concept.

SMART

MANAGING

Choose Your Battles

Since the headline makes or breaks your ad, use great care in writing it. Small changes in the wording of your headline can make a huge difference in results. In direct response ads, a one-word change in one headline has occasionally been shown to make more than a 1,000 percent difference in sales response. Therefore, when it comes to writing, editing, discussing, testing, and defending your advertising copy, it is worth it to spend more time and money on your headlines than to sweat every little word in your body copy. If you are facing an advertising approver who can't resist making his or her mark on an ad, let it be in the body copy, not the headline and main visual. Choose your battles—and headlines are worth the fight.

Headline Generator

Use these 18 proven approaches to writing a headline. (For more detail, see my book *Perfect Phrases for Sales and Marketing Copy*.)

TOOLS

1. State a tangible benefit involving time, money, or ease.
   - Our college graduates earn 20 percent more.
   - Reduce your chances of burglary and theft.
   - New tool requires less muscle effort.

2. State an emotional benefit that fulfills a desire or alleviates a fear.
   - Feel 10 years younger.
   - Never worry about sewage problems again.
   - Find the career of your dreams online.

3. State a problem and provide a solution.
   - Too many debts? Consolidate them and save.
   - If you are losing customers, our loyalty programs can help.
   - Dirty chimneys cleaned cheap.

4. Provide a demonstration.
   - Even at 120 below zero, this car battery starts right up.
   - Which one is the drawing and which one is the photograph?
   - This console is so simple to use, even a three-year-old can master it.

5. Announce news.
   - Expanded summer hours beginning June 1.
   - Announcing a breakthrough in business consulting software.
   - Weather forecast for tomorrow is ice and snow. Time for snow tires.
6. Flag the prospective customer.
   - Thinking about getting divorced? Call our lawyers first.
   - Introducing a health clinic for women, by women.
   - If you think an applet is a small apple, don't apply for a job at our company.
7. Ask a question.
   - Who says you can't take it with you?
   - Why do we triple-reinforce our truck shocks?
   - When is the right time to buy a house?
8. Offer savings. (Make sure your lawyer previews your promotional offers.)
   - Buy one, get one free.
   - Save up to 50% with this coupon.
   - The lowest price—or we'll refund the difference.
9. Offer freebies.
   - Get a free safety inspection with every oil change.
   - The first 50 callers also get a free T-shirt.
   - Sign up for our rewards program and get preferred customer benefits.
10. List helpful how-tos.
    - Ten ways to reduce your income taxes this year.
    - The year's 20 best gift ideas for teenagers.
    - What to do when your customer won't pay you.
11. Tell a story.
    - When Dr. Smith is not doing surgery here in town, he's volunteering to help the poor in Calcutta.
    - The plumber and the diamond ring.
    - How we turn the world's best beef into the world's tastiest sandwich.
12. Shock and surprise.
    - You may have cancer and not even know it!
    - The average kitchen cutting board wouldn't pass a restaurant food inspection.
    - Ten things your accountant will never tell you.
13. Use humor.
    - If you don't have a good accountant, may we suggest a good lawyer?
    - Our printing quality is a lot better than this newspaper ad.
    - Optometrists with vision.

14. Use drama. (Think of a situation where the stakes are higher than usual.)
    - It's 3:15 am. Your factory line has just shut down. You're losing $1,589 per minute. How soon can you get a replacement part?
    - 15 minutes after the tornado flattened our house, our agent was there with food and water.
    - Without the carbon monoxide detector, the Smith family would have died on Christmas Eve.

15. Use an expert endorsement.
    - All our mechanics are ASE-certified as Master Auto Technicians.
    - As seen on television.
    - Named the city's number-one employment contractor by *In-Town Magazine*.

16. Use a customer testimonial.
    - "We drive over 100 miles just to get our hair cut there." —Willa and Bob Smith
    - Why Carl Virona has been coming to our restaurant every Friday night for 23 years, minus sick days.
    - "They have integrity." —Reverend Malcolm Washington, First Baptist Church

17. Work with a typical customer objection.
    - Not all mechanics are out to rip you off.
    - Most advertising doesn't work. Ours does—and we can prove it.
    - Introducing a radical idea: computer technicians who speak plain English.

18. Associate with a good cause or organization.
    - For every dollar you spend on purchases this December, we'll donate a portion to Orphans Without Toys.
    - PTA members can save 20% on book purchases at this event.
    - Show us your AARP membership card and get an instant 10% off all prescription drugs.

Tagline

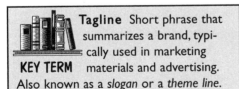

KEY TERM **Tagline** Short phrase that summarizes a brand, typically used in marketing materials and advertising. Also known as a *slogan* or a *theme line*.

A tagline, slogan, or theme line is a short phrase that summarizes your brand and signs off your communication. It usually accompanies your brand name: before, after, or next to your name.

For example, in my print ad or on my Web site, you might see:

CorPROV™

Corporate Improvisational Training

But in my TV commercial, you might see and hear:

VIDEO	AUDIO
FADE UP TAGLINE: Corporate Improvisational Training	ANNOUNCER (voiceover): For corporate improvisational training
FADE UP LOGO: CORPROV™	Corprov.

In any communications medium that uses audio or video, your tagline may also be accompanied by a memory device called a *mnemonic* (pronounced "nee-mahn'-ik). The purpose of a mnemonic is to burn the name and tagline into your memory through repetition.

There are several types of mnemonic devices. One is a repetitive sound and motion, such as the Energizer Bunny pounding on a drum with the

> **Mnemonic** Anything (especially a verbal device) used to help remember something. For example, **KEY TERM** SMART goals—specific, measurable, achievable, relevant, and time-bound.

tagline, "Energizer. Keeps going and going...." Another is a sound effect, such as the echoed double note that accompanies each major edit point in the TV show *Law and Order*. Another is an instrumental jingle under the spoken word, such as the music notes suggesting percolating coffee in Maxwell House commercials. Another is a jingle in which the words to the tagline are sung to a recognizable melody, such as the "Zoom Zoom Zoom" Mazda song or "Rattle rattle thunder clatter boom boom boom, Don't worry call the Car-X man." In some cases, the call to action may be incorporated into the tagline in the form of brand name and phone number sung to music. Music is an excellent memory device. If you can do it, it is an excellent idea to incorporate your brand name into your tagline; for example: "With a name like Smucker's, it has to be good.®"

It's like hitting a lottery jackpot when a tagline becomes a popular

---

THE STAYING POWER OF A GREAT TAGLINE

FOR EXAMPLE

Fill in the blank on these famous and powerful taglines, some of which no longer run. (Answers upside down below.)

A. _____. Because a mind is a terrible thing to waste.

B. The few, the proud, the _____.

C. You're in good hands with _____.

D. Got _____?

E. I'm cuckoo for _____.

Answers: A. United Negro College Fund, B. Marines, C. Allstate, D. Milk, E. Cocoa Puffs.

---

catchphrase used by entertainers and in everyday speech. For example, today, when people do something wild they want to keep a secret, they say, "What happens in Vegas stays in Vegas." That tagline exceeded the expectations of the Las Vegas Convention and Visitors Authority.

A great tagline should stick to your memory like duct tape. But the vast majority of taglines are utterly generic and forgettable: e.g., "People

---

FOR EXAMPLE

THE TAGLINE THAT INCREASED SALES 70 PERCENT IN ONE YEAR

I talked about this in Chapter 2, but it's appropriate here as well. An accounting firm client approached our agency with a very specific request—make our firm stand out. The brochures and Web sites of the firm's competitors showed that they were all doing, saying, and showing the same thing: professional-looking computer montages of four-color photos of handshakes to connote partnership, baronial mahogany boardrooms to suggest stability, and multiethnic groups of people gathered around computer screens to suggest teamwork. The taglines were rife with industry generalities such as "responsive," "professional," "prudent," "quality," and "responsible." You could have switched the logos out on almost any brochure and no one would have been the wiser.

Our agency created a new tagline, "Think Black Ink," to emphasize the core strength of strategic thinking and the chief benefit of helping clients stay in the black and out of the red. I have never seen a client run with a tagline like that firm. The firm got rid of all its four-color printed materials (including its ink pens) and made everything black and white—everything from business cards to office walls. One year later the company president, in an interview in a business magazine, attributed a 70 percent sales increase to the "Think Black Ink" campaign.

helping people with technology" or "Excellence through total quality." Most taglines are so bad that there is a board game called Adverteasing™ in which the object is to match the tagline with the brand name. The sign of a bad tagline is when you can easily switch company names and no one notices the difference.

Your tagline should appear with consistency everywhere your brand name appears. A good tagline should answer one or more of three questions:

1. What do you do?
2. For whom do you do it? Whom do you serve?
3. How are you different from your competitors? What do you do best?

Readers of your advertising are unlikely to go digging for answers to these three key questions. Put your answers into a short, sweet tagline, so readers can quickly determine if your ad is relevant.

This is particularly critical for your Web site. When visitors land, they want to know where they are and what they can do at your site. A good tagline is a time- and space-efficient way to communicate this.

Don't be afraid to be literal and descriptive with your tagline, especially if you are in a new, little-known, or little-understood business or technology category. This is imperative if your name does not indicate what you do, such as "Acme Corporation. Computer Recycling."

All the rules that apply to selecting or creating a name also apply to a tagline. The more concrete, visual, emotional, unusual, specific, and easy to say, the better.

Finally, there is no rule that says your brand *must* have a tagline. But generally, you are better off having one.

Reasons to Believe

According to Barry Callen's Teeter-Totter Theory of Human Behavior™ (presented in Chapter 4), all behavior is the result of balance between fear and desire. In order to avoid fearful things, human beings have subconscious BS detectors operating at all times. We are constantly scanning for negative cues, reasons to *not* believe what someone is saying. While most of our behavior is driven emotionally, we also use our conscious rational minds to double-check our actions or to rationalize what we want.

Tagline Generator

Use these 23 proven approaches to writing a tagline. (For more detail, see my book *Perfect Phrases for Sales and Marketing Copy*.)

TOOLS

1. Ask a question.
   - Why not do it right the first time?
   - What does your suit say about you?
   - Why not you? Why not now?

2. Use alliteration. (Repeat a letter or sound.)
   - Better bids for bigger bucks.
   - Concrete quality counts.
   - Intelligent. Informed. Insightful.

3. Use rhyme.
   - All of the caring. None of the swearing.
   - Unleash your inner winner.
   - Flexible textable messaging.

4. Use rhythm. (Repeat sounds using words with the same number of syllables: "frat rat," "entrance inside," and "merrily-verily" are one-, two-, and three-syllable examples.)
   - We're movers, not shakers. (for a moving company)
   - We know when to leverage what you know.
   - Bridal. Floral. For all.

5. Use an oxymoron (opposites put together).
   - Cool fireplaces.
   - It's stupid not to use the smartest technology.
   - Because the only constant is change.

6. Tie it to a name.
   - Czimaligentri Realty. Hard to pronounce. Easy to work with.
   - Bernard Kutz cuts hair.
   - Susan Golden Investments. When you're with us, you're golden.

7. Position with stereotypical associations.
   - Not your garden-variety nursery.
   - Our lawyers are no joke.
   - Just like mother used to make—but without all the guilt.

8. Position against competitors. (Show how you are different and better.)
   - The area's only 24-hour emergency service.
   - Where the customer is queen.
   - They say it. We do it.

9. Keep it short and conversational.
   - We'll take it from here.
   - Need some help?
   - Just around the corner.

10. Use an analogy, simile, metaphor, or symbol.
    - The top of the mountain.
    - Always have a safety net.
    - As loyal as an old friend.
11. Paint a picture. Tell a story.
    - Modaff's Used Cars. We take the high road to fair prices.
    - Veronshky's Deli. A cut above grocery store meat.
    - Anglon's Advertising. Target marketing for bull's-eye profits.
12. Dramatize it. (Exaggerate the problem, benefit, or feeling.)
    - Make sure you end with more money than retirement years.
    - If it was any more fun, it would be illegal.
    - Don't wait until your car breaks down.
13. Tie it to a physical attribute.
    - The purple wine in the spiral bottle.
    - The little speaker with the big sounds.
    - Look for the man in the sparkling white van.
14. Include your customers.
    - For parents who care about their children's education.
    - The IT department for businesses without IT departments.
    - Honk if you love antique cars.
15. Tie it to a time or place.
    - Weddings and only weddings.
    - It's time you took a family vacation.
    - Montana range-fed beef.
16. Express a feeling.
    - Yippee!
    - I've never done *that* before.
    - Check it off the list.
17. State a position. (Express something you or you customers think or believe.)
    - Where single moms get equal pay.
    - Anything worth doing is worth doing well.
    - There's a lot more to life than business meetings.
18. Call for action.
    - Eat it up.
    - Come back for more.
    - Send a friend a flower.
19. State a benefit.
    - Gifts that get noticed.
    - Get more done in less time.

- The non-jargon get-it-done-today-so-you-don't-have-to-worry-about-it computer repair service.
20. Use unusual words.
   - Ery-vay un-fay ids-kay oys-tay.
   - Doggamit! Dog training for difficult dogs.
   - Bonjour!
21. Make it the voice of a character (a spokesperson, employee, or customer).
   - It's not just my job, it's my calling.
   - Everybody in the pool!
   - My, my, my, but that's tasty!
22. Play with words. (Find a fun way to play with your name or category.)
   - Our massage therapy will rub you the right way.
   - Accounting that measures up.
   - Housecleaning with Kindness (proprietor: Arlene Kindness).
23. Use your category descriptor.
   - Emergency furnace and air-conditioning repair.
   - Robotic manufacturing process software design.
   - Homemade pies for restaurants, delivered fresh daily.

So after you have gotten your prospects' attention and activated their desire, you must then convince them that what you are saying is true and that the risk of taking action is low. That is the purpose of providing reasons to believe.

Usually a reason to believe is a secondary issue. Reasons to believe are irrelevant until you have engaged the prospects' attention and stimulated their desire.

There is a relationship among three factors—the strength of the promise, the risk of the purchase, and the need for a reason to believe. In some cases, the cost and performance risk of buying a product is so low relative to the desire (chewing gum, for example) that we don't even need to supply a reason to believe. But in some cases, the risk of taking action is so great (airplane safety equipment, nuclear power reactor coolant systems, first-time home purchase) that the reason to believe is often placed in the headline or tagline. The reason to believe also becomes a main message in categories renowned for failure, deceit, and lack of performance, such as car repairs, politics, used car sales, and, yes, ... advertising. (I'm an ad guy. You believe me, don't you? Don't you?) In general, the more amazing the promise ("We cure cancer free instantly!"), the more powerful the reason to believe must be. The prospects' reaction is "Oh, yeah. That sounds too good to be true. Prove it!" When it comes to advertising, most people are from Missouri, the "Show-Me State."

Today it is almost impossible to underestimate the cynicism of the American public. We have ceased to trust our government, our religious leaders, our schools, our news media, our neighbors, and even our parents. Why should we trust a profit-obsessed corporation run by faceless, nameless, greedy executives who want to sell us something?

The most powerful reasons to believe are the reasons we need to believe in order to maintain our emotional sense of safety, control, self-esteem, reputation, and perception of reality. Parents need to believe they are doing the best they can for their children, even though this is not always true. Executives need to believe they are powerful and smart, even though this is not always true. The privileged need to believe they are entitled. The downtrodden need to believe they are proud. And so on. Ask

> ### DOUBLE-CHECK FACTS AND LEGALITIES BEFORE YOU MAKE CLAIMS
> **CAUTION**
>
> Make sure you get the necessary legal permission to use names, testimonials, and certifications, or they will come back to haunt you. Double-check your facts to make sure they are true—or you run the risk of permanently ruining your reputation and inviting lawsuits for false advertising. Be particularly careful of superlative claims, like *always, never, guaranteed, promise, forever, permanently, unquestionably, absolutely, the best, better than, superior to, the only, exclusively,* etc.

yourself what your target prospects most need to believe in order to live with themselves, and start there.

A good general attitude for a marketing communicator is this: "Don't brag about it. Prove it." To the extent other people can draw positive conclusions about you, let them do it. Claims from third parties or conclusions drawn by the prospects from facts or demonstrations you supply are more effective than any conclusion you can draw. The more you can demonstrate a point instead of just describing it, the more believable your communications will be. One way to do this is to picture the most cynical person you know reading your ad. What would he or she tell you?

GO LIGHT ON THE LEGALESE

CAUTION

On the flip side, don't let lawyers take over writing your ads. Research shows that the mere presence of legal disclaimer copy in an ad causes prospects to automatically assume the ad is BS. The greater the percentage of space devoted to legal disclaimers, the greater the instant cynicism of the prospects. If possible, put all your legal disclaimers into the body copy of your ad in simple language. Or separate them graphically. Or dial back your claims to require less legalese. The less people trust your category, the more the presence of legal copy damages the credibility of your message. It has become an automatic cue for distrust.

This principle is doubly true in the area of public relations. Perhaps the most cynical people on the planet are news editors. By personal inclination, training, and experience, they are trained to identify and attack lies and mendacity. They love to stick needles in pretentious corporate balloons. They are often the most cynical about whether or not your news announcement is really important news that their readers and viewers will value.

REASONS TO BELIEVE

Use these 16 proven approaches to convincing others that what you say is true. (For more detail, see my book *Perfect Phrases for Sales and Marketing Copy.*)

TOOLS

1. Prove customer satisfaction.
   - 99.3% of our customers plan to purchase a car from us again.
2. Prove leadership.
   - We've put more folks into their first home than any other savings and loan in Mount Carmel.
3. Provide a customer testimonial. (Be sure you get a signed talent release from the people whose names you mention in your commercial, authorizing you to use their names in any medium and any geographic location in perpetuity. For the talent release to be valid, you will need to pay them at least one dollar. Check with your media rep or your lawyer for a sample form.)
   - Four times a year, like clockwork, Harold and Monica M. drive their Chevy S-10 pickup truck to our garage to get it fixed. What's unusual about that is that they live over 100 miles away, in Macarthyburg. We asked them why they drive so far just to get their car fixed here. They said, "When you find a mechanic you can trust, you stick with them."

4. Provide an expert testimonial. (The same legalities apply to this as apply to a regular testimonial. See above.)
   - Nine out of ten dentists recommend using our toothpaste. Ten out of ten of our employees recommend you buy it from us, because you'll save 10%.

5. List credible endorsements. (Many endorsing organizations and certifiers have very specific rules about what you can and can't say in your advertising about their certification. You could lose your certification permanently and risk a potential lawsuit if you violate even minor terms of the agreement. Check with the organization or your lawyer first.)
   - Former five-time convicted burglar and felon "Rambo" Ronson says, quote, "Eventually I learned to walk away from any house with a 'Protected by Booth Security' sign. I knew it would dramatically increase my chances of getting caught. In fact, four of the five times I was caught, it was a Booth Security silent alarm that was the problem."

6. List certificates and memberships.
   - Rama Forrest is a fully certified Reiki Master and one of only three Americans certified in Japan.

7. Offer a guarantee or make-good. (Guarantees have legal ramifications. Make sure you can follow through on your promise, and make sure a lawyer reviews your guarantee. You will also need to calculate the break-even point for your offer and estimate the chances you will at least cover your costs.)
   - If you're not absolutely satisfied with your Garden Grubber, return it within 30 days for a full refund, no questions asked.

8. Prove quality.
   - Our "Death by Chocolate" truffles contain the highest percentage of cacao possible: 90% dark chocolate. Compare that with the 15% cacao in the average candy bar and you'll see what we mean by world-class quality.

9. Offer a compelling or unusual statistic. The more precise, the better.
   - Most lawn mower engines are machined to within 1/100th of an inch. But our lawn mowers are machined to within 1/1000th of an inch. That's hundreds of times smaller than the width of your eyelash.

10. Invite skeptics to see for themselves.
    - Our new Rhinohide Truck Bed Liner is so tough you can beat it with a baseball bat and it will not crack or dent. The liner, that is. You may break the bat. If you try this test, we also suggest you remove the liner from your truck first. We have a supply of bats down at the dealership, so come on down and try it for yourself.

11. State a growth fact.
    - If you put $1,000 in a Local Bank money market CD today, and you leave it in for seven years at an average compound rate, your money will double. That's right: the magic of compound interest can turn $1,000 into $2,000—and you don't have to report to work or lift a finger.

12. List years of experience.
    - Since 1812.
    - Mariposa Realty is now under the third generation of family management.

13. Prove authentic motivation or compassion.
    - When Susan was four, she made a mud pie. Then another. Then 40. The first thing she made in her Easy-Bake Oven was ... an apple pie. By the time she was 12, she could use a real oven and bake a real good peach pie with peaches fresh picked from her family's orchard. At 16, she won the county fair FFA blue ribbon prize for—you guessed it—the best pie, a rhubarb-blueberry compote with graham cracker crust. So it was only a matter of time before she started her own business, the appropriately named "Susan's Pies." You can go there today and have your choice of homemade—or rather, "Susan-made"—pies.

14. Use positive and negative cues in your communication.
    - Bad example using negative cues:
      - *Our fried chicken tastes definitively rural, as any person who grew up in the southern region of the United States can verify.*
      - Details undermine the authenticity of the message to a Southerner. "Definitively rural" sounds like a British anthropologist. "Person," "region of the United States," and "verify" sound too formal, urban, intellectual, and upscale. These negative cues make this communication feel wrong to a true Southerner.
    - Good example using positive cues:
      - Our fried chicken tastes as real down-home country Southern as sweet tea on a front porch swing after church.
      - "Real down-home country Southern" is informal language that American Southerners use to describe themselves. The shared insider details of "sweet tea," "front porch swing," and "after church" signal that this sentence was written by someone who grew up in the South and shares those happy memories with other Southerners. Authentic insider-to-insider communication is more believable. To communicate an authentic Southern feel, you must use authentic Southern language and imagery—positive cues and no negative cues.

- Some target markets, like traditional Southerners, retain their authenticity cues for a long time. Others, like American teenagers, change their cues every six months. If you run an ad with dated language, clothing, hairstyles, or music, they will automatically reject or mock your communication. Cues are powerful reasons to believe. Communications can be tested for authenticity cues.

15. Name-drop. (*Attention, lawyers and readers:* The following example *is not true*. It is provided for demonstration and learning purposes only. Please retain your sense of reality and sense of humor.)
   - Oprah, Madonna, Liza, and Cher raved about Corprov™ in this week's *People Magazine*.

16. Provide a demonstration or dramatization. (From a free sample to a dramatic demonstration, seeing is believing.)
   - We froze this car in a block of ice in Antarctica for one week at sub-zero temperatures. It has the same car battery you can buy. Watch what happens when we start it up. (Engine turns over, lights come on, engine runs.) This winter, consider buying our battery.

Call to Action

Ask the readers and viewers of your ad to take action now. This action could be a change in attitude, a change in behavior, or a search for additional information. You could ask them to call, stop by, order now, request information, contact you, or take advantage of a promotional offer.

It is not always necessary to ask customers to buy your product. Sometimes that request is implied automatically. On the other hand, in direct response marketing, ads that "ask for the order" generally have higher response rates than ads that don't.

It pays to devote some creative thought to asking for the order. As mentioned earlier, asking boat magazine editors to take a baseball bat and beat the living daylights out of a new hull material and then write about what happened was a far more effective call to action than asking them to run an article on the new technology.

In choosing your call to action, your goal is to choose the action with the lowest perceived risk and the highest perceived reward. Asking for a small, low-risk step like finding out more information may be more effective than just asking for the order right away, especially if you are dealing with a big-ticket, high-risk purchase like a house or a retirement investment.

CALL TO ACTION

Use these 19 proven approaches to call your prospects to action. (For more detail, see my book *Perfect Phrases for Sales and Marketing Copy*.)

TOOLS

1. Act now to avoid losing something.
   - Hurry! Offer ends June 23rd.
   2. Act now to gain something.
   - The sooner you order, the sooner you can enjoy your new swimming pool.

3. Take small, low-risk steps.
   - To receive your free booklet on how improv training games can improve your next corporate retreat, contact Barry Callen or Nell Weatherwax at 608.347.8396, at barry.callen@gmail.com, or at *corprov.com*.

4. Remember your name.
   - So remember our name: Blaine Hardware. Blaine. It rhymes with insane, as in our insanely low prices.

5. Remember your phone number.
   - Call 1-800-BUYAPIE. That's one, eight hundred, buy a—B, U, Y, A—pie—P, I, E.

6. Remember your Web site.
   - For more information, visit our Web site at *www.christmastrees delivered.com*.

7. Remember your name and number the next time a need arises.
   - So the next time your car windshield cracks or breaks, remember to call Glassmasters at 555-GLASS.

8. Call now for information.
   - Operators are standing by. Call us toll-free at 1-800-UCALLUS.

9. Order now.
   - Call now to order your own personalized mug and get a free packet of hot chocolate.
   - Get your new Sleeperific king-sized bed right now and enjoy it tonight.

10. Use the product and judge for yourself.
    - We're so confident you will like the quality of our used cars that we're making this special offer. For only $100, you can test-drive one of our used cars for seven days. If you don't like it, you don't have to buy it.

11. Ask a friend or expert about you.
    - Chances are, you already know people who reads our newspaper every day. Ask them what they like about the *Sentinel-News*.

12. Don't miss a limited offer.
   - Hurry. Sale ends this Tuesday at 9:00 p.m.
13. Send for free no-obligation information.
   - Order your free drawing information kit within the next 10 minutes and get a free Conté crayon to keep. No salesman will call.
14. Try a test.
   - Visit our Web site and do a free insurance evaluation for yourself. The test takes only 10 minutes.
15. Enter to win a promotional offer.
   - Stop by this week and enter to win a free Cancun vacation for two worth $10,000!
16. Stop by your store.
   - Drop in anytime and check out our showroom in the new Northtown Mall.
17. Attend a special event.
   - Don't miss the grand opening of our Children's Gourmet Workshop.
18. Support a good cause.
   - This month, Huey's Canoe Outfitters will donate a portion of every purchase to The Rainbow Project for the treatment of child abuse.
19. Know how convenient your location and hours are.
   - The Best Little Restaurant in Texas is only a 15-minute drive from downtown Houston.

Visual

The first or second thing that people are likely to notice in your ad is the visual. It may be a photograph, an illustration, or a design. It may be a color or a typestyle or a material, such as a special paper stock made of ground-up dollar bills.

Together with the main headline, the visual's job is to capture attention in under a half second and generate enough interest to get people to read the ad. The purpose of the visual can be to attract attention (picture the image of a gorilla in a jockstrap), provide relevance (a shot of the product in use), or combine with the headline for an unusual juxtaposition. Long before people read your ad or your Web site, they see the visual all at once and right away. Billboards, which usually have less than four to seven seconds to work, are almost entirely visual. Television ads are better than print and radio at appealing to our nostalgia and taste buds, thanks to moving pictures.

Even radio ads have visuals. The visuals take place in your imagination. In fact, radio enables marketers to create amazing visuals that could never be filmed or photographed affordably, if at all. For example, in radio, a blue monkey the size of the Empire State Building can eat a banana the size of a tractor-trailer truck, slip on the peel, and land in a tub of whipped cream flown in by hundreds of U.S. Army helicopters. Try re-creating that visual in real life.

Visuals have the advantage of being holistic, instantaneous, emotional, and memorable. Visuals transcend language barriers, which is very helpful when you have global product distribution. The best visuals tell a story: something either just happened or is about to happen. Smaller inset visuals are also reader hotspots. The captions you pair with the visuals get above-average readership. Visuals can be used to flag your prospect, demonstrate your benefit, capture attention, or reveal inner technical workings. The new broadband Internet connections now allow the visuals to move and have sounds.

Visuals can easily become dated due to clothing, hairstyles, automobiles, and technology. There are immediately recognizable differences among a black-and-white TV image from 1950, a color image from 1970, and a high-definition image from 2005.

Visuals are usually loaded with positive and negative cues. Visuals can also be used to communicate indirectly what might seem inappropriate to say out loud: "Won't you look rich and successful in this shiny new expensive car?"

Manager's Checklist for Chapter 9

☑ The most common parts of an ad are the name, logo, headline, visual, reason to believe, and call to action. Teaser ads omit many of these parts to pique curiosity.

☑ A great name can increase what customers are willing to pay up to 20 percent. About 94 percent of all words are now legally owned by someone.

☑ A tagline, slogan, or theme line is a short phrase that summarizes your brand and signs off your communication. It usually accompanies your brand name.

☑ Your logo, logotype, tagline, and visual rules can be combined to create your visual identity, a core set of visual communications used inside almost every other communication, from invoices to signage.

☑ By being consistent in your visual identity, you create a recognizable visual equity. A brand standards manual and consistent enforcement are essential to maintain your brand. Visual identities need periodic updating.

☑ Every ad has a main point or headline. The headline and the main visual are the two most important attention-getting features of your ad. This requires them to be both relevant and unexpected, which is hard to do.

☑ In general, the more amazing the promise, the more powerful the reason to believe must be. It is almost impossible to underestimate the cynicism of today's consumer.

☑ A call to action is a request for the reader or viewer to do something, buy something, or feel something. In choosing a call to action, try to find the smallest possible risk and the greatest possible reward. Be realistic.

Media Planning and Buying

C reating ads that will grab attention and change behavior is a job for creative people. Making sure your ads are seen in the right place at the right time is the role of media planning. Of all your advertising expenditures—creating the ads, producing the ads, researching the ads—the vast majority of your dollars are likely to go to the purchase of media. So it pays to know something about media planning.

Media Planning

A media plan guides a series of informed decisions about where to place advertising so that it will be seen or heard by those people most likely to respond. Today, those decisions are being made in a rapidly expanding, complicated, and fragmented environment of media choices.

Media are around us 24/7 and customers depend it as their primary source for news, information, and entertainment. They fall asleep watching Leno and hit the snooze button too many times on a clock radio the next morning. A daily newspaper lands on a fair number of lawns and there's a magazine to feed a hunger for every need, hobby, or desire. Outdoor billboards are ubiquitous and have been elevated to an art form in

This chapter was coauthored with veteran media expert Nancy Bolts, Director of Client Services of Communicopia Marketing Services, Inc.

some areas. People are deluged by direct mail. And time spent on the Internet now rivals time spent with most forms of traditional media as we Google, blog, text, tweet, and post our way through a new and evolving social hierarchy.

Media Objectives and Strategies

Media objectives and strategies define *who* the media plan will target, *what* media will be considered, *where* the advertising will run, *when* it will be scheduled, *how* many people it will effectively impact, and *how much* it will cost. It is an analytical as well as creative extension of the marketing and advertising plan.

The primary objective of a media plan is to drive the awareness that will enhance recall and persuasion, effectively launch a new product, or sustain a brand threatened by intense competitive pressure. Figure 10-1 shows a simplified media plan.

> **Media strategy** A plan that includes deciding *who* will be targeted, *how many* people will be impacted, **KEY TERM** *what* media will be used, *where* and *when* the media will run, and *how much* it will cost. This is usually a written document, an analytical and creative extension of the marketing and advertising plan.

	Jan	Feb	Mar	Apr	May	Jun	Jul	Aug	Sep	Oct	Nov	Dec
TV								▓	▓	▓	▓	▓
Outdoor	▓	▓	▓	▓	▓	▓	▓	▓	▓	▓	▓	▓
Radio	▓		▓			▓						
Magazine	▓	▓	▓	▓	▓	▓	▓					
Newspaper								▓		▓		▓
Internet	▓	▓	▓	▓	▓	▓	▓	▓	▓	▓	▓	▓
Direct Mail										▓	▓	▓

Figure 10-1. Simplified example of an annual media plan

Target Market

The first step is to flesh out the demographics of the best potential customer. Demographics are measurable characteristics that describe people, such as age, gender, race, income level, educational attainment, employment status, and more. Psychographic profiling further defines the target prospects in term of their lifestyle, interests, and values.

Reach and Frequency

Once a target market has been defined, the next step in the planning process is to set communications goals, including reach and frequency objectives. *Reach* is the percent of the target market that will be exposed to the advertising message. It's expressed in terms of *rating points*, with each rating point representing reaching 1 percent of the population. *Frequency* is the average number of times that those who are reached by the advertising message will be exposed to it again. The levels of reach and frequency are determined by the size of the budget and how well the media is planned and scheduled.

KEY TERMS

Reach Percent of the target market that will be exposed to the advertising message, expressed as rating points, with each rating point representing reaching 1 percent of the population.

Frequency Average number of times that people who are reached by the advertising message will be exposed to it again.

In some media the basis of reach and frequency is the number of individual impressions or individual exposures. In broadcast media, the basis of reach and frequency is the accumulation of ratings. The planner estimates the number of gross rating points (GRPs) that will be required, and ultimately a media buyer develops schedules that will deliver those.

The total of GRPs planned determines the levels of reach and frequency that can be achieved. If the communications goal is to reach 70 percent of a target market an average of three times each, the media buyer develops a schedule for 210 GRPs. If more reach is called for, assuming the same number of GRPs (210), frequency will have to be decreased. If heavier frequency is called for, reach will have to be decreased. Those 210 GRPs could be planned in various reach-and-frequency scenarios, e.g., 30 percent reach/7 times, or 10 percent reach/21

EXAMPLE OF REACH

A gross rating point, as explained in Chapter 3, is calculated by multiplying frequency by reach. Here's an example for three TV programs.

TV Program	# of Spots	Rating	GRPs
Daytime Soap Opera	5x	3	15
Evening News	3x	6	18
Primetime Sitcom	2x	12	24
	Total GRPs =		57

The 57 GRPs accumulated in the example schedule do not necessarily reach 57 percent of the target market. That is because some of the viewers would be exposed more than once to the same commercial.

times, 42 percent reach/5 times, 5 percent reach/42 times, 21 percent/10 times ....

Different objectives call for different levels of reach and frequency over different periods of time, and the level of GRPs will be adjusted within the framework of the budget. Generally speaking, a plan will call for the highest possible reach when the objective is to build awareness, such as when you need to launch a new product or communicate new product news. As for frequency, research shows that three times is the minimum level of effectiveness. Less than that and prospects are not likely to recall the message or act upon it. Heavier frequency is in order when advertising to drive persuasion and trial, advertising in a category with low interest, or advertising when the message is very complex. Other factors to be considered when deciding between reach and frequency include brand loyalty, purchase cycle (how often people purchase your product or service), competitive activity, and whether your communication goal is to build a brand image or sell a product.

Geographic Considerations

If a brand enjoys national distribution and sales across all regions of the country, then a cost-effective media plan is likely to include network television and national consumer magazines. If a brand sells better in some regions than in others, then "spot" media will be recommended. Buying spot media allows planners to allocate budget to designated market areas, metro areas, or even more narrowly defined areas that represent the highest sales opportunity.

A complex market by market analysis of a brand's sales strengths and weaknesses can enable the media planner to prioritize media spending. The planner can rank each market based on growth opportunity.

Media planners calculate a Brand Development Index (BDI) for every market under consideration as a tool used when allocating budget. If one market has a higher BDI than another, one route would be to allocate more dollars to that market because of its brand strength relative to what might have been anticipated based on the population.

Planners also look at total category sales when applying a formula to determine a Category Development Index (CDI). These reveal overall demand for a particular product (including competitive brands) in the markets.

KEY TERMS

Brand Development Index (BDI) A measure of the relative sales strength of a brand in a specific market area. It is calculated as a % national population divided by % of households (HH). For example:

Market A

Category Share	8.6%
HH Share	6.3%
BDI	137

Market B

Sales	12.2%
HH Share	15.4%
BDI	79

Category Development Index (CDI) A measure of the sales strength of a particular category of product within a specific market. It is calculated as category sales as a % national population divided by % of national households (HH). For example

Market A

Category Share	11.9%
HH Share	6.3%
CDI	189

Market B

Category Share	9.4%
HH Share	15.4%
CDI	61

In Market A product sales are 89 percent better than in an average market, and in market B sales are nearly 40 percent below average.

Seasonality

Sales analysis also forms the basis for determining wher.
Sales are tracked by month, and money is allocated to those months or
quarters when the brand or category sales are heaviest. In this example,
running media in April through September, the peak buying period,
makes the most sense.

Month	Sales	Percent
January	$30.8	3%
February	$40.1	3%
March	$86.9	7%
April	$110.7	10%
May	$128.5	11%
June	$136.3	12%
July	$149.6	13%
August	$154.8	13%
September	$121.3	10%
October	$80.1	7%
November	$64.2	6%
December	$59.3	5%
		100%

Competitive Spending

What and how competitors are spending is also analyzed to ensure that
the brand will be advertising with an effective "share of voice" (SOV).
Competitive media expenditures in total and by media type are studied
and appropriate decisions made as to how the budget will be allocated.

Share of voice (SOV) Advertising for a specific product or
brand as a percentage of total category advertising. It is calculated as the amount of investment by one company divided by
the total amount invested by all companies. **KEY TERM**
   If three competitors are advertising in a market and Company A spends
$20,000, Company B spends $25,000, and Company C spends $5,000, then
the SOV is 40 percent for A ($20,000 / $50,000), 50 percent for B ($25,000
/ $50,000), and 10 percent for C ($5,000 / $50,000).

Media Mix

Media mix is the combination of advertising media used in pursuing the promotional objectives of a marketing plan. Considering more than one media type can optimize a plan's effectiveness and take advantage of the unique advantages of each type.

- *Television* has tremendous reach and loads of impact. It is considered by many to be the most influential medium. It is also among the most cost-efficient options. Further, it is flexible, targeted, and timely.
- *Radio* can also achieve reach if marketers buy a number of stations in the right combination. And one of radio's main strengths is to increase frequency. Radio allows for very specific targeting, such as advertising during commute time to target working adults who are difficult to reach.
- *Newspapers* are valued for their editorial environment and timeliness.
- *Magazines* are chosen for their affluent, well-educated readers and ability to sustain a message over a longer period of time.
- *Outdoor media* (e.g., billboards and signs) provide reinforcement, heightened reach, and visual impact while accurately zeroing in on a specific geography at a very low cost per impression.
- *Direct mail*, while less cost-efficient, offers the most selective targeting and the greatest measurable impact.
- Presence on the *Internet* is an absolute must.

Media Scheduling and Execution

A media recommendation in the form of a flowchart and budget breakdown provides a means of presentation and a roadmap for the actual purchasing of the media. It provides details such as:

- Spending by media type
- Ad length and ad sizes that recognize creative requirements
- Broadcast daypart distribution and weight
- Print vehicles and insertions
- Scheduling patterns (e.g., continuous media exposure; flighted media to take advantage of purchase cycle, a launch date, special events, pulsing)

■ Anticipated cost efficiencies (e.g., cost per point, CPP [also called cost per rating point], or cost per thousand, CPM [also called cost per thousand impressions])

Media Buying

To varying degrees, all media buying is negotiable. Buyers attempt to meet goals like delivering a cost per rating point (CPP) or cost per thousand impressions (CPM). They look for efficiencies and added value that may be the result of volume discounts or supply and demand. They negotiate whether a TV commercial will appear at the beginning or end (but not middle) of a commercial

KEY TERMS

Flighting Advertising in waves interspersed with periods of total inactivity.

Pulsing Advertising continuously with occasional bursts of heavy advertising.

Cost per point (CPP) Cost of reaching 1 percent of a television or radio audience (one rating point), used as a measure of cost efficiency when comparing broadcast media. AKA *cost per rating point.*

Cost per thousand (CPM) Cost of reaching 1,000 households or individuals with an advertising medium, used as a measure of cost efficiency when comparing print or broadcast media. AKA *cost per thousand impressions.*

break, they negotiate for premium placement in print, and they negotiate for additional free promotions and merchandising.

In the Final Analysis

The analysis doesn't end when the advertising hits the media. It's important to do a post-analysis of what was actually received for the money spent. A thorough post-analysis will reveal whether the ratings stood up to the test of time or to changes in a station's programming or format. It will uncover instances where the ad aired right on the heels of a competitor's ad or appeared in an editorial environment that actually negated its impact. If these or any other media mishaps are uncovered, buyers ask for a *make-good,* as explained in Chapter 3. Remember: it's all negotiable—even after the fact.

If increases in awareness or sales don't meet expectations, consider test markets. Test markets can be specifically structured to isolate media variables like budget levels and alternative plans. If, as Marshall McLuhan

SOME KEY QUESTIONS TO ANSWER IN POST-ANALYSIS

What were the actual ratings achieved versus those that were projected?

Did the ad run at the beginning, middle, or end of the commercial break?

How often did the radio commercial run in the heart of morning or evening rush hour traffic versus around 6 am or 7 pm (which could also count as "drive time")?

Was the ad adjacent to an editorial or surrounded by other ads? If so, what was the article about?

How did the ad look in terms of reproduction quality?

stated, the medium is the message, don't be too quick to shoot the messenger.

Manager's Checklist for Chapter 10

☑ The ways consumers now go about gathering information and seeking entertainment are changing the traditional definition of media.

☑ New media vehicles demand new ways of thinking and a mind open to these as alternatives.

☑ Some traditional principles remain constant: know your target customers, reach them at optimum media levels, and reach them enough times to have your message sink in and be acted upon.

☑ Play to your strengths. Strong sales are a good indication that there are more prospects who are likely to act in a similar fashion if reached effectively.

☑ Don't leave money on the table. Media are negotiable. Foster relationships, ask for more, and make sure you got what you paid for.

Traditional Print and Broadcast Advertising Media

Each advertising medium has different strengths and weaknesses. It pays to have a general idea of what each can best be used for. Almost anything can be turned into an advertising medium (guerrilla marketing), and the number and variety of media are expanding all the time. With the exception of the Internet and perhaps premium items such as printed pens, the most commonly purchased advertising media are discussed in this chapter. (For more information on the Internet, see Chapter 13.)

Traditional paid advertising media fall into two types: *print* and *broadcast*. Print involves printing words and pictures on a surface. Broadcast involves sending a signal with audio or video content to a receiving unit. Traditional print advertising media include magazines, newspapers, brochures, posters and flyers, billboards, Yellow Pages, and direct mail. Traditional broadcast advertising media include radio and TV.

Magazine Display Ads

Magazines can be divided into three types: news or general-interest magazines like *Time* and *Newsweek*, special-interest magazines like *Cat Fancy* or *Easy Rider*, and trade journals like *Adweek* or *The Journal of the American Medical Association*. The first two types are considered *consumer* magazines. The third type is industry-oriented.

177

Most magazines are printed with four colors on a high-speed web offset press in 16-page sections. The sections are then bound or stapled together, often with a glossy four-color cover, and distributed through bookstores, newsstands, or mail. Distribution can be annual, quarterly, monthly, bimonthly, or weekly. Sections can be printed in black and white, in full color, or in spot color. The size and weight of most magazines are usually determined by the amount of advertising space sold, but trade journals tend to carry less advertising because they are financially supported through subscriptions and memberships. The advertising pays for the editorial content of the magazine, but is otherwise kept strictly separate from content development. Magazines can be *paid circulation* or *controlled circulation*, or a combination.

Magazines serve different geographic areas: local, regional, state, national, and international. Some larger magazines offer the opportunity to purchase specific localities. Many magazines also offer discounted ads on their online versions of the magazine.

> **KEY TERMS**
>
> **Controlled circulation publication** Publication distributed nationally, regionally, or locally free of charge to people on a selective mailing list that usually targets specific groups. If reader surveys and demographics can show that the publication is reaching enough people in those target groups, the publication can generate enough income through advertising to cover editorial and production costs.
>
> **Advertorial** Advertisement written in the form of an article or an editorial and often resembling articles in font and format. Advertorials carry a disclaimer identifying them as "paid advertisement." An advertorial is the print equivalent of the broadcast *infomercial*.

Magazines have introduced various tactics to appeal to the advertiser: scented paper, scratch-and-sniff ads, perforated coupons, blow-in coupons and postcards (which often fall out when the reader picks up the magazine), pop-ups, free CDs, a directory of advertisers, 3-D lenticular printing, classified ads, advertorials, and others. But the workhorse of magazine advertising is the display ad, usually full color.

Ad costs vary according to size, placement, and frequency. The bigger the ad, the more noticeable the placement in the magazine; and the more colorful the ad, the more expensive it is to purchase.

Ad costs also vary according to the circulation of the magazine. Here it can get a little tricky for advertisers. Magazine publishers tend to quote numbers for readership or distribution. You should understand what those terms mean and what the numbers are worth. *Readership* is a measure of the number of people who have read or at least looked inside a publication. *Distribution* is a measure of the number of copies of a publication sent to subscribers, prospects, and retail outlets. *Circulation* is a measure of the number of people who have purchased or received a publication.

Advertisers can purchase space in various sizes—an entire section of many pages, a two-page full-color spread, or ads running one page, three-quarters of a page, a half page, a quarter page, an eighth page, or tailored. Ad costs are generally calculated in inches, calculated by multiplying height by width by cost per inch. It costs more to advertise in areas of a magazine that are noticed more. These include the back cover, inside and out, the inside front cover, and any foldouts or special sections—collections of ads and editorial content organized around a theme or subject. Also more expensive is space next to popular features or the table of contents. Discounts are usually offered for long-term contracts. Once the

Readership A measure of the number of people who have read or at least looked inside a publication. *Readership* numbers can vary considerably from *subscription* numbers, because they include *pass-along readers*. On the other hand, circulation numbers include copies that are not read, especially for free publications. Readership numbers are generally estimated.

KEY TERMS

Pass-along readers Readers of a print publication who did not buy or subscribe to the publication (whether paid or free) but rather read copies belonging to someone else. Pass-along readers are also called *secondary* readers, while subscribers are called *primary* readers. Pass-along readership is a relevant factor when evaluating the reach of a publication, but the numbers are unreliable, since they are only estimates calculated by multiplying the circulation figure by a factor such as 2.5 or 5.0 or whatever the publisher chooses to use.

Distribution A measure of the number of copies of a publication sent to subscribers, prospects, and retail outlets.

Circulation A measure of the number of people who have purchased or received a publication. Circulation may be *non-audited* or *audited*, either by the publisher or by a third party.

CHECK OUT THE NUMBERS

TOOLS   If a magazine gives you only readership or distribution numbers, find out more.
If the magazine is audited by the Audit Bureau of Circulation, request the most recent copy. This will provide information, including the number of paid subscribers.
If the magazine is not audited by ABC, check the issue published at the end of the year. Most magazines must publish a "Statement of Ownership, Management and Circulation" once a year, generally November, December, or January. This statement is often tucked away in the back of the magazine and often in very small print. It lists numbers for copies printed, paid and/or requested subscriptions, sales through dealers and carriers, free distribution, and copies not distributed.

space is purchased, it usually can't be changed. You will have to pay for it even if you don't use it. So make sure your ads are ready.

Most readers don't read magazines for the ads. They read articles and look at photographs and other graphics. Your ad must capture their attention in less than half a second as they flip pages. The vast majority of readers will only see your visual and read your headline and then continue on. Other attention hot spots include subheads, inset photos, photo captions, the logo, and the tagline.

The majority of the stopping power of a display ad lies in the combination of headline and main visual. In general, reverse body copy (white type on black background) reduces readership by about 60 percent, so don't do it. Other ways to increase readership include unexpected or relevant headline or main visual, subheads, initial caps, serif typography, lots of white space, shorter sentences or bullets, bolding or underlining (in moderation!), sidebars, and imitating editorial graphic looks and content.

KEY TERMS   **Serif** A term that identifies type fonts characterized by *serifs*, fine lines finishing off the main strokes of the letters. Standard serif fonts include Times New Roman, Courier, and Palatino.

Sans serif A term that identifies type fonts characterized by the lack of serifs. Standard sans serif fonts include Arial, Helvetica, and Verdana.

The layout, typography, and design of the ad should have a clear hierarchy of dominance. Your eye should go effortlessly from one thing to another in a certain order that matches the way you read. Magazine reproduction is usually higher quality than newspaper, so expensive four-color photography or illustrations can make your product look great. Some consumers dream about future purchases, such as home decorations or wedding dresses, and plan for them by going through magazines and tearing out product

MEDIA KITS

TRICKS OF THE TRADE

When considering advertising in a magazine, request a media kit. A media kit will generally include the following:

- Mission and /or positioning statement
- Sample issue of the magazine
- Rate card: pricing, positioning, discounts, etc.
- Specifications: dimensions for the ad sizes, requirements for photographs, etc.
- Circulation information

photos they like. Magazine ads can be split-run (a technique explained earlier in which every other ad has one variable that differs from the control) to test offers, color, and other creative decisions that could affect results.

Newspaper Display Ads

Newspaper ads have a lot in common with magazine ads. However, there are two big differences for the marketer. First, newspapers are usually printed in black and white on rough newsprint stock, which has lower image quality and readability than the stocks used for magazines. Second, newspapers tend to be passed along less and kept around less than magazines—as you know from your experiences in waiting rooms of dentists, doctors, veterinarians, and auto repair shops.

Many people subscribe to newspapers for home delivery, but newspapers are also distributed through newsstands, bookstores, and vending machines. A few newspapers are distributed nationally, such as *USA Today,* *The New York Times*, and *The Wall Street Journal*. Most newspapers are distributed locally, and many newspapers have a monopoly in their localities. Some newspapers also offer the choice of morning and evening editions.

Newspaper formats vary from standard *broadsheets* (pages about 24 inches high by 15 inches wide, although many U.S. newspapers have reduced the width to reduce the cost) to *tabloids* (pages about 15 inches by 12 inches). Most are printed on web offset presses at high speeds.

Some parts of a newspaper—such as free-standing inserts (multi-colored ad and coupon sections usually found in the Sunday edition) and special sections on topics like new home buying—are printed in advance and have earlier ad deadlines than the ads that run in the main part of the paper.

The size of the newspaper is determined by the amount of advertising sold. The traditional ratio is roughly 40 percent editorial and 60 percent advertising. The greater the number of square inches in an ad, the greater the cost. Ads can range from a two-page display spread to a small classified ad. Ads can be selected for printing and distribution into geographic zones (such as a downtown area but not outlying communities). Ads can also be selected for placement into or near specific sections of interest, such as national news, local news, weather, editorial, sports, comics, opinions, cross-words, advice columns, classifieds, food, travel, or entertainment. It usually costs extra to specify exact ad placement. Generally, you are better off with an ad located above the fold or a buy that enables your ad to visually dominate the page. You can also purchase an ad on the plastic sleeve that protects the newspaper on a rainy day or on the card on the front of the newspaper vending machine. Increasingly, newspapers are also offering online versions of their print editions, complete with ads.

People read newspapers primarily for local news, weather, sports, and entertainment. On Sundays, they may read the ads to pull coupons or look for sales. Newspapers are a great place to announce news such as grand openings or new sales and to provide coupons. The great advantage of most newspapers is that they are both local and daily.

As with magazines, the secret to effective newspaper ads is an arresting and unexpected headline and main visual or a local or particularly timely reference: "Hey Chicagoland, it's snowing! Get your snow tires here!" Spot color has also been proven to help an ad stand out and get noticed. Newspapers vary dramatically in their reproduction quality, so don't give them an ad that requires perfect reproduction of an image or that has type that is too small. It can be effective to use a reverse (white type on a black background), but it's usually a bad idea to reverse body copy. Powerful selling words in any medium, but particularly in newspapers, are references to local people and places, references to current seasons or times, and words like "free," "new," "now," "introducing," and "save."

Of all the media you will consider, newspaper readers are the most likely to actually *read* your ad. Increasingly, the Web and 24/7 television have taken some of the newspapers' share of the news market. Newspaper readership has shown declines, and some newspapers have died, at least in print. The growing online practice of skimming information on a screen instead of reading it on a page is causing newspapers to change to formats that make it easier to skim for topics of interest.

Brochures

Brochures are handheld advertisements printed on light to heavy paper stock. Most brochures have multiple panels or multiple pages and are designed as much to inform as to sell.

Brochures vary widely in formats and costs. A brochure can be as simple and cheap as an 8fi x 11 sheet of white paper folded in half (or more commonly, folded into eight panels, four on one side and four on the other) and printed in one color of ink. And it can be as complex and expensive as a hand-assembled book with four or more colors, special cover materials and polished metal fasteners, gold embossing, personalized printing, foil stamping, perforations, perfect binding, and die cuts (using a metal die to cut shapes into the edge). Inks can be scented or metallic or made from environmentally friendly natural dyes. Paper can be thick or thin (measured in pounds); glossy or dull; varnished or unvarnished or laminated; uniform or impregnated with leaves, money, flecks of color, or other objects.

Small quantities of brochures can be printed on a standard press; large quantities are usually printed on a high-speed web offset press. Brochures are usually printed in four-page increments, so your choices are four pages, eight pages, 12 pages, and so on. There are a variety of formats and types of binding and folds, such as Z-folds, gatefolds, and French folds.

Brochures are generally delivered in person and left behind with the prospect (for which reason they're also called *leave-behinds*), sent through the mail (brochures that are mailed without envelopes are called

---

KEY TERMS

Z-fold Shape created when a sheet of paper is folded twice, to resemble a rudimentary folding fan. Also known as a *fan fold* or a *zig-zag fold*.

Gatefold Shape created when a sheet of paper is folded twice, to create a center panel with a panel on each side that's a little narrower than half the size of the center panel. The two side panels can be folded to cover the center panel, and the brochure thus folded can be folded again down the middle of the center panel, so that the brochure opens like a book and then the side panels open outward.

French fold Shape created by folding a page in half in one direction and then folding the folded page in half in the opposite direction. If you ever made a greeting card in elementary school that looked like a little four-page book with two pairs of pages stuck together, you probably made a French fold. Also known as a *rectangle fold* and a *right angle fold*.

---

self-mailers), displayed on racks (in which case only the top of the brochure may be visible), or even stuck under a windshield wiper or handed out to passersby (pamphlets). Some brochures are also used as aids to presentations by salespeople or volunteers.

Brochures are either *interruptive* (meaning the prospect did not ask for the information contained within) or *experiential* (meaning the prospect wants to read the brochure and to enjoy the experience, such as the brochure you might request for planning a vacation trip). For *interruptive* brochures, the front panel and the back panel are critical to success. People will quickly skim the cover headline and visual and perhaps the brand name to determine whether or not to take the brochure or open it. Shorter is better. Use a single dominant theme or idea to attract interest on the outside, and then use details to prove or demonstrate that theme on the inside.

For *experiential* brochures, the physical and sensory experience is paramount. You can maximize that experience with beautiful photography, descriptive prose, and sensory elements such as thick artistic paper stock and unusual sizes, shapes, weights, and inks. Experiential brochures should meet your graphic standards and look similar to your business cards, Web site, and PowerPoint slides.

If your brochure is to be mailed, whether in an envelope or separately (as a self-mailer), make sure you check with the Postal Service first to ensure that it meets postal requirements. This includes things like your indicia, size, shape, flaps, weight, and a host of other criteria. It would be a very expensive waste to print brochures that you can't mail.

> **Indicia** *A rectangle that contains postal* information (usually a special number or bar code) necessary to send your brochure as a self-mailer at a bulk rate.
>
> **KEY TERM**

Posters and Flyers

Posters and flyers are single sheets of paper or cardboard with words and pictures printed on the front side. The major difference is that flyers, like brochures, are intended to be circulated (thus the synonym advertising circular), and posters are intended to remain where they are posted.

Posters are placed on (usually) vertical surfaces for easy viewing from a distance

> **INDICIA AND MAILING PANEL**
>
> **MISTAKE PROOFING**
>
> You must get your indicia from the Postal Service. The USPS is very particular about how the indicia and mailing panel should be laid out on the page and also what information they should contain. The inicia must appear to the upper right of the delivery address and consist of only four or five lines:
>
> *Line 1:* Rate marking
> *Line 2:* The words "US Postage Paid"
> *Line 3:* City and state where the permit is held
> *Line 4:* The words "Permit No." and the permit number

and affixed with glue, paste, tape, staples, or tacks or pressed flat within windowed showcases or frames that hold them in place. Posters are typically displayed where lots of people pass by or congregate. Common poster locations are downtown building walls, street kiosks, plate glass windows, bulletin boards, schools, lounges, cafeterias, and public transportation. Many businesses maintain framed structures for easy placement of posters. Some vendors even offer to display advertising in bathroom stalls!

Posters are often used to promote one-time events. Posters are primarily a visual medium, like billboards, and are designed to interrupt attention from a distance. The visual and headline do the primary work. An attention-getting and powerful visual is the most important part, followed by the name of the product or event. Details are usually placed in easy-to-read bullets below the visual and headline. The most important details, after the name of the event and the headline, are the date, time, place, and cost of the event and the way to order tickets or get more information. Less is more in a poster.

The cost of a poster varies by size (from standard one-page flyer to wall-sized subway poster), number of colors (from one-color type to four-color photography), materials (from typewriter paper to weather-resistant laminate), and quantity. Timing and location are critical to the success of a poster. Most posters must be weatherproof, and generally have a very short life.

Flyers, like brochures, can go anywhere you can find your prospects. You can place piles of flyers in strategic locations, you can hand out flyers in the street, you can mail flyers, and you can stick flyers up like small posters. (In the last case, the difference between a flyer and a poster may be only size and/or construction.)

Billboards

Billboards are large advertisements near highways and streets that can be read by passing motorists (and in some cases bikers and pedestrians). Billboard advertising is also referred to as *outdoor advertising*—although that's a category that also includes ads on and around and inside sports centers and race tracks, and on mass transit vehicles and shelters, on blimps, and on banners pulled by airplanes.

Billboards are primarily a visual medium, and the visual must be clear, attention-getting, and memorable. Barring traffic jam situations, most billboards must be read by passing motorists in seven to 12 seconds, so simplicity is of the essence. It is usually not a good idea to put more than seven words on a billboard, including your company name or logo. One word or no words is even better. Let the visual carry the message and show your product with the logo on the package.

The "one ad, one idea" rule reigns in this medium. Billboards vary from small to large, from printed (usually on vinyl) to hand-painted (sometimes on the sides of buildings), and from flat and rectangular to three-dimensional with shapes extending beyond the border. Billboards can also be illuminated at night, have moving elements (e.g., wind-activated dots and op art movement), or be electronic like a large TV screen (with multiple ads per billboard or with moving pictures).

Billboards are independently rated according to the amount of traffic that passes by. The bigger the billboard, the more special features, the longer the ad stays up (billboards are usually purchased by the month), and the more eyeballs that pass the location, the more the billboard costs.

Billboards are good for products that are easy to understand and for messages that are simple and can be conveyed visually with a minimum of words. Billboards are a good way to reach motorists and business commuters and people who live or work in targeted neighborhoods. Billboards are also good at increasing brand-name awareness (a very simple message: "know our name") and recall (commuters often drive by the same billboard every day).

Billboards can provide a sustaining presence to compensate for the short pulses or flights of TV, radio, or newspaper. Billboards are frequently used to give directions to motorists on highways for restaurants and entertainment attractions at upcoming exits. Very few people write down information while they are driving (thank heavens!), so location and driving directions can be useful information on a billboard.

Billboards can be localized to refer (humorously or otherwise) to buildings, people, or objects in the vicinity and can even have arrows pointing at what they are advertising. Billboards can also be installed in sections to create a teaser campaign that reveals the punch line or sponsor at the very end. A series of billboards along a proven route can be used to build a string of messages from billboard to billboard. Some traffic

---

IF YOU DON'T KNOW WHOSE SIGNS THESE ARE

FOR EXAMPLE

Perhaps the most famous series of billboards was the first— and the signs were not really billboards. In 1925, Clinton Odell, whose family business produced the first brushless shaving cream, started putting up sets of six signs running about 500 feet along stretches of highway. Each sign carried a line of a short poem, and the last showed the product name—although people knew the product as soon as they saw the first small, red sign with white lettering. After all, as one set of signs stated, "If you don't know whose signs these are, you can't have driven very far."

locations are so excellent that billboards must be booked years in advance. Billboards are also an excellent way to claim or own a geographic area with your brand name.

Yellow Pages

Most people who read a Yellow Pages ad have already decided to make a purchase. The purpose of your ad is to get them to pay attention to your company instead of your competitors. You want to be the first one they call.

Unlike most print ads, white space (or in this case, yellow space) is of very little value. It pays to cram your Yellow Pages ad with information. Just make sure that you prioritize the information visually so that what is most important is read first.

Use your visual or headline to dominate attention on the page. Larger ads, unusual and unexpected and emotionally powerful words and pictures, attention-grabbing design such as bold headlines, and products or services that make you different from the competition—all these are more important than your brand name in this medium. Make sure your visuals are not just decorations or clip-art icons. They should attract attention to your ad. They should make potential customers feel something. Your headline should either promise an immediate solution to the problem or state how you are different. After the headline, your phone number is the most important element—even more important than your name and logo.

Don't imitate your competitors. Cram your ad with services and features, reasons to believe, and reasons to call now. Offer potential customers an incentive for immediate action.

Don't reverse out the type in your body copy. Using white (or yellow) letters on a black background can reduce readability as much as 60 percent. Display ads are more expensive than simple listings. Using more words and more highlights is more expensive than using fewer words and no highlights. The greatest expense is to list your business under multiple headings.

Finally, Yellow Pages ads are expensive and last for a year. So make sure you proofread your ad before you submit it for print.

GRAB ATTENTION—AND GET CALLS

SMART

Make the most of your Yellow Pages ad.

MANAGING

1. Select a visual that will stand out.
2. Create a headline. Be brief and emotionally engaging. Use placement and font to make it dominate.
3. Create a subhead. State your second-most important point.
4. Give important information, points of difference, reasons to believe.
5. Get potential customers to call now, immediately.
6. Place your company name and logo. The best locations are lower right or bottom center.
7. Give your phone number—big and bold.
8. Add your slogan. The best locations are just below your logo or at the bottom of your ad.
9. Make sure the pieces all work together. The most important pieces should stand out most. Remember that the Yellow Pages is not like other books: people usually read it without proper lighting and often in a hurry. Make it easy for potential customers to call.

Direct Mail

Direct mail is advertising mailed directly to the prospects' homes or businesses, usually via the U.S. Postal Service. Some mailers are addressed to a specific person, and others are addressed to "occupant" or "resident."

Direct mail divides roughly into letters and self-mailers. Letters are usually sent in a standard business envelope and often appear as a personal or business communication in the form of a typed letter, rather than as an advertisement. Self-mailers are often vivid four-color multi-piece ads that can contain many coupons, images, and promotional offers.

The outside of a mail piece is the most critical portion. People throw away most mail without reading it, judging it in seconds to be "junk mail." To make that decision, they look at the format of the envelope, their name on the mailing label, whether it's addressed by hand, whether it bears a first-class stamp, and who sent it. The more personal and handwritten your mailer appears, the more likely the recipient will open it. Because there's a 50/50 chance the recipient will read the back first instead of the front, you might consider putting your most important message in both places. Because most direct mail is considered highly interruptive and unwanted, it is important to get to the point quickly and offer a strong reason for the recipient to care.

Direct mail can be highly targeted using database analysis and list suppliers to identify zip codes where your customers are most likely to live and where the potential for return is highest. Smart direct mailers continuously test lists, offers, and creative formats. These can be tested one at a time through split-run testing, as explained earlier, or through "recipe testing" of multiple variables with highly sophisticated mathematics. You need a minimum cell size to validate the results. It is not unusual for a mailer to pull .05 percent response, and it is possible for different recipes to pull up to 200 percent more responses than the control. A typical strategy is to find a winner in a small test and then roll the winner out to your entire market.

> **KEY TERM**
>
> **Cell size** Number of returns required for a test to be statistically valid. In practical terms for direct mail marketing, cell size is the number of pieces mailed of each type to each mailing list. Generally, for a test to yield statistically valid results, each cell should consist of at least 1,000 to 2,000 names.

Mailing costs vary from the size and weight of the mailer, the number and sophistication of the printed elements inside the envelope, the postage used, the quantities mailed, the amount of computer personalization, and the economic cost of any discounts or free offers used. Catalogs are a highly sophisticated and expensive version of direct mail, but each product and ad within the catalog can be tested for effectiveness. Coupon and promotional offers can also be tested. In general, if you are making a promotional offer, put it as a headline on the outside of your mailer. It also helps to limit the offer period to encourage people to act immediately. Including a call to action can boost response as much as 20 percent.

Radio

Radio is primarily a news and entertainment medium. Radio stations or programming segments are generally divided into talk and music. Talk stations and segments can cover sports, politics, social commentary, topics of community interest, celebrities, and virtually anything that might interest enough listeners to support the station or the segment. Music stations and segments generally divide by musical genre. Common radio station formats include rock (alternative, progressive, classic, heavy metal), top 40 or pop (music that appeals to the most people), classical, jazz, urban (hip-hop, rap, dance, and rhythm and blues), Hispanic, easy listening, and oldies (songs from the past).

Radio stations divide into two bands of radio frequencies: AM and FM. AM frequency waves can diffract around the curvature of the earth and reach up to a few hundred miles during the day and even farther at night, because changes in the ionosphere enable the waves to transmit differently. The broadcast distance depends on transmitter power (which for commercial AM stations in North America ranges from around 250 watts to 50,000 watts). However, AM radio waves are more subject than FM waves to atmospheric and electrical interference.

Because of this susceptibility to interference, AM broadcasting primarily serves for talk radio and news programming. Also because of the ionospheric conditions at night, most AM stations must reduce their transmitting power to prevent interference from stations with similar frequencies. (Those few stations that broadcast on a frequency that is not shared are known as *clear-channel stations* and can be heard clearly across the United States at night.)

FM stations offer much higher sound quality (fidelity), stereo sound, and less interference. However, because FM frequency waves travel in a straight line, reception is generally limited to about 50–100 miles, depending on transmission power. Since the broadcast radius of FM stations is much smaller, they are more local in reach and interest.

Most radio stations are commercial enterprises that make money by selling commercial time. Services such as Arbitron and International Dynamics measure the number of listeners for each station and generally segments. In general, as you would expect, the more listeners, the higher the cost of airtime. The most typical radio commercial is 60 seconds long, but other lengths include 30 seconds and 10 seconds. The longer the commercial, the more it costs.

Commercials can be entirely produced in a recording studio and then sent via Internet to the radio station. Commercials can also be written as

ARBITRON

TOOLS This company dominates the radio ratings game in the United States. It provides local, regional, and national qualitative information that can enable marketers to understand and target consumers more effectively. Some of the information available through the company Web site (*www.arbitron.com*) is free of charge.

scripts and read live by on-air radio talent. A combination is possible: the commercial can be recorded, with a portion of it consisting of music (a music bed), to serve as a background for the on-air talent to talk live from a script. This enables marketers to tailor commercials to local markets and event promotions. Some radio stations will arrange for their talent to set up a live remote recording to promote an event such as a store opening.

Creatively, it is possible in radio to create images in the mind of the listener that you could never afford to shoot in a TV commercial, using creative copywriting, voice acting, music, and sound effects. Music can be used to create emotion or drama or humor or in a jingle that can help listeners remember your name, your slogan, or your phone number. Make sure your commercial is appropriate to the genre of programming during which it will be played. A commercial using country music will stand out on an urban rap station—but not in a good way.

Because people don't listen to radio stations for the commercials, it is important to be entertaining or to provide useful information. The first few seconds of your commercial will determine if people listen, tune it out, or change stations. The last few seconds will determine what they remember and how they feel about your message. In general, it is not a bad idea to repeat your brand name several times within 60 seconds.

With the exception of local radio, most radio advertising buys are made through advertising and media agencies, which develop a buying strategy based on audience reach and frequency numbers, negotiate the price and any perks (such as announcements on the radio station Web site or live remotes), check to make sure the ad actually ran, and, if not, see that there is a make-good.

Television

Almost all broadcast television in the United States is digital, as of June 12, 2009. Digital broadcasting offers much higher-quality images and sound, which can make marketing more effective—or make less sophisticated ads stand out in a bad way. Most television stations are locally operated and affiliated with one of the major national networks. The distribution of TV programming through coaxial cable instead of broadcasting has enabled advertisers to buy spots with much more specific targeting, geographically, demographically, and psychographically.

A single national broadcast TV commercial can reach millions of people. Local commercials, depending on the time and the program and the broadcast area, can reach hundreds or thousands of people. TV stations generate revenues through subscriptions (cable TV), or selling commercial time (broadcast), or both. The commercials underwrite the cost of the free broadcast programming. The most common TV commercial length is 30 seconds, but you can also purchase 60-second commercials and even longer commercials, called *infomercials*. Some infomercials imitate television program formats as they attempt to sell their products.

Until the advent of the Internet (online marketing is covered in the Chapter 13), television was the dominant communication medium in the United States, exceeding all other media combined in number of viewers, time spent viewing, and advertising expenditures. TV shows are carefully rated by services like Nielsen to determine the number of viewers reached. The more viewers and the greater the demand for a specific commercial time slot, the higher the price. A 30-second spot on the Super Bowl can cost millions of dollars, but it can reach tens of millions of viewers. TV programming time slots can also be selected based on audience types or market segments. Database companies can identify which shows your prospective customers are most likely to watch.

> **Infomercial** Advertisement broadcast in the form of a program, generally lasting five minutes to an hour and often including an interview, a discussion, a story, and/or a demonstration. An infomercial is usually identified by a disclaimer, such as "The following program is a paid advertisement." Also known as *paid programming*, an infomercial is the broadcast equivalent of the print *advertorial*.
>
> **KEY TERM**

NIELSEN MEDIA RESEARCH

TOOLS

This company (*www.nielsenmedia.com*) dominates the TV ratings game in the United States. It uses People Meters, set-tuning meters, and paper diaries to track TV watching.

The People Meters are boxes that are attached to each TV set in a national sample composed of a cross-section of nearly 10,000 representative homes throughout the United States. They also measure some of the largest local markets.

Set-tuning meters are used in mid-sized to large local markets. These meters give information about set-tuning only. In these markets, demographic information is provided by a separate sample of people who fill out seven-day paper diaries.

Paper diaries are used for smaller markets. Every week diaries are mailed to homes, and recipients are asked to keep a tally of what is watched on each TV set and by whom. Each year the company processes about 1.6 million paper diaries from households across the country for the "sweeps" ratings periods.

Because people don't watch television for the commercials, it is important to make sure your commercial content is either unexpected or useful. Television is primarily a visual medium, and most great TV commercials can be reduced to a single visual image or key frame. As on radio, the first few seconds of the commercial must hook the viewers and the last few seconds will determine what they remember. TV affords the ability to tell stories, show the product in use, personify your brand with celebrities, build appetites and desires, trigger emotions such as nostalgia, entertain with humor, announce information, and provide convincing demonstrations. Most brands attempt to end their commercial with some sort of consistent memory device, such as a sound effect, jingle, catchphrase, animation, action, gesture, spokesperson, or recurring image that is tied to their name or logo.

Combining Media

Most advertisers use a combination of media to hit their target markets with the right reach (number of people) and the right frequency (number of times exposed). Some media are flighted or pulsed, while others provide a continuous presence. (See Chapter 10 for more information on how to combine media for optimum effect.)

Manager's Checklist for Chapter 11

☑ Each traditional advertising medium has different strengths and weaknesses.

☑ Most advertisers use a combination of traditional media to reach their target.

☑ In general, the cost of a traditional media buy goes up with increases in reach (number of people), frequency (number of times exposed), amount of time exposed, duration of exposure (days, weeks, months), and demand from competing advertisers.

☑ Traditional paid advertising media fall into two types: print and broadcast. Traditional print advertising media include magazines, newspapers, brochures, posters, and direct mail. Traditional broadcast advertising media include TV and radio.

☑ Until the Internet, the dominant advertising medium was TV.

Public Relations

Public opinion is everything. With public sentiment, nothing can fail; without it, nothing can succeed. —Abraham Lincoln

Public relations paves the way for you to build and maintain successful relationships with everyone who has or needs to have a connection with your brand. Whatever business you're in, you're dealing with multiple audiences who have the ability to shape perceptions others have about your brand. Public relations programs help you develop solid relationships with the audiences that matter most to your company, shaping positive perceptions of the brands and the organization.

Some of the most successful brands started with public relations campaigns that built the brands through third-party endorsements, media buzz, and consumer word of mouth long before they began their advertising campaigns. Starbucks. The Body Shop. Amazon.com. eBay. Palm. Google. Prozac. Viagra. Botox. Red Bull. Microsoft. Intel. Beanie Babies. The people behind those brands knew that the power of positive endorsements could create a groundswell of brand support. And it did.

Does it really matter what other people say about your organization? You only need to look at the headlines to see what happens when organ-

This chapter was coauthored with veteran public relations practitioner Barbara Hernandez of Hiebing Marketing Communications.

izations fail to protect their reputations. For instance, what are your employees saying about your company? Are they ambassadors for your brand, or are they rumor-mongers who delight in sharing company secrets with family and friends? Do your vendors represent your brand values, or will their bad behaviors reach out and bite you? Are you dreading a call from *60 Minutes*, or are you looking forward to a feature on your newest innovation?

Stockholders? Competitors? Customers? Prospects? The list is endless; yet each of these audiences has power to shape perceptions (negatively or positively) about your company.

Communication of any kind, particularly when influencing purchasing decisions, cannot be effective unless it is believable. This involves not only the means or vehicle, but also the organizational "voice" behind the communications. Corporate executives are only deceiving themselves if they believe that financial performance alone drives stock price. Today, more than ever, effective communications with all audiences is paramount to achieving business success.

Public Relations Is All About Credibility

Do you believe everything you read in the newspaper or hear on television? Most people do not. In fact, many people believe that advertising messages imply the opposite of what the advertiser intended.

Credibility is about believability, trust, and confidence. Credibility has long been a presumed component of communications. Honesty and integrity used to be the cornerstones for successful companies. But credibility cannot be taken for granted; in fact, it must now be earned, built, and maintained through honesty and integrity.

Without credibility, you might as well save your breath, your money, and your time.

With credibility you can shift attitudes and opinions and obtain the kind of behavior you want to achieve your desired results—whether that's raising funds, getting volunteers, or trying to raise awareness of your activities.

So, what's the best way to do public relations effectively? It depends entirely on what you're trying to achieve: you must choose the correct tool to do the job and make sure the correct message hits the right target at the right time. It's really about being in the right place at the right time.

This chapter will cover some of the basic public relations elements that every marketer should become familiar with, including:

■ Working with the media to tell your story
■ Creating effective press materials
■ Developing memorable events to maximize publicity opportunities
■ Getting started with crisis communications

Working with the Media to Tell Your Story

Media relations is about knowing how to get, and hold, the media's attention.

If handled wisely, media interviews can be valuable opportunities to articulate your brand essence. A media interview and the ensuing story can help you reach a large number of people using a channel that is more credible and far less expensive than paid advertising.

First, you need an objective and a good story to tell. Then you need to find the best way to tell the story. Sometimes figuring out the best way to tell a story is the hardest part, because you need to stand out from a crowd of people who also want to tell stories.

There's an old saying in the media business—"If it bleeds, it leads." If you have "hard news," it's a pretty easy sell. If you have breaking news in a category, you just need to designate the right outlet (print or broadcast) to tell the story.

If you have only "soft news," it's more difficult to interest the media in your story. Media people get stacks of press releases and other information each day from companies and service organizations that believe they have a great story—or at least want the media people to believe so.

Usually the only way to interest media people in telling those stories is by developing relationships with the editorial representatives of your target media. Develop a list of those media people who can help you tell your stories. Go to the meetings they attend and greet them socially. Go meet with them when you don't have a story to sell, to provide them with background on your organization or your resources. Send them periodically information that may help them do their jobs better or at least more easily—a story in a publication, an interesting fact sheet, or a hot tip on a related topic.

Stay informed and current on the topics they're covering. If they know you're following their work, they're more likely to consider you as a possible resource. And when they call, there are a few tips that will help you get the most from your time with them.

Preparation for Meeting with the Media

What are reporters looking for?

A great story! And a great sound byte. To become a good media spokesperson, you must understand the media's perspective and be able to give them what they need. If you can do this, you have a better chance of establishing a good relationship. Media people appreciate anyone who is able to provide accurate information in advance of deadlines. And they're most likely to call upon you repeatedly for interviews once you've established a connection.

Impact. You must tell a story that appeals to a sizable or important segment of the media's total audience. Don't hesitate to help the reporter understand the mass appeal—and state the same facts during the interview. For example, if one in three consumers could save hundreds of thousands of dollars every year, then say so.

Accuracy. Be as specific and succinct as possible. Stick to the facts and make sure you always get them straight. The media look to you, as a spokesperson, for a factual interpretation of an issue. Keep your personal opinions to yourself.

Promptness. Reporters work on deadlines that are sometimes only minutes away. When a reporter calls, ask about the deadline. Either honor it or tell the reporter up front that you cannot, so he or she can go elsewhere. Knowing the deadline is also helpful when you need five to 10 minutes to collect your thoughts and review your notes so you can comfortably answer the reporter's questions. It's OK to request permission to call back. Just agree on a time frame—and then make sure you call back within that time frame.

Important points. Just because a reporter doesn't ask the right questions doesn't mean you've lost the opportunity to share key information.

Reporters are busy, they may be covering multiple beats, or they may be unfamiliar with the types of questions to ask. Be prepared to transition from the reporter's questions to provide responses and/or statements that convey your key messages.

Interview Strategies—in Person or on the Phone

Keep the following guidelines in mind during interviews, whether for a newspaper, magazine, radio station, or television channel.

Make your points early. The beginning of an answer gets the most attention, so put your strongest point first. If you start with a long preamble, you may be interrupted before you reach your important point.

Be concise. Summarize the essence of your message. Use simple, hard-hitting phrases that paint a picture for the readers, viewers, or listeners and leave them wanting to know more. You'll also be creating a natural opportunity to share more information pertinent to the topic.

Watch your language. Avoid jargon, professional buzzwords, and abbreviations. Although the interviewer may know what you mean, such terms often do not create a clear mental image for the readers, viewers, or listeners. They will tune out if the language is too technical. By using simple, colorful words, you can make your message clear.

Be positive. If asked a negative question, do not repeat the negative language in your response. Instead, begin your answer by rephrasing the question in a positive manner and then make your point. For example, if the reporter asks, "Don't you agree that people who begin retirement planning after age 50 will never be able to retire?" you might begin, "Planning can begin at any age ..."

Simplify statistics and put large numbers into context. Statistics are hard enough to understand, so make your numbers people-friendly. Large numbers can be difficult for many people to visualize, so put them into a context. Consider making a statement that paints a visual image. For example, rather than simply mentioning that 500 tons of paper is wasted during tax season, you might say that the 500 tons of paper wasted during a typical tax season would fill Yankee Stadium 10 times over.

Stay "on the record." There is no such thing as "off the record." The minute the reporter walks through the door or calls you on the telephone, he or she is already gathering information and impressions that may well be used in the story. Rule of thumb: don't say anything you don't want to see on the front page of *The Wall Street Journal.*

Location, location. When working with a television reporter, remember that the

NOTHING IS "OFF THE RECORD"

Don't say anything you don't want to see on the front page of *The Wall Street Journal.*

There is no such thing as "off the record" or "off camera" or "off mike" when there are reporters around. Everything you say or do is on the record. Everything.

camera sees everything. You may be making a visual "first impression," so if you're choosing the location, make sure it's appropriate.

Don't guess. Always tell the truth. If you don't know the answer, say so. Then promise to get the information as soon as possible—and keep your agreement. Media people may push for information that doesn't exist. Stick with the information and facts that you have.

If a line of questioning leads into "confidential" territory, simply say, "That is confidential information that I am not at liberty to share." It is also better to state that information is confidential than to simply say "no comment," as the reporter and the readers, viewers, or listeners are inclined to believe you are hiding something.

You don't have to tell all you know about an issue, but never lie to media people.

Don't speculate a situation or what others have said or might say. Encourage the reporter to check with the people in question—but take the opportunity to say what you know or transition to your key messages. The reporter may push you for information or speculation; stay focused and on message. And don't bring up any topics that you don't want to discuss or you don't to become the story.

DON'T GUESS

Don't guess or speculate with a reporter. It's OK to admit you don't know the answer to a question. It's OK to offer to find out the answer and get back to the reporter later. Make a wrong guess and you risk appearing on the record as either an idiot or a liar.

Be professional. Be polite and helpful. Don't lose your temper

MEDIA INTERVIEW TIPS

TRICKS OF THE TRADE

- Wear professional attire.
- Speak slowly and clearly.
- Focus on your key points.
- Summarize your key points at the end of the interview.
- Thank the interviewer.
- Follow up with the interviewer to see if you can help with anything else.

or give smart-aleck responses. And avoid sarcasm. If you don't understand the reporter's questions, politely ask him or her to repeat it or rephrase it.

Silence is OK. If there's a lull in the interview, don't yield to the urge to fill it or offer an off-the-cuff comment. The reporter may simply be finishing writing your comment or hoping you'll jump in with an additional comment. Once you've answered a question, wait patiently for the reporter to ask another.

Creating Effective Press Materials

Two critical public relations tools are the *press release* and the *press advisory*. Each serves a different purpose and will have different impact on the intended media targets.

A *press release* is a written message designed to alert the media to a good story or to serve as the basis for a story. Sometimes media people use the press release verbatim; other times they take the release and use pieces of it for another story that might be in development.

Releases are written in an inverse pyramid style of straight news reporting (who, what, where, when, and why). The most important information should always be in the first paragraph. Historic and contextual information should follow. Few releases should be more than two pages in length. Creative use of language and relevant context are also important to break through the clutter of dozens or hundreds of releases that are put in front of editors each and every day.

Most press releases are sent out immediately following a news event, especially if it's hard news. For soft news, there is often some flexibility, but you should send it as close to the news event as possible.

A *press advisory* is similar to a press release, but it is to advise the media of an upcoming event that may be of interest to readers, viewers, or listeners. Press advisories are often sent to the media prior to press conferences, trade shows, or consumer events that will help the media tell a more compelling story with multiple resources.

Advisories are typically one page in length. They contain critical information about an upcoming event, including why the media outlet (and its readers, viewers, or listeners) would be interested in information presented at the event. It's important to include specific times, location, and contact information for the day of the event (often cell phone numbers). Many advisories include directions to ensure the media people have all the information they need at their fingertips. It's also a good idea to list the names of the individuals who will be sharing information, including titles and company names.

The best time to send an advisory is two to three days before an event. It's wise to follow up the day before or morning of an event to ensure top-of-mind awareness for busy news directors.

Developing Memorable Events to Maximize Publicity Opportunities

Events offer many opportunities to gain visibility with the people that you're trying to influence. As the media channels become ever more fragmented, events are becoming more popular as highly targeted tools

---

HOW TO WRITE A PRESS RELEASE

1. Organize your information.
2. Obtain quotes from key spokespersons.
3. Type your release double-spaced.
4. Place contact information on the upper left of the sheet. Include:
   Name, title
   Telephone number, e-mail address
5. Include the release day (e.g., "For Immediate Release" or "EMBARGO — Not for publication or broadcast before 1 p.m., local time, on July 24, 2009").
6. Write "Press release" or "News release" on the top of the page.
7. Write a grabber headline.
8. Include the dateline to begin the release (e.g., Madison, Wis. — July 15, 2009)
9. Write the body of the release.
10. End the release with "###."

How to Write a Press Advisory

TRICKS OF THE TRADE

1. Organize your information.
2. Format appropriately. Advisories are usually single-spaced, with key information in bold or highlighted, and rarely longer than one page.
3. Place contact information on the upper left of the sheet. Include:
   Name, title
   Telephone number, e-mail address
4. Incorporate pertinent information, including:
   Type of event to take place
   Individuals available for the media to talk with
   Photo opportunities
   Specific time of the event
   Address, including directions and parking information
5. Write "Media Advisory" on the top of the page.
6. Write a grabber headline.
7. End the advisory with "###."

When to Issue a Press Release

SMART

MANAGING

To send a release or not to send a release, that is the question. And here are the answers.

Yes, send a release ...
- Personnel announcements (hires, promotions, etc.)
- Prestigious awards
- Events where your organization will have a key presence
- Breaking news
- Crisis situations
- Financial information
- Public health and safety issues
- New product/service information
- Obituary of prominent corporate official
- New business opening, building dedication
- New technology
- Industry-specific information (for trade media only)

No, don't bother with a release ...
- Internal announcements that don't impact external audiences
- Product news that is more than a few months old

to make a brand statement with impact. Carefully orchestrated events can also be used to garner media attention.

As in all marketing, it's important to establish a primary goal for the event. It's also important to select events that are consistent with your positioning and brand values.

The word "event" means that something important is happening and there will be something for the media people to cover. Whether it's an unveiling of a new exhibit at a museum, the dedication of a new building, or an international dignitary in town for a speech, it's important to assess the likelihood that the media people (and ultimately their audiences) will be interested in the subject.

Events that are most likely to gain the attention of the media, in addition to your other key audiences, include:

- Product launches that incorporate audience or celebrity participation
- Competitive testing, especially if it's in a unique product category
- Opportunities for target audiences to learn about topics or issues
- Events tied to local or national charities or causes
- News conferences that provide interesting imagery and stories
- Groundbreaking or dedication ceremonies
- Sporting events, especially with ties to charities
- Community improvement projects
- Seminars and roundtables

The list of events that connect with your target audiences is endless, but those that provide opportunities for additional publicity require some additional attention to detail.

Getting Started with Crisis Communications

Jay D. Rayburn said, "There are only two kinds of organizations: those who have had crises and those who will." Responsible businesses understand that their actions and communications, both within the organization and among external audiences, within the first hours and days of a crisis are critical. Most companies facing crises are judged not by the crisis itself, but by their response to it.

The great majority of crises involving organizations occur as a result of their day-to-day operations. This means that it is often possible to prepare managers and leaders to take very specific actions to deal with crises.

The other serious crises are the result of such events as natural disas-

EIGHT TIPS FOR MEMORABLE EVENTS

Here are eight tips for getting the most publicity bang for your event buck.

1. Establish realistic objectives against a budget.
2. Plan your event to complement other marketing tools (signage, point-of-sale displays, banners, fact sheets, backdrops, etc.).
3. Identify best time of year, week, and day to ensure best attendance by your target audiences. Timing is critical.
4. Use Internet social marketing tools to create buzz and excitement for the event.
5. Select the best spokesperson(s) to share the message with the target audience(s).
6. Prepare contingency plans against all possible issues, including weather or cancellation.
7. Build in evaluation criteria. How will the event be measured? Media coverage? Leads? Attendance?
8. Seek media, business, or charitable partnerships to help you publicize the event.

GUIDELINES FOR SPOKESPEOPLE IN A CRISIS

In a crisis situation, it is critical to follow all the rules for working with the media that appeared earlier in this chapter. Here are a few additional guidelines to keep in mind if you are responding to a crisis.

1. Tell the truth.
2. Share some facts immediately, even if the news is bad.
3. Act quickly. The first 60 minutes are considered the golden hour—one that may define the entire response.
4. Avoid guessing or making estimates.
5. Express regret if there are injuries to report.
6. Always think before you respond.
7. Stick to approved messages.
8. Provide the media people with what they need to know. Don't bombard them with too many statistics.
9. Use public information officers to assist you in immediate response for health and safety issues.
10. Prepare answers to most likely questions well in advance of an incident.

ters or criminal activity, like product tampering or school shootings. These are highly charged emotional events. Think Katrina or September 11th. These types of events are generally the most difficult to manage and most damaging to an organization's reputation. Practically speaking, a true crisis is a people-stopper, product-stopper, show-stopper, or reputation-definer; or some combination of all four; and it produces victims (people, animals, living systems).

Communication is at the core of a good crisis management plan. In fact, communication in the early phases of any crisis will go a long way toward protecting the organization's reputation as the situation progresses into recovery.

Figure 12-1 offers a few examples of how to categorize the various crises that can impact your reputation. Planning ahead can go a long way toward minimizing the impact they have on you and your organization.

	Local events that could draw attention to your organization	Operating crises	Non-operating crises	Operating/non-operating combination events	Web-based attacks
Activist action/threats	✗		✗		✗
Arrests of senior executives	✗	✗			
Customer complaints	✗	✗	✗		
Drug activity	✗				
Employee violence/job actions	✗	✗	✗	✗	
E-mail/cyber attacks				✗	
Product tampering	✗	✗	✗	✗	✗
Major accident/disaster	✗	✗	✗	✗	✗
Computer failure/security breach	✗	✗	✗	✗	✗
Criminal litigation	✗		✗		
Facility closings/layoffs	✗	✗	✗	✗	✗
Financial disclosures	✗			✗	
Data theft/misuse					✗
Terrorism	✗	✗	✗	✗	✗

Figure 12-1. Crisis category examples

Manager's Checklist for Chapter 12

☑ Public relations is everything you say and do.

☑ Without credibility, your brand has no voice. Your reputation is in your hands.

☑ Public relations efforts must incorporate a dynamic purpose.

☑ The media can help you tell your story. What's new? What's different? What's relevant to the ultimate target?

☑ Use effective tools like press releases and press advisories to help the media tell a dynamic story.

☑ Events can be great opportunities to engage, inspire, and motivate your target groups into action, all while telling a compelling and creative story the media people want to cover.

☑ Crises happen every day. Be prepared.

Online Marketing

What once was a world of computers talking to other computers has evolved into a vast network of people, communications, and devices including video, text messaging, cell phones, and PDAs such as iPhones and BlackBerries. And the opportunities for targeting consumers with marketing messages have become as vast.

E-marketing—also known as Internet marketing, i-marketing, Web marketing, and online marketing—is now the fastest-growing marketing communications area and likely to be the dominant marketing medium in the near future.

As a matter of fact, companies are statistically increasing their online marketing budgets each year to meet the growing demand for online connections and contact with businesses. And it isn't just teenagers with iPods and an online-only mentality. The Internet is mainstream and is often the first preferred point of contact for research, comparison shopping, information, and peer reviews.

The term *e-marketing* is fading as online tactics are simply being thought of as "marketing," pure and simple.

This chapter was coauthored with veteran Web marketer Sandra Bradley.

Be User-Centric

Being *user-centric* means looking at your business from your customers' perspectives and understanding what questions they want answered and what tasks they want to accomplish. It is the actionable and interactive part of the medium that builds this kind of relationship. Why should I do business with you? How can I find the right partner for my business? What size does this come in? Does this product fit others that I own? If businesses can understand the needs of their current and potential customers online and effectively meet them, then they will be highly successful.

It is the understanding of the user that is truly the driver for the kind of tactic (whether online or not) to use to communicate with that user. It is easy to get distracted with new technologies. For example, I hear companies saying, "I need a Facebook page and a Twitter feed and I need them right away!" Just because Oprah now has both doesn't mean these are right for you. Instead, companies should do research on customers to see how many of them are on Facebook and Twitter and use it regularly. They should think strategically about what tactics will work best for their customers. One size does not fit all: the tactics should be based on market, type of business, and tasks to accomplish.

KEY TERMS

Twitter A free social networking service that enables users to communicate through *tweets*. Those are text messages of up to 140 characters in length that a user posts to his or her profile page, from which they are sent to any user who's subscribed to receive them.

Facebook A free-access social networking Web site that is privately owned and operated by Facebook, Inc. Users can join networks of users organized by city, workplace, school, and region.

Use the Advantages of the Medium
Low Cost, Highly Targeted, Global, Interactive

The Web is different in what it can offer over other media. The Internet has brought many unique benefits to marketing, one of which being lower costs for the distribution of information and media to a global market. The interactive nature of Internet marketing, in terms of both provid-

ing instant response and eliciting responses, also makes
the medium highly effective,
as does the ability to target
users based on behavior, history, interests, and geography.

Internet marketing also
refers to the placement of
media along different stages
of the customer engagement
cycle (as described in Chapter
5) through search engine marketing (SEM), search engine
optimization (SEO), banner
ads on specific Web sites, e-mail marketing, and Web 2.0 strategies.

> **WHAT IS WEB 2.0?**
> The terms *Web 2.0*, *social media*, and *user-generated content* are all used interchangeably. Web 2.0 is the "second generation" of Web development, facilitating communication, secure information sharing, and collaboration.
>   Sites such as Wikipedia, LinkedIn, and Facebook are community-built. Other Web 2.0 content includes blogs, comments on news sites, and product reviews.
>   In short, if Web 1.0 is about commerce, then Web 2.0 is about people.
>
> **TOOLS**

As mentioned in Chapter 5, Internet presence is often the first point of contact. Rather than just a Web site destination, company presence on the Web is ubiquitous—in online news channels, YouTube videos, blogs, Flickr images, Facebook pages, and other social networking venues. Managing a brand online is much more complex than ever before.

For example, one toy company I worked with was preparing to discontinue one of its most popular products. Rather than announcing its intent to discontinue, which could potentially ire loyal followers, the company leaked the news to influential bloggers and into related social networks. The result was a subtly PR-driven approach using its evangelists to carry the message that minimized backlash.

As mentioned in Chapter 5, the Internet has made it possible for even the smallest companies to market globally. It has opened the door for products that appeal to tiny percentages of the global population.

One billion-dollar company that has long dominated a particular segment of business-to-business products found that it was being long-tailed out of competition product by product by small specialists that could compete aggressively on price. These tiny players were riding on the long tail of the big company's comet. Competitors it had never considered suddenly aggregated into a competitive threat.

Micro-Marketing

Companies are finding it increasingly difficult to reach their target prospects. As mentioned in Chapter 5, it's no longer enough to blast out a mass message or build a brand in the historical way. Relationships have become ever more important, as has the concept of niche marketing. Users can choose where they go and what they see, what products they interact with, and by whom they want to be contacted. In fact, they are often the ones to initiate a contact, whether through search engines, direct load, or referral.

A Conversation Medium

As mentioned in Chapter 5, top online tactics for businesses are banner ads on specific Web sites, search engine marketing, search engine optimization, and e-mail marketing, all resting on a bed of social networking and based on relationships between and among trusted people. Companies need to understand the potential of these tactics and the concept of one-to-one marketing online space. Above all, the Web can create a place to begin a conversation with a prospect or customer. The relationship built over time is what pays long-term dividends.

The era of one-way communications has given way to a desire to maintain ongoing conversations between companies and their customers. There are great opportunities for companies to listen in, learn, and respond to their customer's needs and to become an everyday part of the fabric of their lives.

Banner Ads

Banner ads are display advertising on specific sites and are typically sold by CPM (cost per thousand views). There are some known problems with banner advertising: While an ad may load, the user may not actually see it, because the page is cluttered, because of its place on the page, or because the user is not interested.

It is difficult to measure direct ROI other than by calculating *click-throughs* on the ad. Many users actively avoid looking at advertising placed in social networking and other spaces.

Click-through What happens when a user clicks on a link in a Web page or e-mail and is sent to a Web page. Click-throughs are used as a measure of effectiveness. The *click-through rate* is calculated by dividing the number of clicks by the number of **KEY TERMS** impressions (e.g., times a banner ad is displayed or number of e-mails sent).

Widget A piece of code that can be inserted in a site in order to do something, to add content that is not static. For example, a weather-tracking widget may display the temperature and other information inline in a site, or a widget of a featured product could enable users to buy from that site.

It is becoming more common to use video or insert *widgets* into display ads to allow for enhanced engagement and real-time interactions. These kinds of ads are more effective than simple graphic banner ads.

Keys to success with banner advertising:

1. Ensure the ad is "above the fold" on the site, placed for better visibility and interaction.
2. Match the content of the ad to actual content placement if possible. For example, if the ad is displayed on a weather page, using an environmental reference will be effective.
3. Always use some kind of actionable message. "Buy now," "Sign up," "Free trial," and "Enter now" are all good actionable ideas.
4. Bigger is better. Use larger formats or interruptive formats (such as drag downs, expand/collapse, or pop over windows) to dominate a cluttered environment.

To make managing many media efficient, there are also tools that can be used to drive social media content into ads. For example, a tool called Shoutlet (*www.shoutlet.com*) is used by some companies to tag social media content, upload You-Tube videos, and publish the same video content into banner space on sites where units have been purchased.

Above the fold The portion of a Web page that visitors can see without scrolling. The size of this **KEY TERM** area varies according to the users' screen size and browser settings. This term comes from newspaper jargon, where it refers to the top half of a page, visible when a folded newspaper is lying face up or displayed. The rest of the page—the part that you have to scroll to see—is known as *below the fold*.

Search Engine Marketing (SEM)

Search engines are one of the most common ways for people to find information and products. Google is the number-one search engine, and (surprisingly) YouTube is currently the number-two search engine, due to a growing use of video for demonstration, communication, and marketing. It is because of this that search marketing or pay-per-click advertising is appealing for businesses. You can quickly present a message when a user is actively seeking your product or service.

Companies now have interesting opportunities to educate. Witness the Auto Credit Express® video on how to buy a car if you have bad credit and the hairstyle tips and curly hairstyle techniques from TRESemmé. These are good examples of wrapping a brand around helpful content without direct selling.

Search engine advertising is appealing because the cost is based on a specific action, or click, which means that a user has actually seen the ad and chosen to interact with it. It is easy to set up a Google AdWords account to create text ads that will display at the top of the page and in the right column alongside relevant keywords in its search. There is also a content-targeted option that displays ads alongside relevant content on news sites, affiliate sites, blogs, and the like.

The placement of the ads is a combination of the amount bid by competitors and the *quality score.* "Quality Score," according to Google, "is a dynamic variable assigned to each of your keywords. It's calculated using a variety of factors and measures how relevant your keyword is to your ad group and to a user's search query." The quality score is a rating of the success of that particular ad; an ad with a higher score is given precedence over other ads. This helps search engines understand what is working and whether the ad is relevant.

Search advertising is immediate, actionable, and effective. And it is highly accountable, with direct metrics that can work toward successful integration of search advertising into campaigns.

Search Engine Optimization (SEO)

Search engine optimization is the process of improving the volume and/or quality of traffic coming to a Web page from *organic* or *natural*

MISTAKES WITH PAID SEARCH

These are some mistakes to avoid with paid search:

- *Not matching ads to keywords.* Use keywords in the headline or body copy.
- *Not matching landing pages to the ad.* Ensure that the ad leads to a page that deals directly with the advertisement or promotion, not just to a generic site page or home page.
- *Not being competitive enough.* A placement of position 1–3 (in the right column of search results) is critical to garner sufficient return on investment.

LANDING PAGE

A landing page is any page on a Web site to which users are sent. The structure, design, and copy should prompt users to take a certain action.

For example:

- Users are sent from a pay-per-click search marketing campaign (e.g., Google AdWords) to any of multiple landing pages, each specific to a search keyword.
- Users are sent from a banner ad to a landing page specific to whatever the banner is advertising.
- Users are sent from a link in a Web site or an e-mail to a landing page designed to provide information or prompt users to take some action.

searches—search results generated by Google, Yahoo! Search, or other search engines.

As mentioned earlier, Google is the leading search engine and the focus of most optimization efforts. Google search is highly targeted by keyword and uses *IP detection* to deliver relevant geographic results.

Appearing on the first page of search results is ideal. However, unlike paid searches, which allow specific placement for a fee, there is no guarantee of placement in natural searches. There are several types of factors that impact placement of sites in natural searches: popularity, content, and structure.

Search engine optimization Process of improving the volume and/or quality of traffic coming to a Web page from the results of *organic* or *natural* searches through search engines such as Google, Yahoo! Search, and Microsoft Live Search.

KEY TERM

KEY TERMS

IP detection IP stands for Internet protocol. Here it's shorthand for Internet protocol address, the numeric address of a computer on the Internet (four numbers separated by periods). These numbers are usually assigned to Internet service providers in blocks by region, so an IP address can often be used to identify the region or country from which a computer is connecting to the Internet.

Link farm A Web site or a group of Web sites that contain a large number of links, so as to raise the index ratings used by search engines.

Popularity. Google in particular relies on links to determine which sites are credible, relevant sources and which are not. Google applies a metric, *Page Rank*, which measures the overall relevancy of sites based on the links to each site. Google uses an algorithm to determine the relative value of links and weight them accordingly.

Cultivating quality links to your site from partner sites, blogs, media, and social sites, such as LinkedIn and Wikipedia, is a good practice in terms of increasing Page Rank. The key is to do this slowly and strategically and to avoid *link farms* or other low-quality services that will garner poor results.

Content. Search engines love good content and lots of it. If you use a focused set of keywords high up on the page, use the keywords many times, and emphasize landing pages, you help search engines rate each page of your Web site. Keyword position and density on the page are translated in terms of importance. Search engine optimization strategies make Web copywriting a fine balance between providing a positive user experience and providing enough content to search engines to be ranked higher in more searches.

Structure. The structure of the site, including code construction and linking, makes it easier for search engines to access content. Search engines love links, so using strong keywords in text links is a good search engine optimization practice. Avoid using technologies that get in the way of search engines, such as JavaScript, frames, and Flash (although Google can parse text files if Flash files are constructed to pull text rather than have content compiled in the Flash).

E-Mail Marketing

Even with a poor reputation due to Spam, mailbox clutter, user fatigue, and overuse, e-mail marketing remains a viable marketing tool if it is permission-based. Permission is key: purchasing lists, sending e-mails blind, or delivering any other unwelcome content simply doesn't work.

Building a strong opt-in program should be a core part of any long-term marketing program. What this means is giving users a reason for giving you their e-mail addresses and permission to market to them. The incentive can be the promise of valuable and useful content regularly or occasionally, the chance of winning a sweepstakes, an offer to provide notifications of discounts and sales, or a subscription to an e-mail newsletter, to mention a few popular examples.

The key is giving users control over how often you will communicate with them, allowing them to select relevant content, enabling them to manage the relationship, and then delivering the content that they consider relevant.

There is a growing trend of using e-mail for behavioral marketing. For example, if a visitor to a site has placed items in a shopping cart but not checked out, an e-mail might be sent to remind the visitor of the shopping cart contents or if visitors have made purchases through a site, a promotion might be sent to mention items that are similar to the items purchased.

The main point in making e-mail successful is personalization, relevance, and user control. All these create a welcome relationship over time that will bear fruit.

Don't Stalk

Some online retailers track movements of visitors to their sites. Then they send e-mails to those visitors based on the pages visited, with a message such as "Because of your interest in YYY, we thought you'd be interested in this" and information about other products, related to YYY or not so much. This form of behavioral marketing may be seen as the cyber equivalent of a sales clerk spying on store visitors and then chasing them down the street yelling, "Hey! I noticed that you were looking at ...."

Social Media

Social media (or Web 2.0 or user-generated content) is really the underpinning of many of the tactics we have just discussed. Banner ads may be

CAN-SPAM RULES
Be a responsible e-mail marketer. In the United States, it is important to become familiar with CAN-SPAM regulations and abide by them. To find out about CAN-SPAM, go to *www.fcc.gov/cgb/consumerfacts/canspam.html.*

placed on blogs or on Facebook pages, paid searches can appear on affiliate sites or around news content, and e-mail can be used to pass links virally. Many social sites have surpassed the popularity of news sites and are becoming a primary source of placement for marketing messages.

Social media have given the individual as much power as traditional media have had in the past. If one person likes a product and starts spreading the word, the result can be free publicity that reaches more people and with greater effect than thousands of dollars could buy in ads. On

SMART MANAGING

VIRAL MARKETING
"Viral," usually a scary term in the computer world, is something good in "viral marketing." It simply means spread by word of mouth, creating buzz and interest. Viral marketing uses strategies that cause people to pass along marketing messages to others. The result can be an exponential spread of the message.

the other hand, if one person hates a product or a brand, the result could do so much damage that it could take thousands of dollars and months of advertising to repair.

Recognizing that the Web has become a conversation medium, marketers are concerned not only with the conversation between themselves and their customers but also conversations among customers about their companies, listening in, and then benefiting from what they learn.

Social media have changed the game in terms of how people get their information and turned around the perception of what managing a brand means. In short, the most successful companies are the ones that allow users to manage their brands and to create their own experiences, rather than trying to create a company-driven brand perception.

When we talk about social media, we're talking about much more than blogs: we're talking about Twitter, the large open directories such as Facebook and MySpace as well as YouTube videos, and social bookmarking on sites such as Digg.com and Delicious.com (formerly del.icio.us).

BENEFITS BEYOND MEASURE

SMART

What kind of return on investment is received in the social media space? It's difficult to measure. Consider some of these main benefits of using social media marketing:

MANAGING

Customer engagement	Marketing research
Direct customer communications	Credibility of the "crowd"
Speed of feedback/results	Reach
Learning customer preferences	Lead generation source
Low cost	Customer service
Brand building	

Social bookmarking A Web site that enables Internet users to store, tag, and search through bookmarks (links to Web pages), by category, by tag, or chronologically. Users can share the bookmarks they contribute, either privately (with specified people or **KEY TERMS** members of specified groups) or publicly (with anybody who accesses the Web site).

Podcast A series of digital media files, usually digital audio or video, delivered over the Internet through an *RSS feed* to subscribers, who play the files on their computers or portable digital audio players, such as the iPod.

RSS feed Delivery through any of a family of Web feed formats used to publish audio, video, news headlines, blog entries, etc., in a standardized format. RSS is generally understood as meaning "Really Simple Syndication."

This area also encompasses podcasts, RSS feeds, and widgets.

The main point is that it is the users who choose what they want to see. Digg.com is a place where people decide what the top headline of the day is based on what they want to see. RSS feeds are selected content. Twitter connects people one-to-one or one-to-many based on choice.

Online marketing is an interesting mix of global opportunity and tightly knit communities. More and more marketing messages are being filtered through peers before being considered or even seen. Leveraging these relationships in a positive way is one of the leading challenges and most important tasks for marketers.

SMART

MANAGING

FIGURING OUT SOCIAL NETWORKING

The array of social networking opportunities is dizzying, and companies often don't know where to start. Here are a few good ways to begin to make the most out of social networking:

Before doing anything, listen. Find out where your customers like to spend time and where they are open to conversing with you. Listen to the way they talk and learn the language. Social networks have cultures, and it is important to learn the tone, jargon, and overall etiquette appropriate to each network.

Be completely transparent. Never pretend to be anything other than you are. Authenticity and transparency are paramount in terms of credibility.

Offer something useful. Develop content that people will want to share or bookmark. Provide information they need or advice that can help them make decisions.

Go slowly. Focus on a few top target sites or tools and master those before branching out. Follow your customers and gravitate to where they are.

Manager's Checklist for Chapter 13

☑ E-marketing—also known as Internet marketing, i-marketing, Web marketing, or online marketing—is now the fastest-growing marketing communications area.

☑ Internet presence is often the first point of customer contact.

☑ Be user-centric. Look at your business from your customers' perspectives.

☑ The Web offers advantages over other media. The Internet is low cost, highly targeted, global, available 24/7, and interactive.

☑ Top online tactics for businesses are search engine marketing, search engine optimization, banner ads on specific Web sites, and e-mail marketing, all built on a foundation of relationships.

☑ The era of one-way communications has given way to conversations between companies and their customers. Successful companies allow users to create their own brand experiences.

Market Research

What Is Market Research?

Very simply, market research is learning everything you can about your current customers and your prospective customers and about how they view your products and services.

Without this information, you risk being out of touch with your customers and prospects. They often have a very different view of your products, services, and advertising than you do. They have a very different point of view from your board, your distributors, your retailers, or anyone else familiar with your business from the inside out.

For example, 55-year-old males who don't cook aren't likely to be familiar with the needs of a working mother who comes home after a long day and has to prepare dinner in minutes for her children. But research can uncover these needs and which products or potential products can solve the dinner problem. Without the objective understanding of your market that research can provide, you risk making expensive marketing mistakes.

Countless products have been introduced to grocery stores without a shred of consumer testing. Companies have invested hundreds or thousands or millions of dollars developing products, creating packaging, and

This chapter was coauthored with veteran market researcher Donna E. Fletcher, Donna E. Fletcher Consulting, Inc.

securing distribution—and then no one buys the products. Why? Well, there's obviously something wrong with the product or how it's being marketed. But what? Do the marketers know even the most basic information about the target market? Do they know how the target consumers reacted to the product, the name and the packaging, or the price? Without this knowledge, a company can't even begin to fix its "problem child."

Where Does Research Fit in the Marketing Process?

To avoid creating "problem children," you must conduct upfront research among your target prospects. It has to be completed before you launch a product or an advertising campaign.

CAUTION

IGNORE UPFRONT RESEARCH AT YOUR OWN PERIL

Clients often design new packaging for retail products. Often they don't bother to conduct basic testing that can help determine if consumers can "see it on the shelf." This test involves setting up the product in the new package on shelves surrounded by competing products, to replicate the actual retail shelf as closely as possible. One at a time, consumers view the shelf for a few seconds, move away from the shelf, and then are asked which brands they remember seeing.

We recently read of a multibillion-dollar company that overhauled its packaging at a cost of hundreds of millions of dollars. Within weeks of the launch, it was reported that consumers could no longer find the specific varieties of the products and felt the package looked generic and not differentiated from competing products. The company plans to change its packaging again. Up-front research could have spotted this potential problem in time to prevent it.

You should also use market research throughout the life cycle of your product or service. As a brand develops and grows and ages, new questions and opportunities arise. Research is the way to get unbiased answers and evaluations.

For example, a company might offer a successful line of shampoos and conditioners. The company may have data that indicate a segment of its female customers have severely dry and damaged hair resulting from overuse of blow dryers and curling irons. The company comes up with a product idea to create a more effective conditioner to treat badly damaged hair. The first research step is to ascertain the appeal of the *product concept* for this conditioner.

> **Product concept** A short description (several sentences) in consumer language of a product under development. Typically, it includes a descriptive name (e.g., conditioner for dry damaged hair) and describes its benefit (e.g., makes dry damaged hair shiny and soft) and its key attributes (e.g., thick and creamy, penetrates the hair, rinses out easily).
>
> **KEY TERM**

If consumers respond positively to the product idea, you then should conduct tests on alternative formulations of the conditioner. Which one works the best? Which one best meets the expectations of the product concept? With this knowledge, a company greatly improves its odds of success in the marketplace.

How to Approach a Market Research Project

You must set objectives. What is it you want to know and how do you intend to use the information? What decisions do you want to make? Write these goals down. If you're working with a brand team, get agreement on the objectives.

You might want to conduct research on a proposed new advertising campaign for a sinking product. This research project will tell you if the commercials under consideration communicate the intended message, such as whether your brand tastes better than the store brand. Based on the results, you will be able to determine which commercials best communicate the message and/or identify what content needs to be changed to improve communication.

However, other team members may want to gain insight into some basic questions about the brand. For example, why are people buying the store brand instead of your brand? This research should precede development of the commercial and be used to shape the message that the ultimate advertising will communicate.

You should get agreement from the entire team before proceeding with a project. Otherwise, the research might not answer the questions that are important to the team members.

Types of Market Research

Market research consists of two broad categories: quantitative and qualitative.

Quantitative, often called surveys, is the technique that tells "how many." How many people use my product? How many users are African American? How many prospective customers live in rural areas? How many live in the city? How many people rate my product as outstanding in quality? Designed and administered correctly, a survey can produce reliable, statistically sound data.

Qualitative research seeks to understand the "how" and "why" of consumer attitudes and behavior, not to count how many have a specific belief or purchasing habit. From qualitative, for example, you would learn why people like and buy a particular brand of deodorant, but you would not learn how many people or what ages of people buy the brand. Or you might learn why the graphics on one package get attention more than an alternate design, but you would not learn how many people prefer one design to the other. Qualitative research uses a small sample size (usually fewer than 50 people), so it is not statistically reliable. The basic qualitative techniques are focus groups and in-depth interviews.

Surveys

All legitimate surveys try to achieve two objectives: produce reliable results that represent the population sampled and produce reliable results as data that can be replicated. In other words, if the survey is designed properly, you should expect almost the same results if it is administered twice. For example, if two surveys each poll 400 adults representative of the U.S. population using the identical questions about dental care, and the surveys are reliable, both surveys would report that approximately 93 percent of adults brush twice daily and 80 percent see the dentist at least once a year.

Surveys use structured questionnaires. This ensures that everyone is asked exactly the same question, so that the results aren't affected by any variation in question wording. Even a wording difference as subtle as "50% off" versus "save 50%" can render the survey results unreliable. The ques-

> **Statistical significance** Degree of certainty that an observed difference (e.g., between means) or relationship (e.g., between variables) actually exists and that it is not the result of chance. Generally market researchers use the 95 percent confidence level, which means there is a 95 percent likelihood that the difference or relationship between two numbers is statistically significant. A related term is *margin of error*.
>
> **KEY TERMS**
>
> **Margin of error** A statistic expressing the amount of random sampling error in a survey's results. Random sampling error is simply the uncertainty that results from surveying a sampling of a population rather than the entire population. The margin of error represents the accuracy of survey results. The larger the margin of error, the less confidence that the results from the sampling are close to the figures for the whole population.

tions are asked identically. Then the answers are tallied to determine "how many" people gave which answers to which question. Statistical tests are then performed to determine if differences in numbers are significant enough to be meaningful.

DENTAL SURVEY

FOR EXAMPLE

In a survey of a sampling of 400 adults representative of the U.S. population, the results show that approximately 93 percent of adults brush twice daily with a margin of error of 4 percent. This means there is a 95 percent likelihood that the true percentage in the population is between 89 percent and 97 percent.

An issue that always arises when designing a survey is how many people to interview. The larger the number of people surveyed, the more reliable the results. Generally for marketing studies, the convention is that a sampling of 400 to 500 total respondents provides acceptable reliability. Total sample size also depends on the subgroups you wish to analyze, such as adults with preschool children or senior citizens. To provide any degree of reliability, a subgroup should contain at least 75 to 100 respondents. For example, if you wish to analyze senior citizens' usage of a product and they constitute 20 percent of the population, you would need a total sample size of 500 people (500 x .20 = 100 seniors).

Often there is disbelief that a survey of a few hundred people can be truly representative. A related misconception is that the larger the population sampled, the larger the survey sample must be. Think of it like the blood sample taken when you visit a doctor. One vial—a tablespoon or two of blood—is sufficient to analyze many measures of health, such as cholesterol, lipids, and blood sugar. A quart of blood won't reveal any more than a tablespoon. Keep in mind that reliable polls of national elections are conducted with as few as 1,000 adults, which is less than 0.000444 percent of the total U.S. population of adults 18 years of age or older, which is close to 230 million.

In addition to survey *reliability*, survey *validity* is an important consideration. Valid surveys contain valid questions—that is, questions that fully accomplish their intended purpose. Survey questions sometimes fail the test of validity, usually when they're written by inexperienced, amateur researchers.

Suppose, for example, that the goal is to assess a public library for the quality of its staff. You know that staff is evaluated by library patrons on two primary criteria—courtesy and knowledge—so the following question is written for a mail survey of patrons: "How do you rate the courtesy and knowledge of the library's staff … as excellent, good, fair, or poor?" This question fails the validity test on two counts. First, a respondent can't answer the question if he or she considers the staff courteous but not knowledgeable or knowledgeable but not courteous. Second, a respondent can't answer the question if he or she has no opinion about the staff or is neutral. This question fails to achieve its intended purpose. It needs to be rewritten by an experienced professional.

How to Administer a Survey

There is no one best way to administer a survey. Depending on your marketing situation, surveys can be conducted legitimately by phone, mail, or the Internet. Each method is viable, and each presents pros and cons.

Phone surveys offer excellent control over qualifying the participants. "Qualifying" means making sure the desired demographic and groups are included in the survey. For example, if you want to conduct a survey among dandruff shampoo users, the phone interviewer will start the interview by asking the respondent: What types of shampoos do you use? If dandruff shampoo is not mentioned, then the person does not participate further in the interview. That way you are not getting data from people whose opinions might be useless or misleading.

You can also set and control quotas for particular types of people. For example, if you are conducting a survey of 500 people and want the sample to include equal numbers of men and women, then you instruct the interviewing firm to interview 250 men and 250 women.

Phone surveys also provide the opportunity for random sampling. The idea of a random sample is that every consumer in the population has an equal chance of participating in the survey. Typically, computers generate random phone numbers for either a particular area or the total U.S. This ensures that both listed and unlisted numbers are included in the sample, which makes the sample more representative of all consumers.

Phone surveys are relatively quick to complete. Once the questionnaire is designed and programmed into the computer for the interviewers, interviews can usually be completed in one to four weeks, depending on sample size and on the difficulty of finding qualified respondents.

This method also makes it feasible to conduct surveys among English- and non-English-speaking consumers. Bilingual interviewers can quickly ascertain which language a respondent feels most comfortable using and then conduct the interview accordingly.

A downside to phone surveys is cost. The cost per interview may be $50 to $80, depending on the difficulty of locating qualified respondents.

Online surveys are rapidly replacing phone surveys. They offer several key advantages.

First, online surveys are faster. Once a questionnaire is approved and programmed onto a Web site, all the data in many cases can be collected in a few days.

Second, online surveys offer the ability to locate hard-to-find targets affordably. Or in research terms, they can reach a "low incidence target."

Using e-mail blasts, thousands of people can be quickly and inexpensively contacted and then screened to see if

> **Incidence** The percentage of population or households that fits a particular specification. For example, if 75 percent of homes have a computer, the incidence is 75 percent. If 20 percent of women have used a prepared stuffing mix in the last six months, the incidence is 20 percent. Incidence affects the price of many research studies. The lower the incidence, the more costly it is to locate the desired segment of the population in phone, mail, or focus group studies. This is much less an issue for online surveys.
>
> **KEY TERM**

FINDING THE ELUSIVE BUYER ONLINE

FOR EXAMPLE A few years ago, when flat-screen TVs were just beginning to become popular, our client wanted to survey consumers who owned flat-screen TVs of a particular size. We figured this was only about 2 percent of the U.S. population. If we had tried to recruit 300 of these people by phone, we would have had to contact about 50,000 people, which would not have been feasible. By using an online panel, we completed interviewing in less than one week.

---

they fit the specifications of the study.

There are limitations to online surveys, however. If you need to conduct a survey among residents in a relatively small specific geographic area—such as a town, city, or county—there are no representative Internet samples available.

Some organizations, such as public libraries, have posted surveys on their Web sites. Unfortunately, such surveys are of poor quality because the respondent selection is highly biased. They are getting information only from people who access the organizations' Web sites. Typically these surveys are also not password protected, so the same person could take the survey many times and "stuff the ballot box." In effect, you have the Chicago phenomenon of "vote early, vote often."

Mail surveys are one of the oldest techniques. Depending on your business, they can yield very useful information at an efficient cost. The costs for distributing a survey are printing and postage. Typically this runs around $1 per questionnaire (less if you have a not-for-profit postage permit). You could print and mail 15,000 surveys, for example, for less than $15,000. If 5 percent are returned, the cost per return is $20, far less than the cost of a phone interview.

Mail surveys are particularly attractive for local tax-funded entities, such as communities, schools, park districts, and libraries. If a community has 30,000 or fewer residents, it's often affordable to send a questionnaire to every household. Including all households has a distinct public relations advantage, allowing the taxing body to say that it solicited every household's opinion.

A downside of a mail survey is timing. From start to finish, the process can take three months: approving a questionnaire, printing the questionnaire, mailing the questionnaire, and receiving and analyzing the questionnaires. Generally, participation rates are low for a mail survey—5 to 7 percent—particularly if it's for a commercial product or service. There are important exceptions to this generality, however. Our experience with public libraries finds that a 15 to 20 percent response rate is common. Suppliers of community surveys also report high response rates.

PARTIAL LIST OF TYPES OF MARKETING SURVEYS

An *attitude and usage study* determines attitudes and product purchase and usage within a population of interest (e.g., men, women, teenagers). These data are fundamental to understanding target markets.

TOOLS

A *tracking study* provides data on awareness and product purchase at different points in time. For example, an advertiser might conduct a survey to determine level of awareness prior to running television commercials. After the advertising has aired, the study would be repeated to determine the effect of the advertising on awareness and purchase.

A *concept study* determines the interest in purchasing a new product. It generally uses a short description of the product and may include the anticipated retail price.

Product testing can include everything from sensory taste tests to consumer usage tests of small appliances and beta tests of new software.

Advertising tests of commercials and print ads either before or after production can uncover what the ads communicate and how consumers respond to the ads.

Focus Groups

You no doubt have heard of focus groups, and you may even have participated in some. This technique consists of moderated group conversations. Led by a trained facilitator, the discussion groups can focus on almost any topic, from jarred pasta sauces or shampoo to insurance or advertising. If the study is for a casual dining chain, the groups might explore a variety of questions: What are their perceptions of different restaurant chains? How do customers decide to visit one? Who (kids, spouses) influences the decision? What impact does the menu have on the choice? What are the strengths and weaknesses of various chains?

Because a focus group is an interactive discussion, it should be small enough to allow participants to interact. Generally, a group with six to 10

CORRECT USE OF FOCUS GROUPS
Focus groups are a small sample, so they are not statistically reliable. However, they can provide excellent insights for marketing ideas, communications, and product development. Ideally, what is learned from focus groups should be confirmed by a quantitative study.

respondents works well for most topics. More than 10 limits the interaction, and less assertive participants are more likely to not be as active. Fewer than six works well if there's need to get into a topic in great depth and to help avoid *groupthink*. Limiting the size facilitates more focus on individual responses. A skilled moderator will often ask participants to write down privately their individual reactions to an idea (e.g., for a new product or a marketing campaign) before any member of the group has a chance to influence them.

WHAT'S IN A NAME?
If you are looking at new names for a product, you might explore consumers' reactions to a range of names. You'd learn what each name communicated, what people associate with it, and if it sounds like other names in the marketplace. The comments would not only tell you which ones are received more or less positively, but also reveal what about each name worked or didn't work. You might learn that "Crispy Oats" cereal sounds tasty and healthy, but "Crunchy Oats" sounds hard to chew and so healthy that it won't taste good. This information can help refine the names further. It's likely some names will receive a more positive response than others. However, before making a final decision, the preferred names should be tested quantitatively to determine which name creates the greatest interest in purchasing the product ("purchase intent" or "intent to purchase").

Focus group sessions generally run 90 minutes to two hours, although some are as short as an hour. In Europe, they often span three hours. Americans generally won't participate in a study that lasts that long.

Critically important to the success of a focus group is its composition. It is essential to decide who should be in the group in terms of product and brand usage, age, and gender. Figuring out the most relevant targets to include in the study makes for more useful results. If you want to understand the role of pasta sauce in weekly meal preparation, for example, you'd likely want to talk

with women who prepare dinner for the families four or
more nights per week and
purchase pasta sauce regularly. It would be of very limited value to interview women
who buy take-out for dinner
or prepare frozen entrees

> **Groupthink** Natural ten-
> dency of all members of a
> group to fall into line with
> what the majority think or **KEY TERM**
> with what the most vocal or influential
> members think. Groupthink is an attempt
> to minimize conflict and reach consensus
> without critically analyzing ideas.

most nights and only occasionally buy pasta sauce.

In general, you want a homogeneous group. That is, you want people who are similar to each other. If you are trying to understand attitudes of different types of auto buyers, you'd have separate groups for hybrid vehicles and for SUVs. If the study is about the role of a community center, seniors will certainly have different preferences than parents of young children. Segmenting the groups leads to a better understanding of the needs of different targets. It also ensures that respondents will be among their peers, which often makes them more forthcoming and more candid in their comments.

How many groups will be conducted on a topic depends on how many different consumer segments you wish to include in the study and how many markets you wish to include. For any one segment, you should conduct two groups. That gives you the opportunity to explore issues more in-depth and gain a greater range of opinions. Conducting only one group within a segment is risky. The group may just be "off" and unable to provide the insights needed. If you have two consumer segments (e.g., users of OTC heartburn remedies and users of prescription heartburn medications) and wish to explore their attitudes and behavior in two markets, then you would conduct a minimum of four groups.

Setting Up and Moderating Focus Groups

After objectives for the study are established, engage an experienced moderator. This is critical. He or she will work with you to design the study and answer key questions. For example, "What are the specifications of the respondents?" "In what market or markets of the U.S. should the groups be conducted?" (This is particularly important if there is a geographic skew to the business.) "How many groups should we conduct?"

KEY TERM
Focus group facility A suite of rooms specially designed for conducting focus groups. Typically it houses one or more conference rooms with one-way mirrors for interviewing the respondents. Clients sit in an adjoining room behind the mirrors to listen and watch the groups. This setup allows the clients to see and hear the respondents as the groups proceed, but not be present in the interviewing room because that could be intimidating to participants.

The moderator will write the screening questionnaire to recruit the appropriate respondents. Typically, a moderator will engage a research facility that has a database of people who have indicated an interest in participating in a focus group as well as a room specially designed for groups. The moderator will also work with the client to determine what areas of inquiry should be included in the discussion. The moderator will write a discussion guide that outlines the areas that will be covered.

Generally, it takes two to three weeks to set up focus groups. The actual groups may be completed in several days. A good rule of thumb is no more than three two-hour sessions in a day.

Entire books are devoted to proper moderating techniques. But there are a few key things to look for in a good moderator. A good moderator has interviewed consumers on many different topics, so that he or she has a broad perspective on consumer response. The moderator relies not only on the words spoken, but also on the excitement registered through facial expressions and body language. The moderator should make respondents feel comfortable and make the discussion about eliciting their opinions, not sharing his or hers. While the session should be free flowing and interactive, the moderator must also control the group, not letting any one participant dominate and keeping the group on task.

CAUTION
DON'T DO IT YOURSELF
A good moderator makes conducting a group look easy. But appearances are deceptive. It takes great skill and experience to lead a discussion without introducing bias through subtle voice and body cues. It takes years of experience to read the body language and voice tone of participants. Don't try to moderate a group without proper training and an apprenticeship with an experienced moderator. If you do it yourself, the results you get could be biased or be misleading.

INTERPRETING WHAT CONSUMERS SAY

TRICKS OF THE TRADE

When testing new products or ideas for new products, experienced focus group moderators know which phrases are thumbs-up and which phrases are thumbs-down.

Three of the most encouraging phrases:

"When will it be on the market?"

"Where can I buy it?"

"I liked the product so much that when I tested it at home, I kept some." (The instructions were to return all unused product to the testing facility.)

On the flip side, some less encouraging comments:

"I'd try it if I had a coupon."

"It would be good for camping."

Those words suggest very limited interest in the idea: "You'd have to buy my interest" or "I'd use the product only very occasionally."

The moderator should provide a report that analyzes the findings and provides implications for marketing. It should not simply be a recapitulation of the conversation. For a moderator to complete a report thoroughly and thoughtfully, allow two weeks.

GOOD REPORTS MATTER

FOR EXAMPLE

A good report explains the reasons behind group participants' responses and provides ways to use the information for marketing. In the case of one pasta restaurant, the participants discussed different casual restaurants and mentioned that the client's restaurants no longer offered a good value. The report explained that participants recalled the chain's long-running advertising campaign that positioned the restaurants as offering a bounty of food. But customers found that the restaurants no longer offered free soda refills or unlimited trips to the salad bar. The report concluded that the dining experience no longer matched the advertising. The clear implication was that the chain should either change its advertising or deliver on what it promised.

Individual Interviews

Individual interviews are one-on-one conversations between a respondent and a moderator. They should be used when the topic is especially sensitive or highly personal (e.g., difficult medical conditions, managing personal finances). Respondents may not want to reveal their experiences and views about these topics in front of other people, but will be forthcoming with an empathetic, neutral moderator. Individual interviews are often preferable for communications testing. If you show your ad or package to consumers individually, you will learn if it communicates the desired message or image. Expose it in a group and the results will likely be influenced by groupthink.

TRICKS OF THE TRADE

TRY TRIADS

While individual interviews almost guarantee the purest results for communications testing, many clients will not commission such a study because it generally takes more time and money than focus groups. So, a decent compromise is *triads*, focus groups of three people. In that situation, the moderator shows an ad and asks each participant to write down the main message and overall reactions to the ad. During the discussion, the moderator should ask participants to refer to their notes. This ensures that each participant shares his or her reactions, and it helps avoid groupthink. At the end of the discussion, the moderator collects the papers and checks whether the written reactions were shared orally.

Individual interviews are a practical way to conduct research among hard-to-recruit targets such as business owners, high-level executives, or physicians. These people tend to be highly time-constrained, so they're more likely to agree to a 30-minute interview (in person or on the phone) than to a two-hour focus group.

A typical individual interview lasts 15 to 60 minutes. It depends on how many topics are covered, how involved the respondent is with the subject, and how deeply the topic can be probed. For example, if you want to learn if a respondent noticed your package on a mock retail shelf, the interview takes no more than 15 minutes. But if you want to interview people who are suffering from chronic sleep problems and find out how those problems are affecting their lives, how they are dealing with the problems, and what they have experienced with various sleep remedies, the interview may last 30 to 45 minutes.

The number of interviews to schedule varies greatly. Generally, you should interview a minimum of 10 to 12 consumers per segment (e.g., current users of a product and potential users of a product). For two segments, you'd conduct a total of 20 to 24 interviews. So, for example, if you wish to explore attitudes in different parts of the U.S. by conducting the study in three markets, then the study would likely consist of 60 to 72 interviews.

When You Shouldn't Do Research

Some ideas simply don't pass the commonsense test and shouldn't command the resources for formal research. Do a quick, informal pitch for friends, family members, and neighbors. Yes, they're biased. No, it's not a real focus group. But it can be a good way to tap into some common sense outside your marketing team.

A Doomed Idea

A well-known brand of power tools—with an image of "for real men," strength, reliability—wanted to determine if there was a market for an electric razor for women using the brand name. What woman would want to shave her legs or delicate underarm skin with a razor carrying the brand name of power tools for men? The answer seems obvious, but costly research was conducted anyway. The result? No interest in a power tool brand shaver for women—and less money available for more useful research.

Selecting a Research Consultant

To find a market research firm, ask contacts who have worked with or hired research consultants. Good leads may come from your contacts at other consumer goods companies, contacts at advertising agencies, or business school classmates. Look for a firm with broad experience in consumer studies.

Then talk with a few consultants (don't rely only on e-mail communications) and explain the project you're contemplating. The consultant should listen, ask thoughtful questions, probe to clarify your objectives, and show enthusiasm for your project.

If you're interested in pursuing the project with the consultant, ask for a written proposal. Read the proposal and call the consultant with questions. How the consultant handles your questions will help reveal his or her style and work ethic. Pricing for research projects varies greatly, so be sure to understand what's included and not included in the proposal.

Different Types of Research Firms

Broadly speaking, there are two types of research firms:

Large global companies that provide a wide array of research services (all types of qualitative and quantitative studies, including sales modeling) in markets all over the world. You'll likely work with an account manager who will coordinate the project, not the people who will actually design, field, and interpret the study.

Smaller firms that generally focus on either qualitative or quantitative research, sometimes with limited capabilities. You'll likely have contact with the people who will design and conduct the research. Some of these firms, particularly ones specializing in qualitative research, consist of a single moderator or several moderators.

Also, some colleges and universities provide research services, primarily for not-for-profit entities. Generally, students under the supervision of a professor conduct most of the project. Quality tends to vary a lot.

Limits of Market Research

Market research is excellent at capturing and measuring what is happening or what has happened. It can be excellent at predicting what is likely to happen based on the present and the past. However, market research has limits, and the wise researcher is aware of these limits.

For example, it is wise not to generalize from focus group or qualitative results. The sample sizes are too small to predict what the population at large will do. You are better off using focus groups to focus your inquiries and then verifying them quantitatively.

It is wise not to ask one group of people to predict another group's behavior. Questions like "Do you think your mother will approve of your musical purchases?" do not produce reliable answers. People are notoriously bad at looking at the world through other people's eyes. Such questions result in guesses or speculations that may involve a lot of wishful thinking

It is also wise not to ask people about their own behavior when there are values or perceptions involved: "Would you rather help an orphan or watch TV?" Most people would rather watch TV, but may state a preference for helping orphans. Most of us want people to think well of us.

It is also unwise to ask people to reflect on their own subconscious motives. We may not really know or we may not want to admit our motives. People may state motives they feel would be more socially acceptable rather than reveal their real motives.

The more an ad or product depends upon the details of the execution (such as how the words are written, how the music is recorded, or how bright the colors are), the less likely the test of a rough ad concept will be predictive. Testing radio as words typed on a page or verbally describing a billboard that depends on the color red will not produce useful results. People have a hard time imagining a finished ad and filling in the details that do not yet exist.

The more radically innovative the product or idea is, the less reliable research will be at predicting its success. Imagine being the first marketer to suggest posting ads in the restrooms of restaurants and bars or installing mirrors that play short video clip ads? How would focus group participants or people interviewed in shopping malls have reacted? The more innovative the idea, the less dependable the research prediction.

Also, the further out in time you need to predict behavior, the less reliable the predictability. For example, American teens change their preference for music, clothing, and language every six months. If a focus group of teens liked a particular TV commercial and it didn't even start running for another six months, the results might not be as predicted by the research.

In the vast majority of marketing situations however, market research can provide a useful and predictive guide to decision making.

One important limitation to most market research is not the data, the techniques, the time, the cost, or the technology. It is the willingness of the client sponsoring the research to understand the results, believe

HEAR NO EVIL

As a group of retail executives sat behind a one-way mirror watching a focus group, the female customers complained repeatedly that the store wasn't carrying the latest and trendiest products and was woefully behind the times. The company vice president, who'd had a bit too much to drink, banged on the glass of the one-way mirror with his fists, disrupting the discussion in the other room, and shouted, "You're wrong! You're all liars! What do you know about retail!" The moral of the story: don't ask your customers any questions for which you don't really want answers.

the results (especially if they conflict with the client's personal point of view), and apply the results. Sometimes managers "shoot the messenger" who delivers news they don't like. Or they rely on research the way a drunk relies on a lamppost—more for support than for illumination.

The true limitation of market research is not the research. It's the people who don't use it properly.

Manager's Checklist for Chapter 14

☑ Market research means learning everything you can about the people in your target market and their views and behaviors.

☑ Market research can be used up front to prevent problems in campaign or product development, and it can be used throughout the life cycle of a product or brand to monitor situations and help make important marketing decisions.

☑ Get agreement on market research objectives ahead of time from all members of the team.

☑ Market research consists of two broad categories: quantitative and qualitative. Quantitative research (surveys) provides results that are statistically reliable for the population sampled. Qualitative research seeks to understand the "how" and "why" of consumer attitudes and behavior.

☑ Surveys can be conducted by phone, mail, or the Internet. Each has plusses and minuses.

☑ Hire a research consultant who has broad experience with consumer studies and who listens to you, asks thoughtful questions, and writes insightful reports.

☑ One important limitation of market research is the tendency of some clients to ignore results with which they disagree.

Index

Index

About the Author

Barry Callen is a marketing consultant, speaker, and teacher who has worked with most advertising media in a variety of roles: graphic designer, copywriter, creative director, strategist, salesman, broadcast producer, focus group moderator, agency search consultant, and client. For over a decade, Barry has been teaching and speaking from the University of Wisconsin Fluno Center for Executive Education in Madison, Wisconsin to Madison Square Garden in New York City. For over thirty years, he has also been applying the principles he teaches in the advertising wars of Madison Avenue at agencies like Ogilvy & Mather; Lintas Long-Haymes & Carr; The Hiebing Group; and Lois-USA. In fact, hundreds of clients like Coca-Cola, Shell, Culligan, Hanes, First Alert, Kraft, Wachovia Bank, and Famous Footwear have invested just under half a billion dollars in media to communicate ideas Barry has

created or creative-directed. In addition to hundreds of creative awards, he is proudest of his Effie Awards for advertising effectiveness.

Barry has been Askme.com's #1-rated advertising expert. He writes a monthly column called "The B.S.-Free Zone" for *In-Business Magazine* and is a frequent talk-show guest. He is the author of another book published by McGraw-Hill: *Perfect Phrases for Sales and Marketing Copy*. Barry invented a successful naming process and the PitchPerfect™ Message Strategy process for finding the most powerful thing to say. After studying improv comedy at Second City and performing with "Without Annette," he founded Corprov™ improvisational training for corporations, which he teaches with partner Nell Weatherwax. They have been known to achieve the highest student evaluation scores in the entire history of a teaching program. Barry has never met an art form he didn't like. He has been struck by lightning. For further information and to download free whitepapers, please visit Barry's Web site at www.barrycallen.com or contact him via e-mail at barry.callen@gmail.com and by phone at 608.347.8396.